Hope For A Culture
Preoccupied With Death

Steven A. Carr &
Franklin A. Meyer

Wolgemuth & Hyatt, Publishers, Inc.
Brentwood, Tennessee

The mission of Wolgemuth & Hyatt, Publishers, Inc. is to publish and distribute books that lead individuals toward:

- A personal faith in the one true God: Father, Son, and Holy Spirit;

- A lifestyle of practical discipleship; and

- A worldview that is consistent with the historic, Christian faith.

Moreover, the Company endeavors to accomplish this mission at a reasonable profit and in a manner which glorifies God and serves His Kingdom.

© 1990 by Steven A. Carr and Franklin A. Meyer. All rights reserved.
Published June 1990. First Edition.
Printed in the United States of America.
97 96 95 94 93 92 91 90   8 7 6 5 4 3 2 (Second Printing, September 1990)

Illustrations © by Chuck Asay. Used by permission.

Illustrations © by Wayne Stayskal. Used by permission.

Unless otherwise noted, all Scripture quotations are from the Holy Bible, New International Version. © 1973, 1978, 1984 International Bible Society. Used by permission of Zondervan Bible Publishers.

Wolgemuth & Hyatt, Publishers, Inc.
1749 Mallory Lane, Suite 110
Brentwood, Tennessee 37027

Library of Congress Cataloging-in-Publication Data

Carr, Steven A.
    Celebrate life : hope for a culture preoccupied with death / Steven A. Carr. Franklin A. Meyer. p.   cm.
    ISBN 0-943497-14-0
    1. Life and death, Power over — Religious aspects — Christianity. 2. Human ecology — Religious aspects — Christianity. 3. Man (Christian thoelogy) 4. Hope — Religious aspects. — Christianity. 5. Christianity and culture. 6. Christian ethics. 7. Social ethics. 8. Church and social problems. I. Meyer, Franklin A. II. Title.
    BJ1469.C37 1990   90-38812
    261 — dc20   CIP

We dedicate this book to:

The God
who creates life

Our parents
who gave us life

Our wives
with whom we share in life

Our children
who will carry on life

Our fellow warriors
for the protection of life

and

The millions of nameless babies
who have been denied life

CONTENTS

FOREWORD

I t is not often that you read a serious book that is so interesting you can hardly put it down. *Celebrate Life* is such a book. The authors have dealt with some "heavy" subjects of our generation—subjects that put most people to sleep. But they explain the facts in such a unique way and present their arguments so well that the reader will be motivated to do what all authors wish for—stay awake and think!

We are all aware that there are several vital subjects that we should know about to stay current in today's confusing generation. But it's too easy to immerse one's brain in "entertainment" or to become so "spiritually-minded" we fail to recognize what is going on around us. This book will entertain you while teaching you the up-to-date facts you need to know—facts that will arm you with answers for confused people.

Just look at some of the issues they deal with: the value of life—the hottest issue of our times, the overpopulation hoax, the so-called environmental doom myth, the "evolution is a fact" fraud; these are all presented here in a most fascinating scenario. Quite candidly, I thought I was well informed on these subjects, but I learned a lot reading this book.

You will also find hope here. Steve and Frank believe it is still possible to turn our culture back to the traditional moral sanity of just one generation ago, but it will require the understanding of the facts that are so deftly presented here. And the authors know what they are talking about.

I have known Steven Carr for five years. I watched him make the decision to leave a very promising business field to do what he could to return our nation to Biblical principles and values. I have spent hours with him on the phone and in person as he hammered out the plan God gave him for The Christian Connection, an organization that has already had a solid impact on his city and state. Now he and his associates are ready to roll it out as a national ministry that will enable thousands of others to "get involved."

I believe in this young man, and after reading this book, must tell you something that he probably would never tell. Several of the fascinating stories of debates or confrontations with people come right out of his own experience. That may be why they are so vivid and believable.

Frank Meyer I also commend for the strong leadership and godly wisdom he has provided in the development of The Christian Connection. His experience as a pastor has been instrumental in the creation of the ministry's educational products and services.

Every parent ought to read this book and then give it to their children. Teenagers will enjoy this book. And be sure of this, when you get through reading it, you will be able to discuss these subjects intelligently with other members of your family and with the misguided people who haven't learned the whole story behind the story.

One thing I can guarantee, you will learn much from the solid information these authors give on subjects that appear in our newspapers and on TV every day. And you will find it easy and enjoyable reading in the process.

Dr. Tim LaHaye

Author, minister, educator,
co-chairman of Celebrate
Life Outreach

ACKNOWLEDGMENTS

This book would not have come into existence without the faith of the publishers, Mike Hyatt and Robert Wolgemuth. They took a risk on the evidence of our word and we are thankful.

Also, this book would not exist in readable form without the skill and dedication of Neil Wilson who took the rough draft and turned it into a message that flowed with a clear sense of direction. More than an editor, he served as a co-writer on this project.

We are also indebted to Dr. Jim Galvin and The Livingstone Corporation as they patiently listened, cooperated, and educated us to the realities of publishing a credibly lucid book.

Behind every successful man is an amazed mother-in-law and a wife who knew he could do it all the time. Our wives and children encouraged us all the way. Peggy and daughter Elizabeth gave Steve lots of valuable insights that added to the storyline. Judith took time from her busy schedule as The Christian Connection's editor to proof Frank's writing, as she has been doing for almost thirty years.

Then there are the others who helped when asked, not because of what they would get out of it but because they just wanted to help. Dr. Julian L. Simon, author of *The Ultimate Resource*, gave us personal encouragement and permission to use whatever material out of his book would be helpful. Lonna Willis proved to be a blessing once again with her excellent proofreading skills. Leanne Geist of the Wauconda library and other librarians in the area assisted us in tracking down needed information. We gained a new appreciation for the tremendous resource of truth that is available in our public libraries.

And where does that leave the authors? With the reality that all we can claim as "our" ideas and thoughts were actually given to us by a host of teachers and writers that make up our current reservoir of knowledge. So on the one hand we are grateful to have a part in creating this book, but on the other hand very humbled with the realization of whose it is and how it came into being. Praise be to our Lord Jesus Christ for the privilege of allowing us to paticipate in such a challenging and life engendering project.

INTRODUCTION

J esus must have looked around the circle of faces before He asked His disciples this question: "Do you bring in a lamp to put it under a bowl or a bed?" After a moment, He gave them the obvious answer. "Instead, don't you put it on its stand? For whatever is hidden is meant to be disclosed, and whatever is concealed is meant to be brought out into the open" (Mark 4:21).

We open this book with the same question on our minds. If you are a Christian, Jesus has placed His light in you. Where are you shining? Looking at what is going on in the world today, how would you describe the ways Jesus wants to shine through you?

This book will help you discover some of the ways Christians are being challenged, changed, equipped, and mobilized to shine out in their corner of the world. You will read about God working through individuals and groups to make a difference in society. In their stories we trust you will find direction for your own life.

This is not a book for fence-sitters. The truths you learn in this book will make it hard for you to remain silent in conversations where you now feel you have nothing to say. What you learn will demand action. The truth will make you free to speak out and accountable before God for what you know.

Our purpose is not to fill your mind with interesting information, but to challenge your emotions and motivate you to become involved in taking God's life-giving truth to a world convinced by "answers" that only lead to death.

1

Within these pages you will discover other resources that can help you to truthfully and compassionately champion the causes of life. You will be introduced to The Christian Connection's ongoing plan of action in which you can become involved at various levels (see Addendum). We are praying that this book will help recruit a vast army of men and women who are tired of being silent fence-sitters watching much of the world literally go to hell. The truth we have as Christians is too precious to be hidden. It must be lived and shared with others out in the open, where everyone can see.

Jesus, who is life Himself, has decided to communicate that life through us. He invites us to follow Him into a world oppressed by death, and in every way possible, to CELEBRATE LIFE.

Steven A. Carr
Franklin A. Meyer

O N E

LIVING YOUR ANSWERS

Key Question: What keeps Christians silent in a society with more exposure to Christianity than any other on earth?

The facts you are about to learn are true. Names have been changed, and fictional settings have been created, but these are only a useful way to bring you important answers you can use. Incidents and conversations similar to the ones you will read take place every day. The battle for life is raging everywhere. The issues surrounding abortion are only part of a much larger pattern of symptoms indicating a desperate condition in our society. The list of symptoms keeps growing. Rampant teen suicide, death education in our public schools, and the growing acceptance of euthanasia are all evidence of a nation and world in deep trouble. Christians can no longer view action as optional. It is the goal of this book to help Christians become effective communicators in friendly conversations as well as in unpleasant confrontations.

This is also a book of answers — answers to difficult questions. Some of the answers in these pages will be very familiar. We hear or read them constantly in the media. We are tempted to accept these answers about the problems in our world because the people giving them seem to know more than we do. But their answers contradict what we know from God's Word. That is why they are called "Myths" in this book. They are answers that have come to be believed widely, but have not been proven true.

As Christians, our challenge is to come up with real answers. What could be better than the truth? People are looking for better answers than they have because many of them realize they don't have the truth. We do have the truth, recorded in God's Word. The Bible is His instruction manual for the human race. Modern news, science, technology, medicine, and education are discovering truths the Bible has said all along. Rather than disproving the Bible's relevancy and applicability, these sources confirm its teaching daily. But in our anxiety over being put on the spot by a question we can't answer, we sometimes miss out on opportunities to help people with the answers we do have. It may be humility that makes us say we don't know *all* the answers; it is not humility when we act as if we don't know *any* answers. It is fear.

Fearful silence is not an option for committed Christians. The world is lost in despair and has come more and more under the control of a "death-style" mentality. In stark contrast to this hopelessness is the Bible's description of the Christian mind, which is filled with Christ. The battle lines are being clearly drawn between those ideas and attitudes that represent what we will call the "death-style" mentality, and those representing what we will call the "life-style" mentality. Christ is the source of life, but our society is focusing on death. The very lives of our children and grandchildren will be deeply affected by the outcome of this battle in our day. We can no longer remain uninvolved.

The apostle Peter said: "Always be prepared to give an answer to everyone who asks you to give the reason for the hope that you have" (1 Peter 3:15). One way hope is vividly demonstrated is by how we answer the challenges and questions life brings. People who see us avoiding or denying the difficult issues in life probably won't think to ask us, "Why are you so hopeful about life?"

Jesus said He is the Truth (John 14:6). We need to develop confidence that the answers that come from a Christian point of view are tied to the truth. The truth is on our side, whether it is printed in a secular source like *The Wall Street Journal* or written in the book of Psalms. We need not be afraid of what others say. Instead, we can take the offensive — we can and must attack the lies that are being accepted by society and replace them with truth. Proclaiming clearly what we believe can be one of the most powerful ways to celebrate life.

How to Read This Book

Each chapter begins with a "Key Question" that will help you understand its topic, then brings you into a different fictional "Setting" where common answers are challenged and the truth expressed. Next is a summarizing "Comment" of key issues covered in the chapter, as well as a section titled "In the News." These quotes, primarily from secular media sources, can be used effectively because they carry credibility with non-Christians. They support the Biblical perspective on the issues in the chapter. Other "Key Quotations" will also be included along with a relevant Scripture passage.

You may wish to enjoy this book by reading the first sections in each chapter straight through, skipping the "In the News" portion. Later, you may want to scan the "In the News" sections to see what information is there. Then, when you need some facts to help present the truth, you can return again and again to the helpful information compiled in these pages.

We may not be able to imagine ourselves proclaiming Christianity in a hostile setting, or a crowded auditorium, or even an office lunchroom. Still, we are each called to bring the gospel, along with Christian answers, into whatever arenas make up our lives. The truth must touch and change friendships, churches, and families. We trust God will use these pages to give you a new awareness of opportunities and responsibilities to bring God's truth to your daily life.

Key Quotations

It was the Lord who put into my mind (I could feel His Hand upon me) to sail from here to the Indies. All who heard of my project rejected it with laughter, ridiculing me. There is no question that my inspiration was from the Holy Spirit, because He comforted me with rays of marvelous illumination from the Holy Scriptures, encouraging me continually to press forward. . . . No one should fear to undertake any task in the name of our Saviour, if it is just and if the intention is purely for His Holy service. . . . O what a gracious Lord, Who desires that people should perform for Him those things for which He holds Himself responsible! Day and night, moment by moment, everyone should express to Him their most devoted gratitude.

Christopher Columbus explaining his voyage
to the New World

Do not merely listen to the word, and so deceive yourselves. Do what it says. Anyone who listens to the word but does not do what it says is like a man who looks at his face in a mirror and, after looking at himself, goes away and immediately forgets what he looks like. But the man who looks intently into the perfect law that gives freedom, and continues to do this, not forgetting what he has heard, but doing it — he will be blessed in what he does.

James 1:22–25

©1982 Copley News Service

. . . that by his death he might destroy him who holds the power
of death — that is the devil. Hebrews 2:14b

THE POPULATION EXPLOSION MYTH

Key Question: Doesn't everybody agree that the world is too crowded?

Setting: Student assembly at East High School

As the auditorium began to fill, the noise of casual conversation gradually became a roar. Looking out from the side of the stage, David Sheffield could see the expressions on the faces of the high school students who were moving to their assigned seats. He identified with these young adults who were enthusiastic and full of energy. The room pulsated with life.

One of three people on stage approached the lectern and an expectant hush settled on the crowd. The sudden silence was electrifying. The students had come for a good show. Anticipation and tension filled the air. The principal introduced the first speaker of the afternoon: Ms. Sheila Turner, representative of Planned Population, would be lecturing on "The Population Explosion Crisis."

Ms. Turner was greeted with enthusiastic applause. As she walked to the microphone, inevitable visual comparisons were being made between her and the next speaker. Ms. Turner was both strikingly beautiful and well dressed. Her tailored gray business suit seemed to give her credibility before she even spoke. Several young men made their impressions of her loud enough to be heard. She gave a glance, smiled at her notes, but otherwise ignored them.

It was immediately apparent that her verbal skills matched her visual qualifications. Ms. Turner commanded the audience with her movements and words. She began with a declaration that we are entering a new era of sexual liberation, intellectual humanism, and family planning responsibilities. As she continued, each reference to sexuality brought scattered applause. As the students leaned forward in attentiveness, Ms. Turner came to her main point: One of the darkest clouds on their bright future was the crisis of population explosion. She then proceeded to lead her audience through a well-orchestrated series of statistics and celebrity quotes, forcefully building a case for the actions that must be taken to curb this population crisis. The students expressed their enthusiasm for her message. Logical conclusions were driven home. There were hard decisions to be made. Abortion, infanticide, and euthanasia needed to be seriously considered as part of a positive solution to the crisis. The students agreed. She pressed her time to the limit plus an extra ten minutes, which meant the other speaker would only be allowed twenty minutes. Given the seemingly invincible strength of her arguments, the difference in amount of time mattered little to anyone but the other speaker.

As Ms. Turner returned to her seat, the students gave her a prolonged standing ovation. Boys were whistling. Girls were cheering. Even kids who hadn't listened thought she looked good enough to be applauded. She was clearly enjoying her overwhelming success.

The principal reluctantly approached the podium, hesitant to intrude on the glory of the previous speaker. He quickly introduced Pastor David Sheffield, who would be addressing the same subject under the title, "Is Population Growth Really a Crisis?"

The audience was suddenly restless, bored. They had already heard the answer. Besides, they were quite sure this religious type couldn't even relate to their world. He felt their resistance. He considered his disadvantage. Not only was his audience prejudiced, there were also strict limits on his own freedom of speech. The principal had made the rules clear: "No religious proselytizing or morals from a Judeo-Christian perspective are to be presented." This in spite of Ms. Turner's repeated comments about narrow-minded religious people who want to interfere with the freedoms of others.

Concerted efforts had been made to keep this from being a two-sided presentation in the first place. Parents and teachers, orchestrated by Ms. Turner and her staff, had vigorously resisted any opposing perspective. The principal had held firm only because the assembly was sponsored by the student government. The president, Mike Jenkins, had respectfully insisted on equal time for another point of view. He was known in school for his vocal Christian faith. If there was any humiliation over this debate, Mike would be the recipient.

No one in the room knew this better than Mike. As he listened to "his" speaker being introduced, Mike felt terribly alone. He couldn't help but wonder if he had made a big mistake. He could hear the whispered comments behind his back. Students in front of him kept turning and looking at him. Mike hoped the emotions running laps around his heart weren't showing all over his face.

David moved to center stage and began by thanking Mike for his invitation. The students were unimpressed with his physical appearance. In their minds, a sports coat and tie didn't compare favorably with the flash of Ms. Turner's outfit. They also suspected what he represented. David continued by expressing his gratitude to the principal for his openness in allowing a contrary opinion to be presented in spite of community opposition. The principal nodded.

David lifted the microphone from the stand. New strength flowed through him. He sensed God's presence. His whole body took on the appearance of someone completely concentrated on his purpose. He began to speak quietly and confidently, purposefully striding back and forth across the stage.

"According to Ms. Turner, if you line up the Chinese people four abreast and march them into the ocean, at the current population growth rate, there would be an endless stream of Chinese people marching into the sea. . . .

"Population explosion bomb posters, magazine articles, television programs, and even billboards send a steady onslaught of messages. After a while they trigger mental neon signs announcing that each new person born is an intrusion and a burden to an already overcrowded global community. . . .

"When people accept this perspective as the basis from which to make decisions, they almost have to agree that the following conclusions are both logical and desirable: Quoting Ms. Turner, 'To preserve an already overburdened human population not only do we need to stem current population growth, but reduce it. As a result of research by four hundred prominent scientists, intellectuals, and government authorities, it has been determined that the earth can only realistically accommodate 2.5 billion people. Therefore, for the sake of future generations, we must reduce current population by fifty percent, and we recommend doing so through abortion, infanticide, euthanasia, starvation, and war.'"

A male voice in the back spoke up, "You got that right!" Others nodded and murmured their agreement. This was familiar territory.

David continued, "This mentality, with its supporting 'facts' has permeated our entire society. It is accepted as truth. But, during these next minutes I will prove beyond a reasonable doubt that it is totally false! And any of you who accept these 'facts' have been seriously misled!"

There was a momentary silence as the statement took hold. Then came the jeers and the hisses. The audience was sure this preacher had just sealed his fate. As David continued he moved closer to the audience. Now he had their complete attention. They didn't want to miss this. They sensed a trap was closing, but they didn't realize who was going to end up getting "caught."

The tone in David's voice abruptly changed. His tone became direct, but friendly. He smiled and said:

"Let's have a little exam to see how well your school and the media have taught you geographical statistics and population growth facts. If we assume all the people of the world (slightly over 5 billion) could gather together in one group, how much area of the world do you think they would cover?"

David's movement brought him close to the bleachers and he stuck the microphone in front of a big, tough kid sporting a letter jacket and a baseball cap turned sideways. "I think they'd cover the Northern Hemisphere," the boy blurted out. Another youth next to him said, "No, just the North American continent."

As he stepped back from them, David said, "What if I tell you that they could all stand together, with a little elbow room . . . (he paused for what seemed to the kids like an eternity) . . . within the city of Jacksonville, Florida."

There was shock and disbelief among the students. The student David had challenged a moment ago was adamant. "No way," he said. David's point would have to be proved. He came back to the bleachers and asked a row of ten students to stand together in a group. Then, he continued, "Now, let's assume that the average student here is two feet wide at the shoulders and two feet deep at the chest. That's four square feet, right? You can see we are being very generous. Now, who out there can tell me how many total square feet we'd need to stand 5 billion people in this way?"

As he waited for an answer, he invited the group of students to sit back down. A girl from the fifth row said quietly, "Twenty billion."

David responded, "Right, 20 billion square feet. Now, how many square feet in a square mile?" No one seemed to know, so he proceeded, "There are 27,878,400 square feet in a square mile. So how many square miles will be required to hold the total world population? That size crowd would cover 718 square miles . . . and Jacksonville, Florida covers 759.6 square miles.

"Here's another example. Let's assume that the average person in the world is six feet tall and two feet wide at the shoulders, and we're going to have a global neighborhood slumber party for all 5 billion people in the world. All, that is, except for this kid right here who snores a lot. (David pointed out a boy who was obviously popular and easy going. He confirmed his character by immediately standing and taking a bow as his schoolmates laughed.) How large a space do you think we would need for this? . . . We can all fit within this county.

"Or how about this one? Let's assume that we can put everyone in the world into families of four. We'll give each family a three bedroom house on a 50-foot by 100-foot lot, with a nice front yard and room for a garden in the back yard. Sounds pretty suburban, right? How much land will we need? Would we have to subdivide the United States? Well, the fact is that we could all fit in the state of Texas, with some space left over for the cowboys and oil wells. . . .

"But, since a suburban lot is really kind of cramped, let's put that family of four on an acre of land. I grew up in a family of eight and we lived on an acre lot in rural Illinois. There was plenty of room for a ball game during the day and 'hide and seek' at night. My family canned over nine hundred pints of fruit and vegetables every year, picked from our garden. Besides that, we ate out of it, and still had plenty to share with our neighbors. The entire world population divided into families of four, given one acre each, could fit within the nation of Australia.

"And, for the real die-hards who like the idea of each person having their own personal space, we could give everyone in the world an acre of land, and using the population projections through the year 2010, could put everyone in the world, with their own acre of land, on the continent of Africa—and still have some room left over for the wild animals. Now remember, this would leave the entire North and South American continents, Australia, Europe, the Middle East, and the huge Asian continent which includes China, India, and Russia."

David paused to let all this sink in. The students were looking at each other in amazement and new understanding. David continued, "We do not deny that there are places in the world where it *appears* that the very numbers of people are the problem, but when we look at the other factors involved we discover that the real crisis isn't a population growth problem. Rather, it is an attitude problem involving economics, politics, religion, and very basic human characteristics.

"Frankly, we live in a nation filled with shame. Entire organizations twist statistics and manipulate people's emotions to make a case for solving problems at the expense of the innocent, helpless, and naive. I have no ill intent toward these people because they also are a part of God's beautiful creation. But I CANNOT and WILL NOT allow their ignorance or diabolic perspective to go unchallenged!"

As he made this closing statement, David carefully replaced the microphone in its stand. He then turned and walked back to his seat. There was a stunned silence.

David glanced over at Ms. Turner who looked embarrassed and perturbed. He couldn't help but think that this would not be his last encounter with Planned Population.

Comment

The Christian debater in this assembly was severely limited. He was prevented from dealing with the central issue: the conclusions being drawn by his opponent based on the supposed population explosion crisis. But, by raising doubts about the "facts" being used, he has started to create questions about the conclusions. The audience hasn't changed sides, but they're not sure if what they have been taking for granted is accurate.

Often, a debate creates more doubts than answers. This in itself can be a step in the right direction. Before a Christian perspective on issues will get any attention, the popular answers need to be exposed to the effects of a critical spotlight. Beliefs that are simply taken for granted may not seem so true in a new light.

The goal, however, must be to create more than doubts. The distortions and lies that are being exposed in this debate need to be pursued to their roots. In the context of a high school assembly this process may only get started. But whenever possible, the doubts must be followed up with further convincing facts that will help people turn away from "death-style" answers.

In the News

Ben J. Wattenberg, a demographic analyst at the conservative American Enterprise Institute in Washington, warns that the U.S. and other Western nations are not producing babies fast enough.

Wattenberg believes the Government should encourage births with cash bonuses of up to $2,000 annually for each child 16 and under, tax deductions for day-care costs and forgiveness of educational loans in the case of graduates with babies.

Conservative politicians and ideologues are supporting Wattenberg's ideas. TV Evangelist Pat Robertson argues that the U.S. could be "committing genetic suicide." He preaches that "depopulation of the West threatens the power of Western industrialized democracies." Republican congressman Jack Kemp of New York seconds Wattenberg's call for birth incentives, saying "People are not a drain on our resources; they are our greatest resource."

Wattenberg, 53, the father of four children, claims, "What I am pushing is a value system that develops economic prosperity and political freedom." A former speechwriter for Lyndon Johnson and campaign adviser to Hubert Humphrey, Wattenberg describes himself as a centrist Democrat who supports liberal immigration policies. Nevertheless, his maverick views have won him a reputation as the conservatives' favorite liberal.

Source: Bowen, Ezra. "Battling over Birth Policy." *Time,* August 24, 1987, p. 58.

ᵢᵃ ᵢᵃ ᵢᵃ

Examples of Proposed People Measures to Reduce U.S. Fertility

Social Constraints

- Restructure family
  a) Postpone or avoid marriage
  b) Alter image of ideal family size

- Compulsory education of children

- Encourage increased homosexuality

- Educate for family limitation

- Fertility control agents in water supply

- Encourage women to work

Economic Deterrents/Incentives

- Substantial marriage tax

- Child Tax

- Tax married more than single

- Remove parents tax exemption

- Additional taxes on parents with more than 1 or 2 children in school

Social Controls
- Compulsory abortion of out-of-wedlock pregnancies

- Compulsory sterilization of all who have two children except for a few who would be allowed three

- Confine childbearing to only a limited number of adults

Measures Predicated on Existing Motivation to Prevent Unwanted Pregnancies

- Payments to encourage sterilization

- Payments to encourage contraception

- Payments to encourage abortion

- Abortion and sterilization on demand

Source: Frederick S. Jaffe. "Activities Relevant to the Study of Population Policy for the U.S." March 11, 1969. (The author was Vice-president of Planned Parenthood — World Population.)

&. &. &.

"A Five-Year Plan: 1976–1980 for the Federation," a manifesto adopted by the membership of the Planned Parenthood Federation of America on Oct. 22, 1975, in Seattle, gives perhaps the most compact presentation of the organization's goals and activities. The preamble to this document declares:

Universal reproductive freedom is a most essential step, if not THE most essential step . . . to solve the most critical problems of hunger, deprivation and the hopelessness of poverty, as well as the deterioration of our water, land and air.

This "universal reproductive freedom," hailed as the panacea for all mankind's ills, is later defined as "making . . . contraception, abortion and sterilization available and fully accessible to all."

Showering these young people with contraceptives and provocative literature results in a tremendous peer pressure that makes teen-agers who do not engage in sex feel abnormal. Through these tactics Planned Parenthood is creating a demand . . . for its own services. Planned Parenthood-style sex-education programs have been found to be ineffective in curbing the two social problems they are ostensibly aimed at eliminating: teen-age pregnancy and venereal disease.

Venereal disease is actually found to increase among children exposed to these programs, because the birth-control pill, the most widely prescribed contraceptive for teen-agers, does nothing to prevent V.D. and, in fact, is said to increase the possibility of contracting it. The apparent reason for these negative results is that the programs stimulate much higher rates of sexual activity among the children subject to them. Yet whenever the problems of teen-age pregnancy or V.D. are discussed, the only solution seems to be more of the same.

Source: Schwartz, Michael C. "Bringing the Sexual Revolution Home: Planned Parenthood's 'Five-Year Plan.'" *America,* February 18, 1978, p. 114–16.

ءæ ءæ ءæ

Through the year 1963, the Planned Parenthood Federation of America—which now is rabidly pro-abortion—distributed a pamphlet which said of abortion, in part: "It kills the life of a baby after it has begun."

So, just 10 years before the Supreme Court declared the murder of unborn babies to be "legal," the PPFA was, ironically, pro-life as regards the unborn baby.

There was even a time when the medical profession officially opposed abortion. On May 3, 1859, in the city of Louisville, Kentucky, the American Medical Association, at its 12th annual convention, unanimously approved a report by its Committee On Criminal Abortion.

Deploring the "general demoralization" occurring in our society, this report cited as one example of this decline "a widespread popular ignorance of the true character of the crime [abortion]—a belief, even among mothers themselves, that the fetus is not alive till after the period of quickening."

Calling the child before birth "a living being," this report noted, critically: "With strange inconsistency, the law fully acknowledges the fetus in utero and its inherent rights."

Pointing out that doctors were "the physical guardians of women" and "their offspring in utero," this report said what was at stake in the abortion issue was "life or death — the life or death of thousands [of unborn babies — J.L.] — and it depends, almost wholly, upon ourselves."

Source: Lofton, John. "And on the Tree of Life. . . ." *Washington Times,* July 28, 1989.

᠃᠃ ᠃᠃ ᠃᠃

An Auckland teenager says a doctor began inducing an abortion on her without her knowledge at the city's main abortion centre.

The doctor inserted a pessary (soft waxy tablet) to dilate her cervix but told her he was performing a Pap smear, she said.

A staff member at the Epsom Day Hospital discovered the abortion was being induced and told the doctor to stop because the woman was undecided about it.

"The doctor removed the pessary and said, 'Your sort can never make up their mind.'"

"I was told I would probably have a miscarriage, but I never returned to the hospital again after another doctor told me there was every chance I could have a healthy baby," she said.

Source: "Abortion Starts Without Consent." *Sunday Star* (New Zealand), November 9, 1988.

᠃᠃ ᠃᠃ ᠃᠃

As our population grows by 3 million a year, where will the new families go? Back to the cities, or into suburban high-rises?

Bill Levitt says no; he envisions new cities, of 50,000 to a quarter-million population, not bedroom communities or satellites or one-company towns but "primary employment towns" — balanced centers of several industries and varied housing, with schools and cultural amenities—located in what are now rural areas.

One day Congress will wake up and provide incentives to help rural county governments attract groups of core businesses. No billions needed; just a sense of the dispersed, mid-sized urban future and the enthusiasm to facilitate it.

Look out your airplane window sometime; there's plenty of room down there.

With the new management technology and the old human need to breathe free, there's no longer a need to crowd together.

Source: Safire, William. "'Future City' Could Resolve Overcrowding." *Daily Courier-News* (Elgin, IL), September 28, 1989.

ฬ ฬ ฬ

Forget the "echo boom"—the idea that the postwar baby boomers are causing a second boom by filling bassinets of their own. Despite much popular speculation that the population is soaring, for nearly a decade the fertility rate in the U.S. has remained at a low of 1.8 births per woman—below the rate needed to replace the parents' generation, says Charles Westoff, the director of the Office of Population Research at Princeton. The only thing that will keep America's population from shrinking, as those of most European countries have done, he writes in *Science,* is immigration.

Only 14 years ago, when Westoff was the executive director of the Commission on Population Growth and the American Future, the commission sighed with relief when the fertility rate began to subside after attaining a peak of 3.8 births per woman. Now, he says, "it is not beyond imagination that the next population commission will be pondering inducements to marriage and childbearing."

"Low fertility is more or less here to stay," Westoff believes, since it reflects not only more effective contraception but also "changes in the status of women that do not seem reversible." Greater economic independence and new mores have led more women than ever before to postpone marriage and childbirth. In 1960 only 28 per cent of women between the ages of 20 and 24 had never married; in 1985 that number was 58.5 per cent. And the mean age for a woman's first birth is projected to be 25.3 by about 1991, nearly three years older than it was 20 years ago.

In 1982 Catholic women reported an average of 1.96 children, compared with 1.92 for Protestant women and 1.79 for Jewish women.

Source: Boxer, Sarah, ed. "Up Front: 'The Notion that We've Entered a Second Baby Boom is a Bust.'" *Discover*, January 1987, p. 8.

Key Quotations

The smiles of heaven can never be expected on a nation that disregards the eternal rules of order and right which heaven itself has ordained.

George Washington

We cannot diminish the value of one category of human life — the unborn — without diminishing the value of all human life . . . there is no cause more important.

Ronald Reagan

Then God said, "Let us make man in our image, in our likeness, and let them rule over the fish of the sea and the birds of the air, over the livestock, over all the earth, and over all the creatures that move along the ground." So God created man in his own image, in the image of

God he created him; male and female he created them. God blessed them and said to them, "Be fruitful and increase in number; fill the earth and subdue it. Rule over the fish of the sea and the birds of the air and over every living creature that moves on the ground."

Genesis 1:26–28

THE WORLD
FOOD SHORTAGE MYTH

Key Question: Aren't there too many people to feed?

Setting: An evening public forum at East High School

The atmosphere in the gym was quite different from the assembly two weeks before. Attendance on this night was by interest only, but interest was obviously high. There were more seats filled, but the crowd was quieter. Students, parents, and others from the community had responded to the invitation for a second debate on population issues.

Mike Jenkins had been asked to serve as moderator. He introduced himself as the student body president and thanked the audience for their attendance. Next, he introduced each of the speakers for the night: Pastor David Sheffield, who had been invited back to defend some of the ideas he expressed in his previous debate, and Mr. James Walker from the National Planned Population headquarters, who was taking Ms. Turner's place representing the concerns of Planned Population.

The presentation began with a summary by Pastor Sheffield of his position. Using several of the same illustrations that had now become familiar around school, David again expressed his argument that population growth figures cannot be used as a valid reason for promoting euthanasia, abortion, and other radical population control measures.

Almost interrupting David's last words, Mr. Walker was on his feet, red faced and scowling. His opening comments were really intimidating shouts, "So what? What have you solved by proving that the earth has enough space for everyone? You haven't addressed the real problems at all. The world situation needs radical solutions, not your fundamentalist propaganda!"

On cue, the lights dimmed and a large video screen came to life. The opening scenes transported the audience out of their comfortable environment and into a place of human suffering. The video was a documentary of a tour to an overcrowded refugee camp in a poverty-stricken nation.

The cameras had no pity. The screen was filled with eyes that looked into the viewer's soul. Expressionless faces of skin and bone caused many to look away. As always, it was the children who drew attention, emotions, tears. Repeatedly, the film crew was surrounded by children, begging in broken English for bread. Their voices and gestures were filled with despair. The reporter pointed out that, for these, life had been reduced to nothing but mere survival—doing anything to live another day. Human value measured in bread. The video was so graphic that quiet sobbing could be heard. There was a general restlessness in the crowd and several people left the room, overwhelmed by these scenes of suffering.

A glimpse of the gate in the background raised hopes that the video was almost over. One last hut to pass by. In the shade sat a woman with three small children. They were huddled on the ground, giving no sign that they were being watched. The camera zoomed into the pitiful, empty stares of the children. Ever-present flies buzzed about. Someone in the crowd voiced everyone's question, "How can they live like that?"

The camera then shifted to the woman's face. How could there be such sadness without tears? Her eyes were dry and lifeless. When the picture became unbearable, the camera slowly dropped its focus down the woman's body to an empty breast where a baby with an abnormally large belly was lying quietly in her arms. Eyes staring; no movement . . . not even breathing. The realization broke like a wave of agony over the audience. The child was dead. The scene faded to hopeless black.

As the lights came back up, Mr. Walker was ready. His challenge was biting: "How can anyone question the crisis of food shortage? Your point that the population can fit in the world is of little comfort if the millions of people can't be fed." He turned to David Sheffield, sized up his athletic frame, and gave his final point of sarcastic confrontation: "It's obvious that you haven't experienced any food shortage. Perhaps I could arrange a trip for you to deliver your 'food shortage myth' concept personally to that mother in the video."

As he returned to his seat, it was clear that he considered his challenge unanswerable. Emotions in the room were at a peak. The audience clearly found Mr. Walker's presentation compelling. They expected Pastor Sheffield to simply agree and end the agony of tension.

David paused for a moment of prayer, then moved to the microphone. He began, "That was one of the most powerful statements of human tragedy I have ever seen. I sincerely hope it will help us do much more than just feel sorry for those who are suffering. The challenge of solving these problems may even become a lifetime work for some of us here tonight."

Then, turning toward Mr. Walker, he said, "You, sir, have a good grasp of the terrible problems created by food shortages in some parts of the world. Would you now care to equally address the problems associated with tremendous food surpluses in other parts of the world?" David returned to his seat.

The audience followed the direction of David's question and noted the stunned embarrassment on Mr. Walker's face. There was an awkward moment of silence. The crowd wondered who would speak first. David mercifully broke the silence by returning to the lectern with his presentation:

"Let's begin addressing the world food surplus problems from the close vantage point of our own country. We pay our farmers in America billions of dollars each year to not grow grain. Please understand, I did not say millions, but billions with a capital "B." In fact, in 1984, we paid our farmers 36 billion dollars because of huge carry-over stocks from previous years.

"Now, at $2.00 a bushel for corn, which is its current market price, we could purchase 18 billion bushels of corn. If we wanted to provide people with a well-balanced diet, we would need to include soybeans, wheat, and oats. That would create a more nutritious diet than most Americans eat. If we assume an average price of $3.00 a bushel for these mixed items, we would have available 12 billion bushels of grain. If I were to tell you we could feed all the people who starved to death in the world last year (13 million including that family we just saw recorded in the video) with a well-balanced diet for the entire year with those 12 billion bushels of grain, would you be surprised? What if I told you we could feed ten times as many people as starved to death (130 million) for a full year with that grain? How many farmers do you think would take me seriously if I told them we could feed ten times more than that with just what we paid them to not grow crops last year? Actually, it's that and more. We can easily feed one-quarter of the world's population with a well-balanced diet (more nutritious than most Americans eat) with just what we pay our farmers to not grow each year.

"The video we saw tonight could be an effective tool to motivate us to help alleviate the suffering of these people and work at future solutions. Instead, it is being used as a tool to convince us that these people, or others like them, are a burden in our world and don't really deserve to live. The real problem is not their need, but our abundance of grain and lack of compassion. The fact is that we can feed the entire world's population with a well-balanced, nutritious diet from just ten midwestern states: Michigan, Ohio, Indiana, Illinois, Missouri, Iowa, Wisconsin, Minnesota, Kansas, and Nebraska.

"And there are other signs of hope. In the last forty years, crop yields have increased four hundred percent while acreage use has consistently shrunk to less than three percent of currently available land. And the agricultural revolution has just begun. Computer advances are already being applied to all areas of agriculture. They monitor animals and crops, ventilate grain, control irrigation, and feed livestock. Gene manipulation is producing bigger, healthier and more productive livestock, grains, fruits, and vegetables. Manipulated microbes to neutralize contaminant chemicals, fight crop diseases, fertilize the soil, and even prevent plant freezing are already available. You can check the library yourself for a book by the Kiplinger Staff entitled, *The New American Boom,* written in 1986.

"The mass application of those advances just mentioned will bring a revolution to farming as great as the introduction and widespread use of powered machinery. This application of technology is already going forward in developed countries. Imagine what can take place when power machinery is made available to Third World countries on a mass scale along with this high technology!

"But, even more critical than providing people with the necessary food to survive year after year, is the practical application of Abraham Lincoln's wise adage, 'I'd rather teach a man to fish than give a man a fish.' In other words, we need to invest in people rather than subsidize poverty. For example, we could easily provide these desperately needy people with inexpensive self-contained growing units which are three feet high and two feet in diameter. Twenty of these units can feed a family of four year round, and because the water condenses at the top and is recycled, the only ongoing necessity would be nutrient packets with seeds shipped year by year. Even inexpensive solar cooking units can be provided to preserve the depleting timber resources caused by firewood usage.

"Beyond surpluses, another real problem behind food shortage is the desperate political situation in many places. Sometimes, food can't even be sent to starving people. At other times, killing people by starvation seems the intention of some governments. For instance, look at Cambodia, where the infamous 'killing fields' have been documented. The Communist Khmer Rouge relocated the entire rural population in the middle of their harvest into urban communities, and moved the urban people to undeveloped areas in the country. The same well-publicized plight has afflicted the people of Ethiopia.

"Another classic example is recorded in the excellent documentary, *Harvest of Despair,* about the experiences of farmers in the Ukraine. People who had just gathered a record harvest in the breadbasket of the Soviet Union in the 1930s in sheer disbelief saw the Soviet army encircle the region, confiscate the grain, and ruthlessly pillage communities while millions of people starved to death to accommodate Stalin's suppression of the Ukrainian nationalist spirit.

"Make no mistake: We do have regional food shortages around the globe. But we also have an even greater world compassion crisis. We, who happen to be among those who have the most, are once again brought face to face with that age-old question a man named Cain tried to use to avoid responsibility before God, 'Am I my brother's keeper?'"

There was scattered applause as Pastor Sheffield sat down. There was a great feeling of concern and a desire to know more. As Mike Jenkins was thanking everyone for their participation, Mr. Walker walked over to David, heatedly informed him that he was ignorant and dangerous, then abruptly left. David and others gathered in small groups for quite a while discussing what actions they would take to alleviate needless suffering and starvation.

Comment

This debate was a not-so-subtle clash between two answers to the very real problems of hunger and abundance. One answer is to find a way to feed the hungry. The other is to find a way to eliminate the hungry. The first answer is compassionate; the second is selfish. The first answer implies that those who have the surplus also have a moral responsibility to help those who don't. The second answer, which uses hunger as a justification for radical population control, actually appeals to our sense of pity while seeking to condone human extermination. Any answer that preserves our affluence and wastefulness at the price of other lives must be challenged. Likewise, answers that deny the duties God has given the human race to be their brothers' keepers must also be rejected.

In the News

Science watchers are already talking about a "second green revolution" and predicting that it will be more dramatic than the original "green revolution"—the one that resulted from the introduction of high-yield strains of rice and wheat in the 1960s. But coming close behind the second green revolution is yet another agricultural breakthrough, more spectacular than pest-resistant tomatoes or farmers irrigating their fields with salt water.

Scientists are working on research that increases the likelihood of people being able to grow food without farms. It is a biotechnological development much closer to being realized than many that are now being worked for and invested in, such as, for example, an AIDS vaccine.

Scientists can now take a slice from a leaf of a tree and put it into a medium of hormones and nutrients that cause it to grow into a callus, a mound of undifferentiated cells. A plant callus is not in itself a particularly inspiring sight — it looks a little like a helping of green mashed potatoes — but it has tremendous potential because every single cell in the callus has the genetic information to become a whole plant. In the proper medium, the callus can produce a hundred — or a million — copies of a single tree.

Source: Anderson, Walter Truett. "Without Farms: The Biotech Revolution in Agriculture." *The Futurist*, January-February 1990. pp.16–18.

ða ða ða

American agriculture is a production miracle. Less than 2 percent of the U.S. population feeds the American people better and at a lower cost as a percentage of income than do the farmers and ranchers in any other country in the world. To do this requires only 60 percent of agriculture's production capability, leaving 40 percent available for other uses.

Perhaps the best — indeed, the only — way to meet this challenge of abundance is to build commercial export markets around the world, country by country. That was done in the late 1950s and throughout the 1960s. The result was strong worldwide demand, followed by good prices in the marketplace.

The drop in U.S. agricultural exports from $43.8 billion in 1981 to $26.3 billion in 1986 is estimated to have cost the U.S. economy $122 billion and tens of thousands of jobs.

The United States took South Korea, Taiwan, Spain, Mexico, and others from bare-subsistence economies and minimum food imports to billion-dollar markets for U.S. agriculture.

Korea, an economic basket case in 1961 with per capita income of $83, now boasts per capita income above $2,200 a year. Twenty-five years of food aid to Korea cost the United States less than it now gets back in a single year of sales to Koreans. And there are many more Korea-type areas out there.

Source: Freeman, Orville L. "America's Agricultural Future." *The Futurist,* September-October 1987. (Orville Freeman is a former U.S. Secretary of Agriculture and is currently president and chief executive officer of the Agricultural Council of America.)

≈ ≈ ≈

Most likely your turn-of-the-century dinner will look the same as it does now. But scratch below the surface and you'll find a wealth of hidden changes. Right now, in food-technology labs around the country, researchers are tinkering with foods we've been eating for years. With test-tube breeding techniques they are creating improved fruits and vegetables. They are combining ingredients in novel ways to develop harmless forms of fats. They are designing edible food packaging to extend the shelf life of perishable goods.

Such advances are not so far away from your local supermarket.

Source: "Meals for the Millennium." *Discover,* November 1988.

≈ ≈ ≈

When he formulated his theory, Malthus ignored the ingenuity of man. But the human population is not a mathematical monster, and we are not all starving next year.

Malthus and his ghost are wrong in asserting that population growth rules out a rising standard of living.

The Club of Rome at least packaged its scare-mongering in a scientific-looking computer study done at MIT, which dutifully declared: "The limits to growth on our planet will be reached sometime within the next one hundred years."

As early as 1967, studies by Simon Kuznets had shown that even rapid population growth was no impediment to rapid economic development, as Thailand, Mexico, Panama, Ecuador, and Jordan illustrate. Blaming poverty on population density will not work either: Julian Simon found high density to be associated with high living standards.

His [Simon's] basic idea is that, in the long run, man produces more than he consumes.

With human beings, scarcity is the mother of abundance. In India between 1951 and 1971, cultivated land was increased by 20 percent. Even now, India is not densely populated. Measured by the number of persons per acre of arable land, Japan and Taiwan—hardly examples of starving populations—are about five times as densely populated. Everyone has heard of Holland's reclamation of land from the sea, and Israel furnishes an instructive example for those who face the barren desert.

Both the prophets of doom and the somber pessimists have foundered on the rocks of scientific research. Population growth does not impede but actually contributes to man's rise from poverty and hardship. The more people there are, free to exploit their own and the earth's resources, the easier it is to feed them.

Source: Percival, Ray. "Malthus and His Ghost." *National Review*, August 18, 1989.

ia ia ia

Coming soon: a vast increase in American agricultural productivity, far more than enough to offset losses of cropland to erosion, development and water salinity or scarcity.

This surge in productivity will be the result of accelerated mechanization of farming and breakthroughs in genetic engineering. American farms—fewer, larger, employing fewer people, and using less water—will continue to produce more food than this country alone can consume. There will be surpluses aplenty for export, but the demand for this surplus will be unpredictable among countries that will also be experiencing productivity gains.

So commodity prices and consumer food prices will stay low, probably lagging the rate of inflation. The variety of foods—including some you may never have heard of—will be almost endless, and the quality will be excellent.

Whatever the problems faced by American agriculture, meeting demand won't be one of them. This will continue to be the best-fed country in the world. We'll still have enough to sell and give away abroad.

Source: Kiplinger Staff. *The New American Boom.* Washington, D.C.: The
Kiplinger Washington Editors, Inc., pp. 120, 129.

ﺵ ﺵ ﺵ

An innovative processing system developed by scientists at the University of Illinois could result in high-protein bakery products.

Researchers with the International Soybean Program (Intsoy) are producing an array of tasty, baked products made with 12 to 25 percent soy flour from the process. All of the products — from cakes and breads to cookies and pizza dough — contain 50 percent or more protein than counterparts made from only wheat or other cereal flours.

"The meal or cake produced from our process has about 50 percent protein and 5 percent oil," says Alvin Nelson, an Intsoy utilization program leader. "It is so nutritionally valuable that it really should be used for human food."

Nelson says the new soy flour does more than just increase the quantity of protein in baked goods. It also improves the quality of the protein by balancing the lysine and sulfur-bearing amino acid contents.

"When we put soy and wheat flours together, we get synergism," he says. "We end up with a protein quality slightly higher than for soy alone. But most importantly, it's much higher than for wheat alone."

Source: "Soy Flour Gives Baked Goods Protein Boost, Scientists Say." *The State Journal-Register* (Springfield, Illinois), November 24, 1988.

ﺵ ﺵ ﺵ

The drought that gripped North America in 1988 is being compared with the Dust Bowl of the 1930's — and with good reason. The news that the Mississippi River had reached its lowest level since record keeping began over a century ago was probably the most startling single measure of how dry the continent's agricultural heartland had become. This lack of rainfall is contributing to what almost certainly will become the steepest one-year drop in world grain stocks ever recorded.

The drought reduced the 1988 U.S. grain harvest by nearly 90,000,000 metric tons from 1987. With the damage to Canada's crop,

North American grain production is likely to be down by some 100,000,000 tons—over 25 percent. In China, which ranks a close second to the U.S. as a food producer, severe drought conditions easily could reduce the harvest by 10 percent, or 30,000,000 tons. *China Daily* described the drought in one province as the worst in 20 years, in another as the worst in a century. In addition, the USSR suffered a 15,000,000-ton drop in grain production.

Only once in recent decades has the world faced such a tight food situation—in 1972, when the Soviet Union decided to offset a crop shortfall by importing grain at the same time the U.S. was holding a record amount of land out of production.

[Author's note: Despite these gloomy predictions, our 1988 harvest gave enough grain not only to meet our domestic needs, but also to meet our export commitments.]

Source: Brown, Lester R. "The World Food Crisis." *USA Today,* March 1989. (Lester Brown is president of Worldwatch Institute, a Washington research organization, and former administrator of the U.S. Department of Agriculture's International Agricultural Development Service.)

Key Quotations

The choice before us is plain, Christ or chaos, conviction or compromise, discipline or disintegration. I am rather tired of hearing about our rights and privileges as American citizens. The time is come, it now is, when we ought to hear about the duties and responsibilities of our citizenship. America's future depends upon her accepting and demonstrating God's government.

Peter Marshall

For the Christian man to reason that God does not want him in politics because there are too many evil men in government is as insensitive as for a Christian doctor to turn his back on an epidemic because there are too many germs there.

Erwin W. Lutzer

The King will reply, "I tell you the truth, whatever you did for one of the least of these brothers of mine, you did for me."

Then he will say to those on his left, "Depart from me, you who are cursed, into the eternal fire prepared for the devil and his angels. For I was hungry and you gave me nothing to eat, I was thirsty and you gave me nothing to drink, I was a stranger and you did not invite me in, I needed clothes and you did not clothe me, I was sick and in prison and you did not look after me."

They also will answer, "Lord, when did we see you hungry or thirsty or a stranger or needing clothes or sick or in prison, and did not help you?"

He will reply, "I tell you the truth, whatever you did not do for one of the least of these, you did not do for me."

Then they will go away to eternal punishment, but the righteous to eternal life.

Matthew 25:40–46

F O U R

THE DISTRIBUTION INCAPABILITIES MYTH

Key Question: How can we get needed food from "here" to "there"?

Setting: A family experiences the personal side of the hunger solution.

P astor David Sheffield leaned back in his office chair and closed his eyes. Anyone passing by his open door might have thought he was praying. Actually, he was thinking. It was almost time to go home. Tomorrow would be a day off.

"Julie and the kids have sure been patient with my schedule lately. We need this time together without interruptions. The debates these last two weeks have taken up most of my energy, too. But I can't forget that my family is part of my calling. Winning public battles won't mean much if I lose those I love the most. Since what I'm fighting for is really true, it has to be just as true at home as it is on stage during a debate."

He sat forward, and as his eyes opened they settled on the photographs of his family, smiling at him. "I want to be the best husband and dad I can be," he thought. "But I do want them to understand and feel as

I do about this world and the God who made it for His purposes. . . ."
At this, David swivelled his office chair away from the desk toward the
picture window behind him. Outside, a light wind was blowing under a
bright, sunny afternoon. Leaves were waving, rooftops shimmering, and
cloud-waves were rolling across the sky. David's eyes looked beyond
these things. Someone walking by the door just then might have thought
Pastor Sheffield was lost in thought. Actually, he was now lost in a
prayer of praise to God for the wonder of life.

Savory smells and children's noises greeted David as he came in the
door from work. As she hugged him, Julie said, "Supper's almost ready.
Would you help get the troops lined up?"

"Judging from the aromas, we're in for a real treat! I'll get the
kids," said David. As he entered the family room, he noticed his children were captivated by something on T.V. It was a spot for a relief
agency asking for funds to send food to one of the areas in Africa struck
by famine. As usual, the pictures of suffering children were troubling.
"Dad's home!" he shouted. Three sets of arms were around him in a
moment. Jacob, eight years old, seemed to get taller every day. Katherine, all of six, seemed to ask a question with every breath. And Tim was
having fun just being a four-year-old.

The next moments were a flurry of hand washing, how-was-your-
days, and I-love-yous. Then Mom gave the signal and it was supper
time. The family held hands as David offered a brief prayer of thanks
for the food. As if on cue, Katherine initiated the discussion for the
evening. "Daddy, can I have some money?" she asked.

As he poured the milk, David answered, "Now, what does my favorite six-year-old need some money for?"

His daughter was quite serious. "I want to send some food to those
people who are starving in Africa that we just saw on T.V."

Jacob, always the adventurer, chimed in, "Yeah, and we could travel
over there and take it to them!"

Julie and David exchanged glances. They could both feel the obvious irony of the situation. David was touched by his daughter's tender-
heartedness. "Katherine, I think that's a wonderful idea," he said. Then,
as he took his next bite of food, he had an idea of his own.

After supper, David asked everyone to stay at the table. He began to
explain his plan. "I like Katherine's idea of sending some food to the

people in Africa. I also like Jacob's idea of taking it over there, but I'm afraid we can't afford that. However, I think it would be good for us to know what it is really like to be there."

It was Jacob who couldn't wait. "How can we do that without going there?" he asked.

"I'm glad you asked that," answered his father. "Here's a way I think will help. Why don't we send them some of our own food?"

"What will we eat, then?" asked Jacob.

"We won't eat anything, Jacob. That's how we'll know what it's like to be over there," David continued. "It would be easy for me to give Katherine money to send food over to Africa. But that won't help us understand how bad the problem can be. If we give some of our own food, and we go without, then we will feel what they feel."

Jacob was quick. "I know. Let's send them tonight's leftovers!"

"We could," said David, "but I have a different idea. Tomorrow, we are going to have a famine at the Sheffield house. We're not going to eat anything all day. We can drink water, but no food will be served. Then, what we save from not eating tomorrow we will send to Africa to help others. What do you think?"

Tim, who had been quiet up until now, suddenly spoke in an almost fearful whisper, "Will I look like one of those kids with the big tummies on T.V.?"

David wanted to laugh and cry at the same time. He took his little boy in his arms and said, "No, Tim, you'll look just like you are, but your tummy is going to hurt by tomorrow night." With supper still a recent memory, the family found it easy to agree to this new adventure. The rest of the evening was taken up with games and stories. No one mentioned food.

Tim was the family alarm clock on Saturdays. Each family member, in their own way, experienced the shock of the famine. For David, the early morning cup of coffee was a time-honored tradition. He wandered into the kitchen where Tim was seated at the counter, coloring. David had filled the pot with water and was reaching for the coffee when he heard his son say, "That's a no, no, Daddy." Julie was the only one who found delight in the arrangement. No cooking, dish washing, cleaning up for a whole day. . . a real vacation! Katherine greeted the reminder that there would be no breakfast with a shrug, but Jacob had to be informed several times that "food" meant anything and everything edible.

Between the mowing, the flowers, and the yard toys, the morning went quickly. Around noon, the family found themselves instinctively gathered once again in the kitchen, around a very bare table. Julie saved the day. "Let's go somewhere together this afternoon," she offered.

Jacob began suggesting various fast-food restaurants. He had a rationale. "We wouldn't be eating our food there. . . ."

They settled on bowling instead. The next several hours did go quickly, though everyone agreed that they had never realized bowling alleys were so filled with the scent of food. After a walk in the park, they started home. All three of the kids reported they were hungry. Conversation became food-centered. Favorite foods and restaurants were compared. The anticipation of the next morning's breakfast was on everyone's mind. But as food filled their thoughts, the emptiness of their stomachs grew. Tim cried softly once or twice. Katherine said she wished she hadn't had this great idea. Jacob was silent and stoic with his suffering.

Waiting for them on the front porch at home was Mike Jenkins, David's high school friend. He wanted to tell David his parents had agreed to let him travel to a science convention David had been invited to attend the following week. They asked him in, and told him about their ongoing family adventure. Mike was very interested. Everyone except Jacob was enjoying telling their hunger stories. When he finally did speak, he was angry. The pain in his belly had gotten his mind moving. He was experiencing some questions he had never had before.

"I don't see why we should have to be hungry to feed those people. Why doesn't God feed them?" said Jacob in a clipped, frustrated tone of voice.

David had prayed there would be an opportunity like this. Now that it was here, he wasn't so sure he had the right answer. He silently asked God to give him the words.

"Jacob, I'm so glad you asked that question. Every Christian ought to ask himself that question. We also should know the answer, son. God does love those people, and He has already provided all the food those people need, and the wisdom to help them grow their own, besides. The thing is, though, that He stored most of this food in our country and a few others. He has trusted us to make sure they get it. We probably don't have to go hungry to feed other people, though we should be willing to if they are worse off than we are.

"Jacob, you suggested last night that we send the people in Africa our leftovers. You were right. That's what I've been trying to tell anyone who will listen. We can feed the world with our leftovers!

"I know that doesn't take away the hungry feelings you're having right now, but I hope we will remember these hurts in our stomachs when we hear about famine and hungry people. Some places in the world, people feel the way we're feeling all the time."

Mike jumped in with a question.

"That reminds me of something I've been wondering about, Pastor David. Even if our country decided to give away all this extra food, how could we ever possibly get it to the people who need it so badly? It seems like the cost of the transportation might be the biggest problem of all."

"That's a great question, Mike," said David. "Some friends of mine have been working on that one for a while." He was amazed by the sharpness of the young man, and by how much he was maturing in his thinking and faith.

David continued, "We have recently sent a report to one of the committees in Congress in Washington D.C. asking them to take seriously some proposals that could not only help with the world hunger situation, but at the same time actually save us tax dollars. Here are a couple of examples, Mike. We've been cutting up excess supertankers for scrap in the Gulf of Louisiana. Those ships could be turned over to organizations that literally have tons of food stockpiled to help others, but lack the shipping they need. Or, how about the incredible amount of unused or outdated military equipment like ships, trucks, and planes that are rusting in storage. Much of this could be turned over to needy nations to use for food transport. Or, how about the suggestion that we give corporations tax benefits for donating space in their transports to carry grain to neighbors in need?

"Changing things may seem expensive, but we need to realize how much we are actually spending leaving things the way they are. Paying farmers not to grow grain and paying expensive storage costs for all this idled equipment is costing more than the stuff is worth. Sure it may be outdated by our standards. In most other countries, though, it would be welcomed as first class help!"

After a moment's reflection, David continued, "There's a common saying, Mike. 'Where there's a will, there's a way.' More often than not, it's true. The biggest problem behind crises like hunger is not a lack of ability to solve the problem, but a lack of caring enough to invest time and effort in the solution. When we enter into a war as a nation, we find ways to transport millions of tons of soldiers and supplies every day from one corner of the globe to the other. But when it comes to placing the same significance on the lives of starving children in Africa, we are failing. The rest of the world and God Himself are going to hold us accountable as a nation for what we fail to do. Don't forget, Mike, 'As you have done it to the least of these, you have done it to Me.'"

Katherine had been sitting quietly on her father's lap throughout the conversation. At the mention of the Bible verse she suddenly chimed in, "Jesus said that!"

The next morning was a family celebration. By a unanimous family vote it was decided that breakfast had been the best, the tastiest, most appreciated meal they had ever had together! And they walked together to the mailbox down the street so Katherine could mail the envelope with their food money to the hunger relief agency. And at church that morning, several people noticed how they seemed to stick a little closer together as a family.

Comment

Truth must make a difference at home as well as is in the debate setting. Children need to have the opportunity to understand both the facts and the feelings behind the problems they will have to face and solve. They also need to realize they can make a difference, even as children. So, a family chooses to experience hunger while they are providing others with food. And some unique suggestions for transportation are mentioned. Once again, the underlying problem has to do with our depth of caring. And training in caring starts at home.

In the News

Some ship graveyards are not exclusively repositories for old tonnage. Nearly half the 400 surviving Very Large and Ultra Large Crude Carrying supertankers built since 1970 are in lay-up fleets. These thousand-foot-long behemoths, the world's largest ships (some are more than three times the gross tonnage of the Queen Mary) were expected to revolutionize shipping when they were introduced. But that was before the sharp run-up of oil prices a few years ago drove down the demand for Middle East crude and large tankers to carry it. Some of these mammoth ships made only one voyage before entering lay-up. Although there is talk of a revival in shipping of crude oil, it will come too late for hundreds of supertankers that have already made their final voyage.

The largest number of idle ships in the U.S. belong to the government's National Defense Reserve Fleet (NDRF). The silent ranks of sealed freighters, tankers, troop transports, and other assorted craft are maintained in a state of readiness to be returned to service in five to 30 days. For most ships, the NDRF has been the last anchorage before being towed to the breaker's yard.

Source: Serig, Howard W. "Ship Graveyards." *Oceans Magazine,* January-February 1987.

           : : :

When the U.S. Navy looks at its aging ships, it sees rusting hulks destined for deep-sixing as missile-practice targets or artificial reefs. But Florida salvager William Justen sees a floating bounty of fluorescent-lighting fixtures, file cabinets, galley grills, aluminum bunks, mattresses and ice machines. Awarded a government contract last year to sink the USS Rankin for use as a reef off the Florida coast (to foster fish breeding), Justen was astounded to find the 44-year-old cargo carrier stocked with an inventory he estimated at $300,000. His whistle-blowing prompted a Defense Department investigation which concluded that the Navy had been "derelict" in the management of its surplus, allowing $17 million worth of salvageable goods to go under with old vessels.

Says Michigan Rep. William Broomfield, who is sponsoring legislation that would require the Navy to hire outside contractors to strip outmoded ships, "America may be the most wealthy nation in the world, but we are not so wealthy that we can afford to dump millions of dollars worth of sophisticated equipment to the bottom of the ocean floor."

One vessel alone, an Army dredge with extensive brass and copper on board, has a scrap value of $2.3 million.

Stung by bad publicity, the Navy plans to begin a pilot program in the fall to allow competitive bidding on its old ships by commerical salvagers. The inspector general's report has identified 64 old Navy ships with an estimated $40 million in usable equipment and goods.

Source: Clift, Eleanor. "Millions of Dollars on the Ocean Floor." *Newsweek,*
August 28, 1989, p. 30.

ᨠ ᨠ ᨠ

About five years ago, with the supertanker business in the doldrums, the Loews Corporation bought seven large tankers for about $5 million each—basically, their scrap value. Now those ships are carrying crude oil between the Middle East and the Gulf Coast for up to $3 million for just one voyage, operating at considerable profit. And if the Tisch family, which controls Loews, ever decides to sell them, it could get close to $40 million apiece.

Source: Salpukas, Agis. "For Supertankers, Super Profits." *The New York
Times* (Business Day), December 5, 1989.

ᨠ ᨠ ᨠ

Northwood had set in motion the greatest operation for the mobilization of civilian shipping in support of the Royal Navy undertaken since the Second World War. The Admiralty's STUFT cell was expanded. Commander Brian Goodson had held his posting as fleet logistics coordinator at Northwood for just a fortnight, yet it was now his responsibility to determine what ships the constantly expanding task force would need to maintain itself at sea. The list was awesome: storeships, tankers, dispatch vessels, hospital ships, repair ships, container ships — some fifty-four from civilian sources alone before the operation was complete, 500,000 tons in all. The Directorate of Naval Operations and Trade was expanded from one commander to four, and began the huge task of deciding which British ships were suitable to operate with the task force, then feeding these requirements to the government broker to supply through the charter market, or if necessary by requisition. About half of the ships for the South Atlantic were finally obtained by each method.

Source: Hastings, Max, and Simon Jenkins, *Battle for the Falklands* (New York: W. W. Norton and Company, 1983).

ن. ن. ن.

Malthus was wrong. Malthus posited that 1) Populations are limited by available food and subsistence resources, and 2) Populations always increase when the means of subsistence increases. There are food surpluses in many nations, and few have true famines. Most famines in recent decades are due to maldistribution of available food. Population growth is declining the quickest in societies with the greatest abundance of food/resources, the complete opposite of what Malthus claimed. In fact a better case can be made that an increase in population numbers will increase the availability of subsistence resources.

That's the argument of population heretic Julian Simon, who maintains in *The Ultimate Resource* (p. 51) that population growth has long-term benefits. He traces the variable rate of population growth in the past (ancient Egypt and Babylon were at one time as populous as in the 1960s) and shows how a rise in population is linked to a rise in inventions and innovation throughout history. He goes on to relate the historical and continuing drop in real costs for all resources including energy, and finally argues that the wealth of any society is in its population. People are not drains on the wealth and resources of a nation, but the producers of it. If a person produces more than they consume after society invests in their 20 years of childhood and education, then that person is a net gain — the more of them, the bigger the collective net gain.

In reality, properly cultivated by institutions that work, hefty populations are the engine of sustainable human advancement.

Source: Kelly, Kevin. "Apocalypse Juggernaut, goodbye." *Whole Earth Review,* Winter 1989, pp. 38–39.

ია. ია. ია.

Between 1980 and 1985 total population increased by 9 percent; between 2020 and 2025 the increase is projected to be only 4 percent.

What are the natural limits, and what do they imply? Malthus assumed that the limit was food, but agricultural progress during the past two centuries has thrown that assumption into question. Food surpluses exist in many nations, and even when famines do occur the cause is much less the absence of food than its maldistribution—which is often accentuated by politics and civil war, as in the Sudan.

Source: Keyfitz, Nathan. "The Growing Human Population." *Scientific American,* September 1989, p. 119.

ია. ია. ია.

Dese, Ethiopia—Comrade Chairman Mengistu Haile Mariam, the military ruler of Ethiopia, stares down from a mural in the center of this squalid town and issues a stern warning to everyone who passes by:

"We have to die for our motherland."

That is exactly what hundreds of thousands of Ethiopians have done during the 15 years that Mengistu's repressive Marxist regime has held power. But they haven't been noble, patriotic deaths.

Perhaps a million people—no one really knows how many—died slow, agonizing deaths from starvation during 1984–85.

This spring 4 million to 5 million face a similar fate.

Today, Ethiopia—one of the six poorest countries in the world—produces 20 percent less food than it did a decade ago, and Western analysts hold Mengistu responsible for most of that decline.

The other major cause of death has been Ethiopia's interminable civil wars in the north. Troops in Mengistu's press-ganged army of 300,000 have been dying at a rate of 10,000 to 20,000 per battle, according to Western diplomats.

No one volunteers for the army, people in Dese explain. "Recruiters" make nighttime sweeps through the streets and kidnap young men for service.

Those soldiers are then made to fight to keep Mengistu's empire from splitting apart.

Source: Witt, Howard. *Chicago Tribune,* April 12, 1990.

Key Quotations

To the kindly influence of Christianity we owe that degree of civil freedom and political and social happiness which mankind now enjoys. In proportion as the genuine effects of Christianity are diminished in any nation, either through unbelief, or the corruption of its doctrines, or the neglect of its institutions; in the same proportion will the people of the nation recede from the blessing of genuine freedom, and approximate the miseries of complete despotism.

Dr. Jedediah Morse (April 25, 1799)

"It is just as I said to Pharaoh: God has shown Pharaoh what he is about to do. Seven years of great abundance are coming throughout the land of Egypt, but seven years of famine will follow them. Then all the abundance in Egypt will be forgotten, and the famine will ravage the land. The abundance in the land will not be remembered, because the famine that follows it will be so severe. The reason the dream was given to Pharaoh in two forms is that the matter has been firmly decided by God, and God will do it soon.

"And now let Pharaoh look for a discerning and wise man and put him in charge of the land of Egypt. Let Pharaoh appoint commissioners over the land to take a fifth of the harvest of Egypt during the seven years of abundance. They should collect all the food of these good years that are coming and store up the grain under the authority of Pharaoh, to be kept in the cities for food. This food should be held in reserve for the country, to be used during the seven years of famine that will come upon Egypt, so that the country may not be ruined by the famine."

When Jacob learned that there was grain in Egypt, he said to his sons, "Why do you just keep looking at each other?" He continued, "I have heard that there is grain in Egypt. Go down there and buy some for us, so that we may live and not die."

Then ten of Joseph's brothers went down to buy grain from Egypt.

Genesis 41:28–36; 42:1–3

_____

_____

_____

THE "ALL SCIENCE IS EVIL" MYTH

Key Question: Why are Christians afraid of science when it documents the validity of God's Word?

Setting: A scientific convention of Christians is the context for a philosophy of Christian involvement in the sciences.

L ike children in a candy store, Pastor David Sheffield and his young friend, Mike Jenkins, quickly moved from booth to booth at the science convention. Eyes wide with wonder, hands full of pamphlets, and minds awakened to new possibilities, they were both having the time of their lives. A mutual interest in science had originally sparked their friendship. Mike had noticed how often David used examples from science to illustrate his sermons. His curiosity and questions had led them into many hours of deep conversation.

David still remembered one of Mike's first questions. "Pastor David, since you seem to like science so much, why didn't you become a scientist?"

David hadn't expected that question following a sermon, but he laughed out loud. "Actually, Mike, I do consider myself a scientist. Theology is one of the oldest sciences and was even called at one time 'the queen of the sciences.' It is my privilege to study my Creator, and observe the directions He has given about how we should treat His creation. I even get to study the special relationship that can exist between the Creator and His creation. I find it challenges every scientific molecule in me!"

David was pleased to have found friendship with someone so young, yet so eager to learn. In the following months, as the pastor had been drawn into the battle for life, the two friends had been able to encourage each other along the way. Now they were having the chance to take part in a Christian symposium on the sciences.

Besides rubbing shoulders with over three hundred scientists at the conference, Mike and David would be having a chance to hear Dr. Rachel Girard, an outstanding scientist in the field of genetic engineering. In fact, it was hearing her name that temporarily stopped their tour of the science booths. The public address system alerted everyone to the session about to begin in the meeting hall. Space was filling up rapidly by the time they entered the auditorium, but they were able to find good seats toward the front. As they sat down, Mike said, "From what I've learned about science at school, I wouldn't have guessed there were this many scientists in the whole world who are Christians!"

After opening the session with prayer, the moderator introduced Dr. Rachel Girard. There was a sense of anticipation in the air. Dr. Girard was known for her ability to speak clearly on ethical issues in science, but her passion was for the protection of human life. She was a committed scientist, but deeply troubled by much that was being done in the name of science. There was a slight echo as her words filled the huge room.

"America is at a crossroads. Indeed, if I may be so bold, the world is at a crossroads. Never before in the history of mankind have humans held in their grasp the power with which to either build up or to destroy the planet. God demonstrated His intentions for our role in His creation when He told our first parents to be fruitful, multiply, fill the earth, and subdue it. God is not intimidated by our inventions and discoveries. On the contrary, these are nothing less than what He planned from the beginning. That's why we call them 'discoveries.' God has left us an almost inexhaustible supply of 'covered' things for us to discover. In fact, sometimes after I hear a proud announcement of one of our latest discoveries, I think I can hear Him asking one of the angels, 'What took them so long, anyway?'

"I'm here to ask the same question today. 'What has taken us so long?' As scientists who know their Creator we ought to have greater motivation to pursue excellence in our chosen fields of research. Are we pursuing the discovery and application of the treasures of creation like people who have the owner's permission and command?

"Let's make no mistake about it. Even today there is a force and power in the world that is opposed to any progress that would make life more enjoyable for mankind. Unless we realize the scope and intensity of this opposition, we may find ourselves thrust into another Dark Ages that will make the previous one seem like an age of enlightenment in comparison. Ironically, the same capacity for science that should be helping people grow in their awareness of the awesome nature of God and His creation is being twisted to work toward the destruction of that creation and denial of its Creator.

"But if we saw ourselves as God sees us, our apprehensions would all fade away and we would pursue science with a vigor never before imagined. We would realize that in a very real sense we have been created in the image and likeness of God. Our hands, our minds, in fact all that we are and all the we have are meant to be a human expression of Godlikeness. God made us to be a unique reflection of His dignity and creativity. Therefore, when humans discover and invent, they are actually being faithful stewards of the talents and gifts God entrusted to them in the first place.

"Unfortunately, humans are capable of taking those same God-given abilities and using them to promote evil. For every evil is the misuse of something with the same or equal potential for good. The splitting of the atom can be used to provide inexpensive energy for an entire nation such as France, or it can be used to make bombs with the capacity to literally obliterate mankind from the face of the earth. Genetic engineering can be used to create astonishing crop yields, or it can be used to prevent crop growth altogether.

"Given these possibilities, there have always been some who suggest that because the potential for evil application of these new discoveries is so great we need to place restrictions on scientific development itself rather than on the applications of scientific development. Friends, this is a modern-day version of a shortsighted plan in which the technological baby is thrown out with the bath water. It reminds me of that group of pessimists and doomsdayers who approached President Woodrow Wilson in 1917 and encouraged him to shut down the patent office because they were convinced that all the worthwhile inventions had already been discovered.

"God is not opposed to progress. In fact, God is the force behind all progress that enables humans to be the faithful stewards God first entrusted us to be on this garden planet. And I am convinced that one day each of us will stand before God and give an account of our individual stewardship. We cannot afford to forget for a moment that there is a cosmic struggle raging in the spiritual realm that manifests itself every moment of every day here in the world. We choose sides every day. Unless we see ourselves as God's representatives in this cosmic struggle, we may not only live to see the forces of evil gain the upper hand in our own culture and around the globe; we may also find that we have actually helped the enemy's cause by our failure to act or our failure to think appropriately before we act.

"Jesus Christ addressed the seriousness of this evil presence when He described this enemy of humanity as one who comes only to kill, steal, and destroy. Satan has found an effective means to accomplish his goals by twisting the use of science and technology. In this way, evil has also invaded every area of life. Science and technology are the building blocks of such diverse areas as business, sports, media, art, and medicine. In each of these we can see evil or good produced by the use or misuse of science. What comes out of our laboratories does make a difference, my friends!

"One key 'litmus' test we can use to constantly evaluate our work is to consider whether our product or service promotes life or death. Another way to do this is by regularly asking ourselves this question: 'Will the application of this product or service result in a constructive or destructive effect on humanity?' We are also bound to ask ourselves who will control this new technology and what are their goals. Yes, the questions are difficult, but avoiding them is not a responsible Christian alternative.

"We need to realize that the great potential for good through an invention is often accompanied by a frightening potential for evil. Hitler's use of the V2 rocket is a clear example of this fact. The original application of that new technology was terribly destructive to human life. Decades later, we realized that, although the missile was used for evil, without it, there would be no space shuttle or jet travel. The invention was morally neutral in nature. But the applications were morally and diametrically opposed.

"We have been commissioned by our Lord to be missionaries in the constructive application of science. This is our calling. It is just as real a calling as the call to be missionaries of the gospel in a foreign land. If we fail, we will witness our tools and ideas used to accomplish the goals of the enemy of human souls. It is happening already. I see it almost daily in my own field of genetic engineering. Diabolical applications of science that Hitler only experimented are becoming a regular practice right here in our own nation. Hitler began using abortion in his plan to 'purify' the Germanic race. Besides the millions of men, women, and children who were murdered in the extermination camps, we have no way of knowing the countless others who were murdered before being born. Yet we live in a nation that dwarfs those statistics by its brutal slaughter of over 26 million pre-born babies who were created, like us, in the image and likeness of God. We have unofficially even taken the next step only theorized by Hitler by killing an estimated ten thousand newborn babies each year, called infanticide, according to former Surgeon General C. Everett Koop's estimates.

"All this because the children did not 'look right,' or were the 'wrong' sex according to the parents' and doctors' expectations. These horrors are taking place in hospitals and clinics just down the street from where we live. In some cases these helpless, 'unwanted' humans have taken as long as twenty-six days to starve to death while Christians have done little or nothing. Our society is not only seriously contemplating euthanasia, but actually encouraging it by attitudes like the one expressed by a former governor of Colorado who said, 'Older people have the duty to die to make room for the young.'

"What has happened, fellow scientists? Our country was once proud to be a place where the poor and destitute were welcomed. We were once considered the protectors and promoters of life and liberty for all. What reason can we give for the change?

"The reason, as I see it, is that we, who know the Author of life and have been charged by Him with the responsibilities to protect life and to apply knowledge in constructive ways, have retreated before the forces of death. We have been intimidated by that one who roars like a lion. We have forgotten whom we serve. And unless we reclaim the same truths that gave boldness to believers who have gone ahead of us, we will continue to retreat. Christians in the past have been harassed for their unpopular stands for truth; we're in danger of being Christians who never really took a stand for truth at all.

"We have failed to make a compelling case for the truth that the promotion of all life is actually far better for the human race than attempting to regulate or 'improve' life with contemporary 'Master Race' techniques. In the packets of material that you received when you entered this meeting, I have provided undeniable and conclusive proof that, contrary to fears of a population explosion, growth in the number of people on this planet has actually led to an increase in the standard of living for humanity as a whole. You will see that we have hardly begun to tap our food production capabilities. Evidence shows that humans should not be portrayed as a drain on the system — every person is a potential contributor to the welfare of all others. More people means having more mouths to feed, but it also means having more minds to advance technology. I often wonder how many 'Einsteins' and 'Beethovens' have been lost to us through abortion and infanticide. You will also read a variety of proposals for facilitating the distribution of vast resources that are presently being wasted to those areas of the world where those resources are desperately needed. God's people need to reclaim a reputation as being champions of life. Positive problem solving can be a significant tool God uses to break the grip that the 'death-style' mentality has on our world. If we are not bold in eliminating problems, we will be overrun by those whose solution is to eliminate people.

"As scientists, if we fail to understand and vigorously advocate this 'life-style' mentality, then our discoveries and inventions, though intended for good, will be more and more often applied to the ends of death.

"Let me close by reminding all of us how the Bible describes our challenge: 'For our struggle is not against flesh and blood, but against the rulers, against the authorities, against the powers of this dark world and against the spiritual forces of evil in the heavenly realms' (Ephesians 6:12). The most important thing to remember from this description is the truth that our struggle is not against people, it is against powers and beings whose goal is the destruction of humans.

"Have you ever wondered why Satan is so intent on our destruction? After pondering this question for some time I have come to the conclusion that the motivation behind Satan's efforts to destroy us is his consuming hatred for God. He has set out to hurt God by hurting those whom God loves. Think about it! If I want to deeply hurt you, isn't it more devastating to attack your children than to attack you directly? That is what Satan is doing, and he is often using people as his tools. We need to have compassion for these people who knowingly or unknowingly are instruments of Satan's 'death-style' crusades. If we lose compassion, we run the danger of also becoming Satan's instruments.

"Our mission is nothing less than to re-capture the initiative in this war of worldviews. The future we give our children and grandchildren depends on our success. May we constantly depend on God for the wisdom and endurance we will need as we seek to obey Him in our critical mission field — science!"

Dr. Girard had hit the mark. Applause exploded from the audience as they rose to their feet. David turned to Mike as the clapping died down and whispered his question, "Do you still think you want to be a scientist?"

Mike's answer came with conviction, "More than ever! I've been trying to figure out how I could be a scientist and find time on the side to serve God. Now I realize that science may be just the place where He wants me to serve. I feel like I'm already on my way!"

Comment

Creation is filled with insights, inventions, and truths to be discovered. Once these treasures are discovered, a new responsibility emerges. How will they be used? Scientists who are Christians need to be deeply involved in the study of the creation whose Creator they claim to worship. Teaching others to treat that creation with respect becomes part of their mission. Christians who are scientists should remember more often that their vocation need not conflict with their faith. Rather, their scientific efforts should have a distinct authority and direction based on their relationship with the Author of the creation they are studying.

In the News

For scientists, and possibly for all humanity, a watershed event is about to take place. Biologists have long been closing in on a goal that is both alluring and frightening: to alter the genetic code of a human being. They have transplanted foreign genes into bacteria, fruit flies, even mice. Now medical researchers at the National Institutes of Health are ready to take the big step: within the next two months they will perform the first authorized gene transplants into humans.

The doctors intend to inject cells containing a gene from the bacterium *E. coli* into cancer patients at NIH. The gene itself will have no therapeutic power, but it will help the researchers monitor the effectiveness of an anti-tumor treatment. More important, the transplantation techniques being developed for the experiment could someday be used to cure several genetic ills, possibly including Huntington's disease, sickle-cell anemia and some types of muscular dystrophy. Says NIH director James Wyngaarden: "We have reached an important milestone in medical history."

Source: Thompson, Dick. "Coming: A Historic Experiment." *Time,* February 13, 1989, p. 64.

ﺎﻣ ﻣﺎ ﻣﺎ

"Over the next 20 to 40 years we will have the potential for eradicating the major diseases that plague the American population," declares Leroy Hood, the Lasker Prize-winning California Institute of Technology biology chairman and physician who specializes in inventing high-tech machines to find and decode genes.

"Our goal is not to help people live forever," Hood says. "But we will let them stay healthy and productive through their entire natural lifetimes."

"I honestly foresee a day when the first thing that happens to a newborn child is a DNA [genetic] profile," says David Beach, a biologist at the Cold Spring Harbor Laboratory on Long Island. "Not only will it be able to predict his future, but it will be able to change it through prevention.

"Right from childhood we will be able to tell which people can eat eggs and which ones can't. We can tell which children are genetically susceptible to alcoholism and so should never drink, as well as those who are at risk for cancer, mental problems, and almost all other disorders," Beach says.

The growing ability to know one's own genes raises important questions that Americans soon will have to deal with. What if you have genes that increase your risk for certain diseases? Whom do you let know? Would you be employable? Would you be eligible for health insurance coverage? What guarantees can protect the privacy of your DNA profile?

Source: Kotulak, Ronald and Peter Gorner. "Gene hunters fighting disease at the source." *Chicago Tribune,* April 12, 1990.

ᵃ ᵃ ᵃ

Japanese researchers are joining scientists worldwide to develop a tiny tube-on-a-chip that could lead to ultrathin high definition television screens, dazzling supercomputers, and super telecommunications gear in the late 1990s.

"Vacuum microelectronics might be the leading-edge electronics of the 21st century," says Henry F. Gray, a physicist of the U.S. Naval Research Laboratory in Washington, D.C. Gray developed the world's first vacuum microelectronic device using photo lithography and etching techniques in December 1986.

Vacuum microelectronic devices have potential operating speeds, switching on and off, of less than 1-trillionth of a second.

Similar to integrated circuits, 10 billion of these tiny tubes, or so-called emitters, are etched onto a single, five-inch wafer equal in size to electronic devices in today's computer chips.

The vacuum tubes are measured in microns, or 1-millionth of a meter (thin as a strand of human hair). The devices are similar to semiconductors but operate faster since electrons travel much faster in a vacuum than through solids. In such devices, electrons are fired through the air a micron away from one point to another without encountering an obstacle.

These micro devices could process data relayed through optical fibers or lasers.

"Cathodes made of silicon or metals are more reliable than semiconductors," says Yasuo Nannichi, a physicist at Tsukuba University, who envisions the technology becoming the basis for electro-optic computers.

Source: Pidge, Dennis. "State-Of-The-Art Frontier." *Mainichi Daily News* (Tokyo, Japan and San Francisco), July 11, 1989.

ɩↄ ɩↄ ɩↄ

Oil and gas deposits that were inaccessible or uneconomical only a few years ago suddenly have become gold mines for the moribund U.S. petroleum industry, thanks to recent breakthroughs in technology that could boost America's proven reserves.

Technological innovation is occurring in every phase of the industry, from geological surveys and exploration to final production. Last week, Shell Oil Company announced plans to develop a promising oil and gas field at a record depth of 2,860 feet. The project, called the Auger field, exceeds the world record set last month for deep-water production by more than 1,000 feet and will cost $1.1 billion. New methods of constructing huge offshore drilling and production platforms make tapping such reservoirs feasible.

"Horizontal drilling is to the petroleum industry what the semiconductor was to electronics," declares Philip Crouse, president of Philip C. Crouse and Associates, a Dallas consulting firm. "It represents a 50-year advancement."

Untapped potential: Some experts maintain that horizontal drilling's true potential has yet to be realized. The technique could be used, for instance, to glean more oil from aging fields and increase production from larger, unfractured reservoirs. Consultant Crouse predicts that horizontal drilling could pump an additional $175 billion into the petroleum industry over the next 15 years.

Source: Sheets, Kenneth R. "Oil Fields of Dreams." *U.S. News and World Report*, December 18, 1989, p. 35.

ta ta ta

The World Health Organization estimated DDT saved 8 million people and 100 million illnesses. But Dr. Joseph W. Still (Health Department) estimated "there are one billion human beings living today healthy who would be either sick or dead without DDT."

In *Silent Spring,* by Rachel Carson, though not a scientist and though her data was not based on facts, Carson proved no ill effects of DDT to humans but said there might be. She claimed fish and birds disappeared.

In 1971 Franklin Russell, a natural historian, reported in *LIFE* magazine: "Rachel Carson's terrifying description of the disastrous overdose of DDT in New Brunswick forests, which killed about all insects, birds and fish in some areas, did not include the fact that two years later nearly all life systems there appeared back to normal."

Several eminent scientists noted that over 100 million species of animals and plants have become extinct. Except for a few dozen, all disappeared long before the advent of chemical pesticides.

On February 12, 1971, the World Health Organization issued a report, praising DDT. "Over one billion people are safe from the risk of malaria in the past 25 years." They said that DDT was no risk to humans. However, people listened to Rachel Carson who was not a true scientist. Instead of DDT causing cancer, tests indicated it may have "an anti-cancer producing potential," according to Dr. Edward Laws, Johns Hopkins University.

Source: Grayson, Marvin J., *The Disaster Lobby — Prophets of Ecological Doom and Other Absurdities,* (Chicago: Fallet Publishing Company, 1973), 24, 34–35, 37–38.

ᶓ ᶓ ᶓ

The U.S. Hubble Space Telescope is scheduled for launch aboard the space shuttle Discovery sometime this year.

Once in orbit, 368 miles above the earth and far from the distorting effects of the atmosphere, Hubble's 94.5-inch mirror will make images 10 times sharper than any earth-based telescope. This will be the greatest jump in astronomers' ability to see stars since Galileo first viewed the heavens 381 years ago.

"For astronomers, it will be like the receipt of the Bible," says John Bachall of the Institute for Advanced Study in Princeton and a father of the Hubble telescope.

Hubble will focus on stars 20 times fainter than any seen with existing telescopes. Even fainter stars at the outer reaches of the known universe will be visible in sharp focus.

Hubble will also examine areas that appear vacant from earth to see if they are populated with faint stars. It will also search for planets outside our solar system.

Source: "An Eye in the Sky." *The Plain Truth,* January 1990.

ᶓ ᶓ ᶓ

The National Space Society was founded as the National Space Institute back in the early '70s by Dr. Wernher von Braun, whom a lot of us consider the father of the American space program.

All of the technological and scientific knowledge has come out of the space program.

It's created a lot of jobs.

We've got to have something to explore. When we first came to this country, we didn't stop east of the Appalachians. We wanted to find out what was on the other side of the Mississippi River.

In medicine, it means new drugs and physiological advances like artificial hearts. Space technology has brought new light-weight materials that are strong and fire resistant.

The electronics industry greatly benefited from the space program.

The space station holds the greatest key for our future.

We'll also be able to conduct materials-processing experiments in space. There are many materials that you can make in space that are impossible to make on earth because of gravity. There's also the opportunity for additional research on solar power.

The National Space Society is a co-supporter of a lunar prospector probe. A lot of the moon was not studied in terms of the distribution of its resources. In the International Space Year, 1992, we'd like to be able to launch this satellite into orbit over the moon that will thoroughly map lunar resources. So, when we do establish commercial facilities on the moon, we will know where the valuable resources are, be they metals or chemicals or even water.

Source: Zeldes, Leah. "Space Society Works for Future." *Voice* (Schaumburg, Illinois), May 31, 1989.

" AND WE'LL HAVE A COTTAGE IN THE COUNTRY, A WHITE PICKET FENCE, A ROSE GARDEN, FROZEN EMBRYOS IN THE FREEZER ... "

Key Quotations

The fact is, your world view is a life and death issue. Why? Because ideas have consequences. Our world view either consciously or unconsciously shapes our ideas, thoughts, attitudes, beliefs, and values. Ideas produce preferences and convictions which lead to action or inaction. That can have dramatic consequences.

Bill Bright and Ron Jenson

When I consider your heavens, the work of your
    fingers,
The moon and the stars, which you have set in place,
What is man that you are mindful of him,
    the son of man that you care for him?
You made him a little lower than the heavenly
        beings
    and crowned him with glory and honor.
You made him ruler over the works of your hands;
    you put everything under his feet.

Psalm 8:3–6

THE ENVIRONMENTAL
DOOM MYTH

Key Question: Is this the autumn before the nuclear winter?

Setting: A letter to the editor becomes the start of a new relationship.

S hortly after the science symposium, Mike Jenkins had an opportunity to put many of the things he was learning to good use. He was reading the morning paper in study hall one day when a letter to the editor caught his eye. It was entitled "Youth Depressed Over Environment." The author's name wasn't familiar, but she claimed to be a student at East High School. As it turned out Wendy Peterson had recently moved to town and was one year behind Mike in school.

The letter began, "Dear editor, I'm a junior in high school and I don't feel like I can do much about what is happening to our world, but I have to speak up! I don't like to think about the future because it seems hopeless. Day after day in my classes I hear about all the ways we are filling our world with trash. I get depressed about spending my life in a giant landfill!"

Mike stopped reading for a moment and looked around the room. He wondered how many of the other students around him were feeling that same hopelessness. He felt like standing up and saying, "Friends, I've got good news. The future really looks pretty good!" Then he felt ashamed of his fear of letting others know that he had hope. He knew he needed to do more for his fellow students. His attention went back to the newspaper.

"What has really shocked me has been the information I've been learning in my social studies class. Some of it even frightens me. Our teacher has done a good job of showing us how fragile our environment is and how quickly we're destroying it. Between styrofoam containers, oil spills, car emissions, and 1001 non-bio-degradable products, we're about to choke on our own trash. It really does seem like we've got too many people and too much garbage for one little planet! It's beginning to make sense that people aren't going to do anything about this crisis unless they have to. It's going to take some radical moves to make this world fit for survivors. Sure wish there was a better answer. . . ."

Several thoughts went through Mike's mind in rapid succession. He was amazed by his new-found ability to see how one-sided the information was that Wendy was being taught. He also recalled a number of contradictory facts he had learned at the symposium that he knew would help Wendy. And he also realized he needed to respond to her letter. He still had half of his study hall left, so he quickly got to work. Afterwards, he felt as if God had helped him put the words together. When he was done, he read it over:

Environment Looks Great!
by
Mike Jenkins, East High School

I'm writing to answer a recent letter to the editor written by my fellow student Wendy Peterson. First, I have to admit that until not too long ago, I had many of the same feelings about the future that she expressed. The future didn't look good to me either. But, I'd like to be able to say a few things to Wendy, and to anyone else who might read this. I'm optimistic about the future!

My optimism started when someone (believe it or not it was the pastor of my church) asked me to seriously evaluate my sources. When I asked him how to do that, he gave me four helpful guidelines:

(1) go to the source of the claims yourself, (2) check to see if the source is reliable, and (3) establish the source's claims as true, (4) make sure the conclusions flow logically from the facts. Things got exciting when I tried this in the same social studies class Wendy mentioned in her letter. Here are some things I found out that I never heard in class.

Never before has the environment of the planet earth been in better shape to serve the needs of mankind. Now, this isn't to say for a moment that we don't have serious ecological problems that must be addressed and solved. But painting a completely dark future by only presenting some of the facts gives a distorted picture at best.

For example, the planet has never seen such reclaimed and maintained green deserts like we find in Southern California and Israel. Never before have we had as many lakes, streams, or ponds with fish and other wildlife to be enjoyed by naturalist and hunter alike. Never before have we been better able to monitor, and therefore take advantage of, weather conditions like rainfall. Never before have we been better able to harness the stored power in our environment for the betterment of humans through solar, wind, and thermal energy. Never before have we been in a better position to stop the extinction of entire species which has happened in the past. Never before have we been able to provide for entire herds of animals or flocks of birds during the difficult winter months when in the past there has been extensive death by starvation. Never before have certain animals, birds, or insects thrived in habitats other than their places of origin. The news about the environment simply isn't all bad.

The facts that are all around us can be interpreted in more than one way. Why have we been so ready to believe those who constantly prophesy gloom and doom as the reasons behind their radical proposals? People like the group Planned Population are the source of most of the one-sided information we get taught as the unquestionable truth in school. We feel threatened by deadly promises of the depletion of the ozone, the greenhouse effect, or the drastic thawing of the polar caps, yet we rarely hear that these are unproven theories, not facts. Does it ever make you wonder why the proposed solutions always seem to boil down to getting rid of people?

Our Creator God made the earth primarily for us. Everything has been provided to fulfill our needs and desires. We also have a clear command to take care of this earth as God's stewards. One day we will have to take responsibility for how well or poorly we have done.

It is important that we never forget that God created the world for humans and not the other way around.

When I see people picket furriers for making a business out of the pain of helpless animals that are slaughtered for the convenience and comfort of people, yet seem not to notice that humans are being torn limb from limb in an abortion clinic next door to the furrier, then I think something is very wrong. We have forgotten the value God has placed on humans when He created us in His image and likeness. When a group denies a family the right to earn a living and survive so that a herd of antelope which are already too numerous on the Great Plains can once again reclaim ground they used to roam two hundred years ago, then our values are out of focus.

I'm convinced that the greatest danger to our survival as the human race is not the environment, but the one-sided, death-style agenda of groups like Planned Population.

I hope this helps, Wendy. It has sure helped me.

Before he left study hall, Mike decided to make a Xerox of the letter so that he would have a copy after he sent his original to the newspaper. He was standing at the copier as the bell rang and a new group of students shattered the quiet of the library. Almost right behind him he heard someone say, "I read your letter to the editor, Wendy. Interesting ideas. . . ." Mike swung around in surprise and neatly unburdened a girl of three large books she was carrying under her arm. Seized by embarrassment, he bent over quickly to pick up the books and their heads almost collided. Somehow, they both managed to herd the volumes, and as they were standing back up, Mike asked, "Are you Wendy Peterson?"

She smiled and said, "Yes, I'm usually recognized by the way I drop books!"

"Listen, I'm sorry," he said. "That was really my fault. You surprised me."

"How did I do that?" she asked with a delightfully curious look on her face.

Mike swallowed hard. He was afraid this wasn't going to come out right. But he also knew it was too late to back out. "You're not going to believe this, but I just wrote you a letter." He realized from the look on her face that she didn't understand. "Your letter to the editor? I wrote you one back." He turned back to the copier and retrieved his original and the copy he had made.

"So, do I have to wait until the paper comes out to read it?" Wendy asked.

Mike found it hard to believe this was happening. He seemed to be watching himself carry on this conversation. His immediate opinion was that he wasn't doing very well. "No, I guess not," he heard himself say. "What are you doing right now?"

"I was just going to drop off these books on the way to lunch, but it wasn't this kind of dropping I had in mind." She answered in a way that made Mike feel like this would be a nice person to get to know. She placed the books on the check-in counter while Mike tried to regain his composure.

By the time she came back, Mike was ready. "If you wouldn't mind joining me during lunch, I'd be glad to let you read the letter," he said, all the while hoping he sounded more casual than he felt. She agreed and they headed for the cafeteria.

Mike discovered that, in spite of her lightheartedness, Wendy was deeply troubled about the future. Her letter hadn't expressed a passing feeling. As they talked, she mentioned several of the facts she had included in her letter. After describing the "impending disasters," she shrugged her shoulders in a hopeless way. "When did you start being scared about the future?" Mike asked.

"I guess it wasn't till after I started my social studies class," was her answer. "It's funny, the teacher seems so nice, but the class is so depressing! I hate going. Every day it's a new reason to check out of planet earth."

Mike said, "I felt the same way when I took the class, that's —"

"You mean I'm not crazy? Someone else had the same reaction?" Wendy interrupted him mid-sentence.

"Yes, you're not crazy, and yes, someone else had the same reaction, and yes, that's why I wrote you this letter after I read yours," Mike said as he handed over his letter.

Wendy pushed her tray aside and placed the letter on the table. As she bent to read, her hair fell down around her face like a curtain, and it seemed to Mike that she was in another world. He thought she was taking a long time to read what he had written, but a slight noise made Mike notice a tear that had landed on the letter. He wasn't sure what to do. He had never written anything before that had caused someone to cry. He waited. Wendy retrieved a napkin from her tray and wiped her eyes. Mike was about to apologize when she suddenly looked up and smiled, tears still shining in her eyes. Her voice was a little strained, but she said softly, "Thank you, Mike. This has helped me, too."

Now he really didn't know what to say. Wendy rescued him by going on, "This pastor you mentioned must be quite a guy. I guess I never thought there could be more than one way of looking at the world. It seemed like I was hearing the same message from everybody."

"You're right Wendy, my pastor is quite a guy. He has helped me look at the world in a different way. But the biggest way he has helped me is by showing me how involved God is in the world," said Mike.

"That's another thing," said Wendy, "I've never thought of religious people knowing anything about the world — like they only cared about God and couldn't see the garbage, or relate to the real world."

"I guess that's true of a lot of people who call themselves Christians," continued Mike, "but Christians claim to worship the God who is the Creator. How can we claim to know the Creator and not care about the creation?"

Wendy thought for a moment and then said, "I don't understand what you mean by 'knowing the Creator.'"

"I'm not sure I can explain it quickly, Wendy, but it's a little like what just happened between us. We started out this day not knowing each other, then we met — I mean we bumped into each other — and began to get to know each other. I can say I know Wendy Peterson now if someone asks. That doesn't mean that I know everything about you, but it means that I know you personally — not just facts about you. Christians believe that God wants us to know him that way, too — personally. It's one of the reasons Jesus came to earth — to show us we could know God." Mike hoped he was making a little sense.

Wendy smiled another one of those smiles Mike was finding he really enjoyed. "So, how do I arrange to bump into this God you're talking about? Is He as clumsy as you?"

Grinning, Mike said, "Think of it this way, Wendy. If He's God, then He's everywhere and should be easy to meet. But He's invisible, so meeting Him has to be by faith. My relationship with God is almost exactly like every relationship I have except for two things: First, it's my most important relationship, and, second, it's a relationship with someone I can't see, but who is with me in a way no human could ever be. The relationship starts when you realize He's there, and what He's really like, and you respond to Him—you tell Him you want to have a relationship with Him." Mike paused as he realized that talking about His faith was actually helping him understand it better.

Wendy asked, "You mean like praying to God? I guess I do that sometimes."

"Almost everybody does that, Wendy. What I'm talking about is a specific prayer when you tell God you want to do more than just talk at Him once in a while—that you want to have a personal, vital relationship with Him," said Mike.

"What do you mean by vital?" she asked.

Mike realized she was listening to every word. "By vital I mean that my whole life really depends on God. I've turned my life over to Him. In fact, my life beyond this life depends on God. The Bible tells me that my relationship with God will last for eternity. That after this life, I will live forever with Him in heaven."

"You talk about heaven like you really believe in it," said Wendy wistfully.

"Knowing God does make life look and feel different," Mike said quietly.

After a few moments, Wendy picked the letter up from the table and said, "I think I want to take your pastor's advice. I'm going to check out what you've been saying myself, and I'm going to ask whether your explanation really takes in all the facts. And I hope you turn out to be right. Could I keep this letter?"

"You can," said Mike, "but it's going to cost you."

"How much?" She flashed another of those smiles.

"How about coming to church with me on Sunday for starters?" said Mike.

Wendy stood up and gathered her belongings as the bell rang. Mike had a brief moment of panic which must have been written all over his face, because she burst out laughing as she said, "I think I'd really like that . . . and thanks again for this letter."

They quickly exchanged phone numbers and went separate ways. Mike had a difficult time paying attention in the rest of his classes that day. But several times people noticed how much he was smiling and thought they heard him murmur something like, "Thank you, Lord." But they shook their heads thinking not even Mike Jenkins would actually pray in school.

Comment

Addressing the problems facing the world can be helpful to motivate action. But, if those problems are only viewed from a life-dishonoring, hopeless perspective, the end result will be to create despair. It is at this very point that the differences between a "death-style" obsession and a "life-style" theology become apparent. The first leads to hopelessness; the second is permeated with hope. If all the answers begin and end with human limitations, the future is in fact filled with despair. But if the answers bring the unlimited wisdom and resources of God into the picture, the future becomes full of hope. It is a hope others should note, even in passing conversations and in our attitudes toward life.

In the News

It has been a bad year for those who worry about the greenhouse effect. It has also been a bad year for worriers in general.

The British, who for two centuries have disregarded Parson Malthus' warning that the world is running out of agricultural space are about to publish a refutation of all doomsday thinkers in the magazine *Economic Affairs.*

Prof. Jacquelin Kasun of Humboldt State University has, in one of the *Economic Affairs* articles, let herself go on behalf of the non-worriers.

Forests, she says, still cover a third of the world's land surface. The big rivers of the world still flow to the sea untouched by man save for a few dams. There is no discernible trend in world climate. Most of the earth is still empty. Prof. Kasun is particularly impressed by Texas, where "all the people in the world could be settled. . . with each person allotted space equal to that of the average American home."

In a final jab at Parson Malthus, Kasun notes that world food output per person has grown 30 to 40 per cent since 1950. Farmers use less than half the available arable land. The world could feed eight times its present population.

Kasun has inspected the mathematical models of the greenhouse effect. They produce wildly conflicting forecasts. There has been an increase in carbon dioxide, but "no measurable effects of this have been observed." Since this can have both cooling and warming effects, its net future consequences remain unknown.

Source: Chamberlain, John. "British Magazine Jabs the Doomsayers." *Human Events,* October 21, 1989.

જ઼ જ઼ જ઼

It isn't clear that the "greenhouse effect" will change the Earth's climate at all, despite all the publicity surrounding it, say three top American scientists. They advised against any government adopting policy changes based on the so-called ecological threat.

The report, "Scientific Perspectives on the Greenhouse Problem," by Robert Jastrow, Frederick Seitz, and William A. Nierenberg, applies the brakes to the dash toward a U.N.-enforced world ecological dictatorship, based largely on claims that there is a heating of the atmosphere underway, due to the release of man-made carbon dioxide and other "greenhouse gases." These will allegedly trap excess heat on the Earth, raising temperatures by as much as 5 degrees Centigrade by the middle of the next century.

Jastrow was director of NASA's Goddard Institute for Space Studies for 20 years. He said that James Hansen, the leader of the greenhouse gang whom he appointed to his present position at NASA, is "the odd man out" in the scientific community when it comes to "greenhouse" claims. Jastrow presented the technical findings of the report.

The three scientists looked at two key issues: the large uncertainty in the forecasts of future climate, and what can be done about improving the forecasts; and whether the 0.5 degree C warming in the past century is a reliable guide to future temperature increases.

Source: Maduro, Rogelio A. "Top Scientists Warn Against 'Greenhouse Effect' Hysteria." *The New Federalist,* June 16, 1989.

ᏧᏧᏧ

Modeling of global climate is being carried out intensively by at least 14 different groups. They have largely concentrated on examining effects of doubling the atmospheric content of greenhouse gases. As might be expected, the answers they get are functions of the models they employ. The spread is from 1.5° to 5°C; that is, there is great uncertainty. In addition, if one examines some of the scientific articles on the subject, one finds virtually unanimous agreement that the models are deficient. For example, they do not adequately incorporate effects of clouds, which are expected to increase with warming. Clouds have both negative and positive effects on warming. Clouds exert a negative effect on temperature in part by reflecting sunlight off into space. They have a positive effect by trapping heat from below. The sensitivity of computer models to the properties of clouds was illustrated in a recent paper. When the water content of clouds was recognized in the model, the predicted global average warming dropped from 5.2° to 1.9°C.

What have been the warming effects, if any, of anthropogenic gases? The typical answer is 0.5°C. But the answer depends on what time interval is chosen. There was substantial increase in temperature from 1880 to 1940. However, from 1940 until the 1960s, temperatures dropped so much as to lead to predictions of a coming ice age. New precise satellite data raise further questions about warming. From 1979 to 1988 large temperature variability was recorded on weekly to multi-yearly time scales, but no obvious temperature trend was noted during the 10-year period.

Source: "Uncertainties About Global Warming." *Science,* March 30, 1990, p. 1529.

ᏧᏧᏧ

Last summer's drought, climatologist Jim Hansen's congressional testimony, and news on the ozone hold combined to tilt world sympathy toward Planet Earth as the underdog in the battle between man and his environment. Mother Earth became Man-of-the-Year on *Time's* cover. And every other publication has felt compelled to declare sides, including *Scientific American,* which devoted its September issue to 11 articles by 16 distinguished scientists and environmentalists on the topic "Managing Planet Earth."

Never mind that Planet Earth has been around some 4.5 billion years while man can claim no more than one or two hours for each of those years: Earth has already been declared vanquished — unless. . . . It is the "unless" that has emerged as the common underlying theme of these latter-day environmentalists.

The biggest current obstacle to making the transition to a sustainable ecology is the holier-than-thou moralism of the environmentalists, which refuses to allow a balancing of costs against benefits. Also involved is the environmentalists' selective presentation of scientific data, overstating some facts and omitting others in an effort to justify the extremity of their solutions.

Source: Ellsaesser, Hugh W. *"Scientific American* on 'Managing Planet Earth': A Review." *21st Century,* November-December 1989, p. 23.

ხ ხ ხ

In an attempt to calm consumer fears about pesticide contamination of the fruits and vegetables they eat, a top administrator of the Environmental Protection Agency March 2 called the nation's food supply "the safest in the world."

John Moore, acting deputy administrator of EPA, said his agency was receiving phone calls from fearful and angry consumers, some bordering "on hysteria," in the wake of reports about the possible links between pesticide residues and cancer.

"The public is being misled by the ominous rhetoric," Moore told a House panel. "I think it is way out of proportion to reality."

On February 27, for example, the Natural Resources Defense Council (NRDC), an environmental group, made headlines by warning of the cancer risks of pesticide on fruits and vegetables, especially for young children.

But on March 1, the National Research Council, an arm of the National Academy of Sciences, released a 1,300-page study urging Americans to eat more fruits and vegetables and declaring there was no conclusive evidence that residual pesticides on food pose a significant cancer risk.

Rep. Pat Roberts, R-Kan., said his seatmate on an airplane recently refused apple juice because she had read that the NRDC report linked increased risk of cancer to Alar, a growth regulator used on some apples.

"She was smoking a cigarette but refusing to drink apple juice," Roberts said. "Clearly, consumers are wondering what on earth is going on. What are we to believe?"

Source: "'The Nation's Food Supply Is Safe,' EPA Official Says." *The Seattle Times,* March 3, 1989.

જ જ જ

"Hydrogen is almost an environmentalist's dream come true," wrote Robert H. Williams and Joan M. Ogden, researchers at Princeton University in a recent study on making hydrogen from solar power.

To make the hydrogen, electric current, which can be generated by photovoltaic cells that tap the sun's energy, is run through water that has a chemical catalyst, in a device called an electrolyzer. The water molecules are divided into hydrogen and oxygen gases. The hydrogen can then be shipped by pipeline for use in many of the same ways as natural gas. For use as a transportation fuel it must be compressed into a liquid or combined with other chemicals, to decrease the size of the fuel tank necessary to hold it. Burning the hydrogen — or recombining it with oxygen in a reaction that gives off heat — produces nothing but H2O and small amounts of nitrous oxide, from nitrogen picked up from the air. These can be easily controlled.

Hydrogen is clean enough, in fact, to burn indoors, without a chimney.

Source: Wald, Matthew L. "Hydrogen: Is It the Clean Fuel of the Future?" *The New York Times,* November 1, 1989.

જ જ જ

We have only ourselves to blame for this environmental crisis. Americans throw out about 160 million tons of garbage a year — 3.5 pounds apiece each day. Where are we going to put it all?

Recycling is gaining popularity, but currently only 11 percent of U.S. solid waste lives again as something else.

Aluminum: Turning bauxite into new aluminum is 10 times more expensive than reprocessing used cans. That's one key reason more than half of all aluminum beverage cans are recycled today—42.5 billion annually.

Glass: Reusing old glass also costs less than forging virgin materials. To date, only 10 percent of it is recycled, but markets are growing steadily.

Plastics: The $140 billion-a-year plastics industry is at last waking up to recycling. Currently only 1 percent of plastics is recaptured.

Paper: Industry officials like to boast that nearly 30 percent of all paper products consumed in this country are recycled—26 million tons a year, turning up in cereal boxes, toilet tissue, even bedding for farm animals.

Busy, distracted citizens also need incentives to recycle. To that end, New York City plans to fine residents who don't comply with its nascent program: $25 for the first offense, $500 for four offenses in a six-month period, with landlords dunned up to $10,000 if their tenants don't cooperate.

Source: "Buried Alive." *Newsweek,* November 27, 1989, p. 67–75.

Key Quotations

I have lived, Sir, a long time; and the longer I live the more convincing proofs I see of this Truth, That God governs in the Affairs of Men!—And if a Sparrow cannot fall to the Ground without His Notice, is it probable that an Empire can rise without His Aid? We have been assured, Sir, in the Sacred Writings, that "except the Lord build the House, they labor in vain that build it." I firmly believe this;—and I also believe that without His concurring Aid we shall succeed in this political Building no better than the Builders of Babel.

Benjamin Franklin to the Constitutional Convention
meeting in Philadelphia on June 28, 1787.

And God saw all that he had made, and it was very good. And there was evening, and there was morning — the sixth day.

Genesis 1:31

The Lord God took the man and put him in the Garden of Eden to work it and take care of it.

Genesis 2:15

THE LACK
OF RESOURCES MYTH

Key Question: Isn't the world running out of everything?

Setting: Christians debate the assumption of rapid decline of resources in a university classroom.

P rofessor Lieborman's letter was obvious in the pile of usual correspondence that might cross a pastor's desk. Quality bond, embossed letterhead, and a matching envelope imprinted with the name of a prestigious university created an air of importance. Dr. Lieborman was cordially inviting Rev. David Sheffield to visit one of the classes at the university and debate certain claims he had made about abundant earth resources. His opponents would be some graduate students. The invitation was coming, wrote the doctor, at the recommendation of several people who had been present at recent debates in which David had been involved.

Invitations like this always created several almost simultaneous reactions in David. One was an instinctive fear of a battle which he knew wouldn't be easy. Another was a sense of caution which always motivated careful preparation. Another was the sheer excitement of a new

challenge. But these all faded into an awareness that this was an opportunity to represent Jesus Christ in a setting where His teaching and the
life He promised were seldom heard.

Because he believed in the value of teamwork, David invited Mike
Jenkins to accompany him to this debate. Mike, in turn, suggested that
Wendy Peterson be allowed to go along, too. He realized how much he
had learned being "in the thick of things" recently. He felt that Wendy
could be helped by seeing Christianity and the affirmation of life pro-
claimed on the front lines. David agreed it was a good idea if it could be
arranged. Then he chuckled as he said, "You sure have been spending a
lot of time with her, Mike." He could almost feel the heat of Mike's
blush coming through the phone line. Then he added, "I think that's
great. I've noticed how she listens in church. All her questions remind
me of someone else I know."

Mike saw his escape and leaped for it. "Yeah, she is neat. I'm glad
I'm not the only one who has to keep up with her questions!"

After suggesting some preparation assignments to Mike, David
called the professor's office and accepted the invitation with the condition that he be allowed to bring along two "assistants." He noted a distinct smugness on the part of the graduate assistant with whom he
spoke. David realized they would be entering an arena where the odds
and attitudes were overwhelmingly against them.

A week later, and brimming with research, Wendy, Mike, and David
drove up to the impressive entrance of the university. On their walk in
from the parking lot, they paused by the corner of the massive academic
building they were about to enter. David asked Mike to pray for their
efforts. Mike prayed that God would give them the right words at the
right time for each challenge they would meet. He asked God to continue to show Himself to Wendy. He also asked God to make them
effective in their presentation of His view of life. He closed by thanking
God for another chance to bring a life-style message to young people
drowning in a death-style view. Ironically, as they opened their eyes,
Mike noticed what he thought was the word "God" on the cornerstone
next to them. He reached out and moved the thick ivy out of the way to
reveal the inscription: "Founded to the glory of God—1823." He said, "I
wonder how many students pass by this inscription every day who have
no idea why this university was started."

Room 220 Hampden Hall turned out to be a large lecture room filled with boisterous students. A curious silence, followed by several snickers welcomed the three guests as they made their way to the front row. The unmistakable Professor Lieborman entered from a side door shortly before the class was to begin. As he approached, David sensed the professor's antagonism and the same smugness he had picked up from the graduate assistant on the phone. The professor sized up Mike and Wendy with a glance and directed his words to David. "I'm glad you accepted our invitation, Doctor . . . . I mean, Reverend . . . I mean, exactly what do you prefer to be called?"

David realized that the abruptness and near hatred he was feeling was not really directed at himself, but at what, or to be more exact whom, he represented. "I prefer to be called Pastor David Sheffield," he responded evenly. Inside, he wondered what might be visible if the people in the room were suddenly given the ability to see the spiritual battle that was already under way around and in them. The forces of death and the forces of life were clearly at war.

"Your two little friends can sit here on the front row while you join several of my students on the stage, Reverend, er, Pastor Sheffield," said the Professor. "Naturally, I won't be debating you myself," he continued in a tone which left no doubt about his expected victory over someone so obviously crippled by religious limitations.

"Let me introduce you to Mike Jenkins and Wendy Peterson. I told your assistant that I would be bringing some associates. I would like them to sit with me during the debate, as we may need to confer," responded David without acknowledging the efforts at intimidation.

"All right, then let's get started," said Dr. Lieborman as he stood and faced the class. "As you know, students, we are in for a real treat today. We've invited as our guest Pastor David Sheffield, a person who would probably welcome the description of being a conservative fundamentalist who gets involved in right wing social concerns." A ripple of laughter passed through the class.

The professor continued by quoting from various articles and books written by David or 'people like him.' The common theme in all his quotes were claims that the world has abundant resources and that God placed us on a garden planet that only needs to be properly cultivated to yield more than ample provision for as many people as God would

allow on earth. His tone of voice conveyed the attitude that these statements could not possibly be true.

To the students in the class it was becoming obvious that the new-
comers were being prepared for a humiliating experience. But few knew
the actual plan. Dr. Lieborman had met with the hand-picked students
who would carry out the debate in order to prepare them and let them
know how important this event was to him. At the close of their meeting, the professor had said, "I want as quick and complete a humiliation
as you can inflict on this man. He doesn't know it yet, but I have a
score to settle with him. He has recently publicly humiliated one of my
brightest and best former students, Sheila Turner. When I heard about it,
I promised Sheila that we would make sure that Reverend Sheffield's
visit to our class would take care of him as a nuisance to her work. No
mercy for him. Let's drive him back into his religious fantasy world
permanently. I want this to be the longest day in his life!"

Following the introduction, Dr. Lieborman asked Jeff Wilson, the
most articulate student in the class, to present his case for the rapid
decline of the world's resources. The young man's presentation was
masterful. Later, Mike, Wendy, and David agreed that they had almost
been convinced themselves by the seeming logic and credibility of his
arguments. In a mere ten minutes, Jeff presented a massive collection of
quotations from newspapers, scientific journals, and research papers. Industrial projections were cited. A brief slide presentation included economic graphs and photographic evidence of depleting stockpiles of rare
metals. Even students from the class, accustomed to gloomy outlooks
that were a part of almost every lecture, were sobered by the grim fate
that seemed closer than the horizon for the human race. Jeff concluded
his presentation with a challenge to David and his friends, "Now, would
you please explain how you can so glibly forecast good things for the
world, when we know how fast it is going downhill toward hell?"

David resisted the temptation of a quick response which would have
included the point that hell is not a place for the world, but for people
who reject God's gift of salvation. Instead he stayed with the original
plan. He and Mike had anticipated this kind of trap. He cleared his
throat and began:

"I'd like to begin by introducing two friends of mine who were neglected at the start of this debate. Next to me is Wendy Peterson, a

junior at East High School who has only recently begun to think that there might be more than the death-style way of looking at the human experience. Beside her is Mike Jenkins, who besides being a senior at East High School, is also president of the student body and a growing Christian in the church where I pastor.

"I confess that I expected to learn some new facts about natural resources today, since, after all, I was going to visit one of the foremost programs of resource studies in the nation. And certainly, the amount of information Mr. Wilson just shared with us is impressive. But, frankly, after listening to his presentation, I seriously wonder if I am in the right place. Is this the science building, or a class on science fiction? Even though I thoroughly enjoy science fiction, I am supposed to be in a debate about natural resources. So far, I've only heard fiction."

Professor Lieborman was on his feet in a rage, his face distorted as he reacted to David's words. His students had never seen their teacher exhibit such anger. His words were darts. "Listen, Sheffield, I don't appreciate your infantile sense of humor. You are very much in the right class, and we will not put up with your diversionary tactics. We're going to nail you, mister. You may be able to get away with those tactics in a high school auditorium with kids in the audience. This, I can assure you, is a very different situation!"

"How did you know about the high school auditorium presentation, Professor Lieborman?" David quietly interrupted.

"Ms. Sheila Turner was a former student of mine. It was at her recommendation that you were invited here today," responded the still seethingly angry teacher.

"I see," said David as the pieces to the puzzle of the sudden invitation began to fall into place.

Struggling to regain composure, the professor said to David, "We are still waiting for your answer to Jeff's rebuttal of your feeble claims."

"Actually, Mike here is probably better prepared to speak to the issues raised by Jeff's presentation," answered David. "I think I'll defer the answer to him."

As everyone's attention shifted to Mike, the young man realized he was being entrusted with an important mission. His throat was instantly dry, and his pulse rate suddenly felt like it had doubled. He knew exactly what he needed to say, but for a few moments wasn't sure he could get the words out. David wondered if he had given the young man too much responsibility and silently prayed for him. Mike began by asking Jeff somewhat uncertainly, "How much in oil reserves did you say were left in the earth?"

Jeff responded, "According to the Petroleum Institute Journal's most recent report, there are only a little under 1 trillion barrels of oil left, and at current world consumption levels, that means we will have completely depleted the oil supply by the year 2026."

"Yes, those were the figures I wrote down earlier," said Mike, with growing confidence in his voice. "I guess this is a perfect example of what Pastor Sheffield was referring to just now when he expressed his opinion that figures like that are much more fiction than fact."

Now it was Jeff's turn to be both indignant and angry. After all, who was this young upstart to question his painstaking research? He mockingly asked, "Are you actually questioning the validity of the statistics on oil reserves in one of the nation's most prestigious journals on resources?"

Mike, realizing this giant of prestigious opinion had an Achilles heel, responded, "With all due respect to your diligent research, Jeff, I have to answer 'yes' to your question. I can't blame you for offering us bad water from a well you didn't know was poisoned." There were obvious gasps and some shocked laughter as the students reacted to Mike's challenge. They had never seen Jeff confronted in this way before, especially by a high schooler obviously not trained in debating.

Before Jeff could speak, Professor Lieborman stood up and said with a smirk on his face, "Young man, if you are not willing to accept the statistics of the world's foremost journal on oil reserves, I believe it is you who are dealing in science fiction and not us!"

David had to restrain the impulse to leap to the defense of his young friend, but he could see that Mike was doing very well on his own. He could also see that Wendy was smiling. She knew where this was headed. David felt as if that look of new hope on her face was what really motivated his own efforts to serve Jesus Christ. In that instant he was thankful for the gift of faith God had given him, and for the opportunities he had to watch people wake up from the hopelessness of a death-style fixation and realize the Author of life wanted to fill them with His own life-style. David found himself smiling too.

Meanwhile, Mike continued, "Jeff, to determine which of us is dealing in the realm of fact or fiction, I need to have you answer two questions, please. First, have you compared the Oil Institute statistics over a period of several years to see whether the supply figures have been steadily declining, as your statements would imply, or have the figures stayed relatively the same in spite of the amount of oil consumption during the passing years? Second, can you think of anyone who would profit a great deal from 'managing' the oil statistics so that it always looks like we're about to run out?"

Jeff was stunned into confused silence. After a few tension-filled moments, the professor reservedly attempted to come to his prize student's rescue. But it wasn't to supply an answer himself. Instead he accused Mike and David of unfair tactics and announced that he was about to call a halt to this debate and dismiss the class.

Now it was David's turn. "Dr. Lieborman, you should understand that if you do what you have just threatened, I am fully prepared to inform all possible media sources of what has happened here and that you and your students were not able to adequately address even our first two questions regarding your views on resources. The fact is, as you well know, the Oil Institute changes their world supply statistics almost monthly, and that they confess in small print that their figures are little more than educated guesses, and I'm afraid, consistently biased guesses at that. There isn't a geologist around who can tell us with clear conscience how much oil exists under the earth's surface. Why is it that in a presentation as well prepared as Jeff Wilson's there is no explanation or even mention of the fact that new oil findings have been outstripping projected usage for years? How can your views account for the fact that a couple of years ago Saudi Arabia increased its projected oil reserves by 50 percent in just one year? What about the improved tertiary recovery methods which are making obsolete all the oil reserve statistics worldwide? A new mammoth oil field in Alaska has significantly changed our own nation's future oil expectations."

The students were looking at each other in amazement. These were not really new facts. They were just facts that had somehow been consistently neglected. Some of these students began to wonder why.

David continued, "The truth is, if you really listen to the news, there is more reporting of an oil glut than on any oil crisis. Almost daily we are finding more and more oil, while at the same time becoming less and less dependent on it. We have more efficient cars, better insulated homes, and more alternatives to fossil fuels. I would suggest, Dr. Lieborman, that you and your class interact more with the factual abundances of the '90s and leave behind the perceived shortages of the '70s."

"Are you actually suggesting, then, that we have no shortages?" asked Jeff Wilson.

David realized it was an honest question as he answered, "No, but I am saying that very often the shortages that we experience are temporary. They are caused more by economic factors and the systems of supply and demand than by actual depletion. At other times, shortages help us do a better job in conservation and development of new ways to accomplish the same tasks. What Mike has helped us see is that what have been announced as dire shortages in the past, like oil supplies, can now be seen in a different light. The underlying point is this: does the past history of resource availability teach us the radical gloominess that we hear so often, or a hopeful optimism that what may be in short supply today will be in surplus tomorrow?

"I also think it is important to point out that never before in the history of the world have resources been as readily available as they are today. In fact, if we trace population growth and resource availability it becomes evident, according to the extensive research of someone like Professor Julian L. Simons, that as the population has increased the availability of resources has kept pace. Shortages are more often due to slow discovery, lack of development of known supplies, and the limitations of our distribution systems."

The debate had degenerated into a free-flowing question and answer time. The professor was helpless to prevent what he had never foreseen. For the rest of the hour, the class and the guests interacted on issue after issue in the field of natural resources. Once the blinders of the death-style view had been lifted, there was a new awareness of evidence for hope. One student actually said she was seeing the world with new eyes. David even had a brief opportunity before the class ended to challenge the students to explore what the real source of truth might be. He asked them to remember how distorted their view of the world had been and to consider that their view of God might be equally distorted. No one noticed when Dr. Lieborman slipped out.

After the class, several students stayed behind. The topic shifted from natural science to spiritual life. There were more questions to answer, and a genuine interest on the part of the students. They set up a time to meet again, and promised to "give David's church a try."

As Mike, Wendy, and David left the building they were ecstatic. They held hands and formed a spontaneous circle on the sidewalk, thanking God for working through them that morning. This time it was Wendy who noticed the hidden cornerstone and said, "I think those people back in 1823 would be happy that God was given proper attention here today!"

Comment

The quality of our thinking is often determined by the quality of our sources. The bumper sticker, "Question Authority," while it originally expressed an attitude of rebellion against authority, nevertheless contains the truth that we need to evaluate the authorities and mentors in our lives. In this debate, students discover that they have been relying heavily on an authority that was biased and inaccurate.

Reliance on God's authority as the source of truth is the goal of Christian thinking. While God has included many specific applications of truth in His Word, the Bible, the bulk of truth available to us is in general form — broad principles that relate to the universe and to humanity. The specific data and conclusions coming from human-centered authority may seem overwhelming in their quantity, but must always be questioned as to their quality. Whenever God is left out of thinking, reliable conclusions will be lacking.

In the News

There is a fundamental message in all this that transcends the oil business. Experience has made a joke of the once fashionable Club of Rome notion that the world is running out of practically everything. It's certainly not running out of oil. The world still has something like 800 billion barrels of recoverable oil in reserves to draw on, over 50 percent more than it had in 1972 and more than 40 years' supply at current rates of consumption. There's nearly twice as much as that yet to be discovered or produced by various kinds of enhanced recovery techniques.

By 1987 the world was consuming 7 percent less oil than it did in the peak year of 1979. According to the International Energy Agency, energy consumption per unit of gross national product fell by 20 percent worldwide over the past decade, and could fall another 30 percent by the year 2000, using technologies that are already in existence.

High prices not only restricted consumption but after a few years they magically created additional supplies. The result was that non-OPEC production went from 22.1 million barrels a day in 1979 to 28.8 million barrels last year, and non-OPEC producers now account for 60 percent of the world's needs, up from 41 percent as recently as 1979.

The real price of oil averaged $14.99 a barrel between 1901 and 1986, as against $27.50 from 1973 to 1986, so that today's $15-to-$18 price may seem high by the standards of a few years back but actually accords pretty well with the industry's long-term experience.

Source: "We're Not Going to Freeze in the Dark." *Forbes,* June 27, 1988, pp. 106–107.

ta ta ta

The stakes are high. The U.S. Chamber of Commerce sums up the issue: "The social and economic well-being of this nation is dependent on the availability of energy."

Future energy crises can be avoided if the American public is willing to accept the realities of the energy situation.

The political arena resounded at that time [after the 1970s energy crisis] with calls for policies that would forever free the U.S. from dependence on foreign sources for energy supplies. But what has happened since the shortages of the 1970s and their symbol — long lines of cars at gasoline stations?

- Oil imports are close to 50 percent of domestic use and could be 60 percent by the end of the 1990s.

- No new U.S. nuclear power plants have been ordered and put into construction since 1973. Indeed, utilities have canceled plans for some 65 plants since the 1979 incident at Three Mile Island. Some operational and nearly operational plants have been abandoned, with investors and utility customers absorbing losses in the billions of dollars.

- The nation's electricity-generating industry warns that existing barriers to construction of sufficient capacity must fall if there is to be enough electricity to support economic growth over the next decade.

- While coal is the nation's most abundant fuel, producers and consumers are warning that pending legislation could curtail its use and sharply increase its costs.

- The hydropower industry says that its efforts simply to maintain — much less expand — its role as a major energy supplier are being hampered by unreasonable government actions.

Source: Bacon, Donald C. "A New Energy Crisis?" *Nation's Business,* February 1990.

꘠ ꘠ ꘠

Energy is not going to be a problem in the next few decades. There will be more than enough oil, gas, and coal to fuel accelerated economic growth at reasonable prices.

But the important point about the distant future of world energy, beyond the year 2000, is that it won't be dominated by fossil fuels. The hydrocarbons of today — coal and oil and gas — are already an aging technology, and the same can be said for conventional nuclear power. The future belongs to energy sources now in their infancy of research and development. Technology will work several small miracles between now and 2000, and "enough" energy may even turn into "too much."

Exotic new materials and some old familiar ones in new guises are going to work wondrous changes in the next two decades, replacing such old standbys as steel, glass, lead, zinc and copper in a number of important applications.

For example: a kind of fiber-reinforced plastic stronger than steel but so light that it can be used for unsinkable boat hulls. Another strong enough to replace high-performance steel in auto drive shafts and leaf springs. And others to serve as bushings, gaskets, hoses and other auto parts that will resist fierce wear, high temperatures and corrosive materials.

And new kinds of ceramics will turn up in many uses requiring high durability and heat resistance, such as auto parts.

Biotechnology — the manipulation of organic processes to make new products — will be the hottest new line in the 90's.

It is going to revolutionize health care, agriculture, fuel production and parts of our industrial complex. The overall result will be an enormous contribution to American productivity and prosperity — something on the order of what computers have done and will be doing at the same time.

There is an interesting parallel building up, in fact, between the micro-organism business and the microchip business: Biotech is today roughly where computers stood 15 or 20 years ago — on the threshold of a takeoff so steep that it left most of the early prophets (and profits) in the dust.

The energy implications of biotech also are substantial. Just now, due to the abundance of cheap oil, the drive to find alternate sources is pretty much on hold. This is understandable enough; folks don't worry about a leaky roof when the sun is shining.

But biotech conversion of cellulose into alcohol is potentially so inexpensive and so productive that it may turn out to be economically feasible even while oil is plentiful. The same may be true for biotech recovery from nominally exhausted fields and of hard-to-reach heavy oils, shales and tar sands.

Source: Kiplinger Staff. *The New American Boom,* Washington, D.C.: The Kiplinger Washington Editors, Inc., pp. 41, 90–91, 96–98.

ია ია ია

You've got an In box and an Out box — now add a Recycling box. American companies are finding they can cut down on trash-disposal costs, and even make a few bucks, by selling their old reports, memos, and computer printouts to recycling dealers.

In New Jersey, AT&T admonishes employees with messages like this: "AT&T's Recycling Program — It's the Law! Virtually all papers are recyclable at AT&T."

The company's program is a direct response to New Jersey's mandatory recycling law. But AT&T has found that the effort also makes good business sense. Cheryl La Perna, the firm's recycling coordinator, reports that in 1988 the company made $190,000 on the 3,800 tons of used office paper it collected. "Ninety percent of our solid waste is paper," says La Perna. "We're a paper factory, no doubt about it."

Other companies are taking similar steps. The Office Paper Recycling Service, part of the Council on the Environment of New York City, has designed 150 corporate recycling programs that together collect 600 tons of paper each month. Merrill Lynch has set up paper-collection areas in its World Financial Center offices; since 1986 the paper has brought in $300,000 and Merrill Lynch has saved $200,000 in trash-hauling costs.

In Rhode Island every employer of more than 500 people is required to submit a plan for reduction and recycling of waste, and some 20 other states are considering comparable measures.

Source: Stambler, Lyndon. "Reach Out and Recycle Something." *Sierra*, November-December 1989.

ﻬ ﻬ ﻬ

The baby boom's population tidal wave — the 76 million Americans born between 1946 and 1964 — is about to enter its most productive years. In 1986, the first boomers turned 40, marking the start of what population experts believe will be a decades-long period of profound change.

First, because people ages 35 to 54 are in their peak years of earning power, the spending implications are awesome. An increase of just 1 percent in the number of people in this age bracket causes added consumer outlays of $9 billion yearly, and their ranks will grow by as much as 40 percent in the next decade.

The baby boomers are likely to spend money differently than 40-year-olds of a decade ago.

People at this stage of life tend to spend relatively less of their rising income and to save more of it. Economist Arnold X. Moskowitz of Dean Witter Reynolds traces the rise of credit card debt to the maturing of baby boomers starting in the late 1960s. With their children growing up and their necessities provided for, these people will become investors, Moskowitz predicts, as they begin to accumulate assets for their later years. He sees trillions of additional dollars being channeled into securities by the mid 1990s.

Investment Implications: Whether they spend or save or do both, the impact will be enormous. . . . Dual-earner families will have "much more income at their disposal."

Source: "Boomers Roar into Middle Age." *Changing Times,* September 1988, p. 60.

ЅА ЅА ЅА

Still Counting: The days for the 6-billionth, 7-billionth, and 8-billionth human beings are anticipated for 1998, 2010, and 2023 respectively, according to U.N. forecasts. By the latter date, the human exodus from the earth may have begun, with small but growing numbers of people living and working in space and on the moon and Mars.

Source: Hamil, Ralph E. "The Arrival of the 5 Billionth Human." *The Futurist,* July-August 1987, p. 37.

ЅА ЅА ЅА

If progress is to be made toward alleviating hunger and malnutrition, agricultural, trade, and food-distribution policies have to be approached from an international perspective and coordinated with monetary and fiscal policies.

The dreadful irony is that, during most of the 1980s, there was enough food to feed the hungry. Before the 1988 drought, food surpluses were five times larger than were needed for this purpose.

Research by the Food and Agriculture program of the International Institute for Applied Systems Analysis (IIASA) has concluded that the problem of hunger amidst plenty stems from a malfunctioning of the world food system. While the economic, trade, and agricultural policies of individual countries may seem rational in the light of national goals toward food self-sufficiency and a viable domestic agricultural sector, taken together as a world food system, such policies are a failure. Nations pursuing their individual goals do not operate necessarily in the best interest of the world food system as a whole or of the world's hungry populations.

Source: Helmuth, John W. "World Hunger Amidst Plenty." *USA Today,* March 1989.

Key Quotations

I ask the Great Creator silently . . . to permit me to speak to Him through the three great Kingdoms of the world which He has created — the animal, the mineral, and vegetable . . .

George Washington Carver
(the scientist who in four days discovered over 100 uses
for the "unusable" peanut)

If you fully obey the LORD your God and carefully follow all his commands I give you today, the LORD your God will set you high above all the nations on earth. All these blessings will come upon you and accompany you if you obey the LORD your God:

You will be blessed in the city and blessed in the country.

The fruit of your womb will be blessed, and the crops of your land and the young of your livestock — the calves of your herds and the lambs of your flocks.

Your basket and your kneading trough will be blessed.

Deuteronomy 28:1–5

THE QUALITY OF LIFE MYTH

Key Question: Is it our right to determine value in human life?

Setting: A P.T.A. meeting focuses on the agenda behind "values clarification" techniques.

B ill and Barb Jenkins were the kind of couple that really frustrate a pastor. They were faithful attenders at church and always brought their two boys, Mike and Ryan. Their marriage was stable. From outward appearances they seemed like an ideal team for leadership roles in the church. But they had always held back. Now their son Mike was blossoming as a young Christian leader, and David wondered how they were feeling. He didn't have to wait long.

David was surprised when his secretary buzzed through to tell him Mrs. Jenkins was calling. But he was even more surprised when he picked up the phone and said, "Hello, Barb." As if his voice were a starter's pistol, Barb took off in a sprinted explanation of why she was calling that lasted several minutes without a pause. She was obviously distraught, and David was able to piece together a situation that was irritatingly familiar. Barb's younger boy, Ryan, who was a fifth grader, had come home from school confused and upset about an exercise that had been part of his classroom experience that day. He and his class-mates had been involved in a "lifeboat simulation game" in which each person was required to take on the character of someone in a group lost at sea. With provisions depleting rapidly, the group was told to decide who would get the benefit of the food and water that was left, and who would have to die. Ryan had been assigned the role of a blind person and had been shocked to be one of the first "sacrificed" by the group, along with several other kids with roles as disabled people. Ryan had tried to describe for his mother what it had felt like to sit there with his blindfold on and hear his classmates calmly decide that blind people didn't really deserve to live as much as people who could see.

There were times during the rush of words when Barb was over-come with tears, feeling for her son's pain, and tears of anger at those who had caused his sense of worthlessness. She stopped and took a deep breath. Then came her questions. "Can they really do this? What's the purpose of a 'game' like this? Do they know how they make kids feel? What are they trying to teach, anyway? How can we stop this?" And then, as if taking a determined step of commitment, "We've got to find a way to stop this. I don't want other mothers to have to discover that their children have been 'educated' in the way Ryan was."

David realized how close his own son Jacob was to being in the same grade. Then he imagined Julie having to comfort their son after an experience like the one he had just heard. He felt his own anger rising. "Barb, thanks for calling me. I share your concern not only as your pastor, but also as a parent. So-called 'games' like Ryan experienced are part of what is known as 'death education' curriculum, and it's being used in far too many schools. It is usually described as a program to help kids understand and cope with death. Actually, beyond causing pain and confusion like Ryan felt, there are deeper problems with this whole approach to life."

Her next question had a steely ring to it, "So, what can we do?"

David guessed he hadn't been the top name on her list to call. "What have you tried already, Barb?" he asked.

"I called the teacher at her home to ask her if other students had reacted the same way as my son. She told me it happens once in a while, but most of the kids just have fun with the game. I asked her if the game was important enough to cause even one student such anguish. She answered that the game was part of an important curriculum in the system, and that any changes would have to be taken up with the principal.

"I couldn't find his home number, but I was on the phone with him at school first thing this morning. Ryan's teacher must have warned him because he was so condescending to me it made me sick! He tried to tell me that mothers often overreact to their children having a bad day and that he had instructed the teacher to make sure the next time the class played the game that Ryan should get a role with better chances of survival. I tried to tell him as calmly as I could that I did not want my child involved in games like these under any circumstances. Then he told me it was not the school policy to exempt children from the accepted normal curriculum of the school, and any exceptions would have to be taken up with the board of education, at their Parents and Teachers meeting. I've found out that meeting is in two weeks."

David whistled softly and said, "Barb, you've done a lot already!"

She sighed as she responded, "I feel like I'm the one who is suddenly having to get an education. I had no idea what was going on. The things Mike has been talking about here at home are starting to make sense. He has sure learned a lot from you, and Bill and I appreciate the time you've spent with him. I'm sorry it has taken something like this to make us realize we have to get involved too!"

David knew they needed to move fast because of the short time before the board meeting, so he asked, "Do you think there are other parents who would share your concerns?"

"You bet they would, if they knew," said Barb emphatically. "And I'm going to make sure they know!"

Before they hung up they decided to have a parents' meeting at the Jenkins' home in two days to discuss how the issue might be handled at the board meeting. David felt like he had just witnessed God flipping a switch inside a person. In spite of the concern and the pain Barb was feeling, it was also clear that she was now filled with a profound awareness that God's value of life is being challenged everywhere and a new realization that God wants Christians to take the offensive wherever those challenges occur.

Two nights later, David could tell Barb had been busy by the number of cars parked in front of the Jenkins' house. There were seven couples gathered in the living room. To David, they seemed like an army. Their presence was proof of what can happen when one person really gets involved. He also realized the group was a little like a hornet's nest. There was great energy in the room that God could channel to benefit many people. But, that same energy, left to run a misguided course, could become ugly, divisive, and ineffective. These people were committed to action; now they needed to clarify the kind of action they should take.

After each parent shared briefly their personal concerns, David laid a foundation for their planning by reminding them from the Bible that God has designated parents as those primarily responsible for the education of their children. That responsibility is not removed by sending children off to public schools. Parents must be involved in monitoring and even changing the system if it is not accomplishing the proper educational goals. Parents should not allow themselves to feel like intruders in the school system. They are simply overseeing those who are assisting in the educational process. When parents make the effort to know who's teaching their children, and what is being taught, they are being obedient to God.

Part of the discussion and planning that night revolved around the importance of having clear goals for what needed to be accomplished at the P.T.A. and board meetings. Several couples volunteered to do specific research on the school curriculum and be prepared with facts should they be needed. Barb was designated as spokesperson for the group, but others were prepared to speak if she needed help. They decided their primary objective for this meeting would be to ask the board to suspend indefinitely the use of the 'death education' curriculum. Barb initiated an open time of prayer at the close of the meeting and David was glad that, although several of the couples were obviously not Christians, there was a common acknowledgement that the group needed God's help to care effectively for their kids.

The next P.T.A. meeting was unusually well attended. Word had gotten out that questions about parts of the curriculum would be raised. David immediately noticed that, besides their group, there was another large group of people sitting with Sheila Turner from Planned Population. The parents with Barb and David had decided beforehand that it would be better if they scattered themselves throughout the crowd. They hoped it would add to their impact to be seen as individual parents with concerns, rather than to be considered as an organized group.

After some minor items of business, an open discussion time was announced and the superintendent recognized Ms. Turner as the first to speak. She began, "Unfortunately, even in today's progressive society, there remains a small but rather vocal group of narrow-minded fundamentalist churchgoers who are attempting to prevent their children from being trained in certain difficult, yet essential realities of life. Furthermore, their efforts do not stop at prohibiting their own children's healthy social development. They are adamant in forcing their views upon others who are committed to nothing less than the best possible education for their children in this new and challenging era. We must all make hard decisions and children will be faced more and more in this age with the need to properly measure the quality of different forms of human life. Not even religious extremists should be allowed to indefinitely shield their children from these basic truths that impact us all. It has been brought to my attention that even tonight someone may recommend that we do away with the essential 'values clarification' curriculum. Some have had the audacity to question the value of an outstanding tool like the 'lifeboat simulation game,' which has so effectively trained children how to deal with placing appropriate value on life. My sincere hope is that we will not allow such a ridiculous perspective to dominate this meeting and I would even suggest that we limit further discussion since there are so many more important items on tonight's agenda."

Surprisingly, the superintendent acted as if the final word had been spoken and was about to move on to another issue, when Barb Jenkins stood and requested the floor. After being acknowledged by the chairperson, Barb began to speak. Those who had spent time with her in the previous weeks could sense the tension in her, and the difficulty she was having in expressing herself with composure. But she forged ahead anyway.

"I am a Christian and not at all ashamed of it. I am also opposed to this school system attempting to teach my fifth-grade son that the lives of human beings can be given different values by creating a cruel game in which children are forced to devalue the lives of others. I cannot see one positive reason for the exercise. What I do see is callous attitudes being confirmed and tender children confused. Do we really believe we can determine that a dentist's life is somehow worth more than the life of a carpenter?

"Who do we think we are that we should make such decisions on behalf of others? I am offended with the way this has negatively impacted my son and I am deeply troubled with the whole notion that children, or anyone for that matter, should be making decisions on who should die first in adverse circumstances. I ask the board to please suspend indefinitely the use of this 'values clarification' curriculum and encourage teachers to spend the added time teaching our children basic skills like reading. The high value of human life has already been established by God."

Before she could explain her last statement, an angry teacher stood, and, pointing his finger at Barb, said, "I'm sick and tired of religious fanatics like you trying to tell the whole world what's right and wrong and how to live our lives." There was actually some scattered applause around the room. Everyone was breathing tension.

The chairperson acknowledged someone in back of David and asked the man to identify himself. David looked back but didn't recognize the person about to speak. He only observed the calm and businesslike air of the man. Then came what David later described as an example of God's unexpected reinforcements. The man identified himself as John Peterson and spoke briefly and powerfully. "It troubles me a great deal that any person in this district who is concerned about the specific instruction our children are receiving in the classroom is automatically labelled and attacked as a religious fanatic or fundamentalist. It is clear that honest questions and recommendations are being discarded without consideration of the merit of the issues being addressed. I'm responding to this in several ways. First, as a non-religious person, much less a fundamentalist, I am offended to see concerns which I happen to share with Mrs. Jenkins dismissed because of her obvious belief in God. The lifeboat exercise is an aggressive attempt to teach certain values, which I believe have been stated by Ms. Turner. In our system, Barb Jenkins has just as much right to defend and promote her values as does Ms. Turner. Second, as a lawyer, I'm seriously wondering about the conduct of these proceedings and the possibility of a case for slander. And third, if I'm not mistaken, Ms. Turner doesn't even have children in this school system. It makes me wonder how appropriate it is for her to be the prime spokesperson for one side in what is supposed to be a parent, teacher, and administrators' meeting.

"I am a professional and a non-religious man who would have probably been all for this kind of curriculum ten years ago. But I have watched the devastating effect this kind of teaching has had on my daughter. We have gone too far. The fact is that the classroom is not a place of neutral values. The values that are being promoted there right now do not reflect mine or anyone else's I respect. I want steps taken to change this. I'm fully prepared to follow up this request with legal action, if necessary.

"I also want to publicly thank Mrs. Jenkins for bringing this problem to light. She deserves the appreciation of all the parents in this district. And as for being a religious fanatic, if mothers like her bring up sons who are as caring and responsible as her son Mike has shown himself to be in my daughter's life, then I say as a father, 'More power to you!'"

The mood of the meeting had taken a new turn. The superintendent realized things were not proceeding as he and Ms. Turner had planned. He tried to salvage the situation, saying, "We still have many items on this evening's agenda, but it is obvious this issue is the main reason many of you are here tonight. So, in the interest of fairness, I want to invite Mrs. Jenkins to present a proposal and we will assign a P.T.A. task force to come up with some satisfactory solutions for all concerned."

Barb stood once again, took a deep breath, and took the next few minutes to share the following. "This school district needs to focus once again on teaching basic educational skills to our young children. Scores on tests our high school students are taking indicate that more attention must be given to the core curriculum. This, however, is not my primary concern. We must realize, as has already been alluded to, that instruction is impossible without values. But because of a widely held myth that the classroom can be 'values-neutral,' few teachers are ever asked to examine or explain their own personal value system. Yet they are teaching that value system, often unconsciously, every day to our children, right along with the dates and facts and figures of education.

"The Judeo-Christian value system is one that exemplifies life and hope. In so many cultures there is a morbid preoccupation with death and despair. This same kind of thinking is influencing our society more and more. Many people, whether religious or not, are becoming alarmed and saying we need to see a change if there is going to be a world worth living in for future generations.

"We need to ask ourselves some hard questions and wrestle with the truth until we have solid answers to why there is pandemic teen suicide and drug abuse. What kind of message are we sending children when they are required by their teachers, who are supposed to be role models, to place greater value on one person's life over another's because of societal status, income, or disabilities? How can an adult, much less a fifth grader, determine the quality of human life as we would compare the value of sacks of flour and wheat?

"If we are going to insist on discussing the possibility of spending thirty days at sea in a lifeboat, then why not put the emphasis on what it would take to keep everyone alive. Or what about emphasizing the beauty of putting other people's needs above our own and the importance of caring for those who are less fortunate than we are? Where are children being given a chance to learn the virtue of self-sacrifice and the joy and fulfillment that it brings to life? What we seem to be teaching is a 'me first,' or 'me only' mentality to this generation. Do we really think it is more important for the dentist to survive in the lifeboat or for the dentist to forfeit the last of the water to the elderly woman or the blind child?

"And as far as dealing with the reality of death itself and not just focusing on an unrealistic situation, wouldn't it be better to remind ourselves and our children that every one of us in this room is going to die? It is an undeniable fact. Beyond that fact it is religion, faith, or speculation, to offer answers. Still, humans, faced with unavoidable death, have to have an answer. The nihilistic belief that this brief earthly existence is all there is offers only one answer. But I find it a terribly disappointing ending to the wonderful story of life if all we have to look forward to is the bottom of a six-foot deep hole. Given the present atmosphere in this nation, I may never see the Christian answer clearly explained as one of the answers in the classroom, but I refuse to accept the present arrangement in which children are only allowed to consider a hopeless humanistic outlook. I'm tired of the anti-Christian death fixation that permeates much of this so-called 'values' teaching.

"The 'death education' curriculum does not accomplish the goals most parents have for their children's understanding of death, or the worth of life. Therefore I am asking again that steps be taken to permanently delete this part of the curriculum. I will continue to work at this until it is accomplished!"

Following the meeting, David made his way back to John Peterson. John spoke first, "I have to tell you, David, my daughter has been a different girl since hanging out at your church and with Mike. Thanks for whatever it is you have done to give her this new perspective. My wife and I have even been thinking about visiting your church."

"You would be more than welcome," said David, amazed at all the ways God was working behind the scenes in people's lives. Then he thought to himself, "The death-style view lost a battle tonight! I'm going to trust God to have the life-style view gain the upper hand in this school and community in the not-too-distant future."

Comment

Significant battles are waged every day in the war against the erosion of truth in our society. Parents, lax in their assumptions about the educational system, are often shocked to discover what their children are actually learning. This is not to say that there aren't vocal Christians within the educational system. However, involved Christian parents have much more say in the content of their children's education than they realize. They may also discover as they begin to monitor their school system, that there are many other parents who share the same basic concern that children should get an education based on truthful and positive values. These shared concerns may be God's way of preparing some parents to hear the gospel for the first time.

In the News

Fallout-Shelter

Purpose: This is a simulated problem-solving exercise.

Procedure: The class is divided into groups of six or seven, who then sit together. The teacher explains the situation to the groups.

"Your group are members of a department in Washington, D.C., that is in charge of experimental stations in the far outposts of civilization. Suddenly the Third World War breaks out and bombs begin dropping. Places all across the globe are being destroyed. People are heading for whatever fallout shelters are available. You receive a desperate call from one of your experimental stations, asking for help.

"It seems that there are ten people but there is only enough space, air, food, and water in their fallout shelter for six people for a period of three months—which is how long they estimate they can safely stay down there. They will abide by your decision.

"You have half-an-hour to make your decision. Then you will have to go to your own shelter.

"It is entirely possible that the six people you choose to stay in the shelter might be the only six people left to start the human race over again. Try to make the best choices possible. Here is all you know about the ten people:

1. Bookkeeper; 31 years old

2. His wife; six months pregnant

3. Black militant; second year medical student

4. Famous historian-author; 42 years old

5. Hollywood starlet; singer; dancer

6. Biochemist

7. Rabbi; 54 years old

8. Olympic athlete; all sports

9. College coed

10. Policeman with gun (they cannot be separated)

Obituary

Purpose: Again, this strategy helps the student see his life more clearly from the perspective of his imagined death. This exercise raises specific issues about the quality of one's life. It reinforces the fact that we still have a life ahead of us to do whatever we want.

Procedure: The teacher says, "We are going to look at life by viewing it again from the perspective of death. I am going to ask you to write out your own obituary.

When everyone is finished, students may volunteer to read their obituaries out loud, or they might share their obituaries in smaller, more personal and supportive groups.

Source: Simon, Sidney B., Leland W. Howe, and Howard Kirschenbaum.
Values Clarification: A Handbook of Practical Strategies for Teachers and Students, (New York: Dodd, Mead and Company, 1972).

ta ta ta

At Children's Hospital in St. Louis, Missouri, a 13-year-old boy with Muscular Dystrophy died when life support machines were turned off and a Doctor gave him an injection of potassium chloride. Potassium chloride is a fatal drug that stops heart activity.

Source: "Euthanasia Exists." *St. Louis Post Dispatch,* September 9, 1988.

ta ta ta

Terminally ill people and their families may soon have more control over how patients spend their last days, under new policies demanded by the Joint Commission on Accreditation of Hospitals.

Beginning in January, the Chicago-based agency, which accredits most of the nation's hospitals, will require health facilities to establish formal written policies on when doctors should stop trying to save patients whose deaths are imminent.

For the first time, many hospitals will have to consider the sensitive medical, ethical and legal issues of whether to withhold lifesaving techniques.

Hospitals failing to comply with the new standards may lose accreditation, the commission said.

Source: Robinson, Tracey. "Panel Aims at Deathbed Issues." *Chicago Sun-Times,* July 27, 1987.

ta ta ta

A man who had been in a semi-conscious state, or coma, since 1978 has now revived to the point of being able to carry on conversations. Michigan resident Earl Lanning had suffered a brain hemorrhage due to an aneurysm.

Lanning has been treated with steroids, which reduced the brain swelling enough to allow the recovery. He now remembers much about his accident, and many of the conversations nurses were having with him during the period he was in a semi-coma.

Source: "Coma Victim Revives After 10 Years." *The New Federalist,* June 3, 1988.

ta ta ta

RIGHT-TO-DIE: Nancy Gamble, paralyzed by incurable Lou Gehrig's disease, died in Nashville, minutes after doctors unhooked her life-support system. They acted one day after Judge Robert Brandt ruled court permission isn't needed to end life-support for disabled people if the patient clearly wants it done. He said disabled patients enjoy the same rights as others. Disabled-rights advocates argued that Gamble, 50, could live at home with attendants.

Source: *Chicago Tribune,* April 12, 1990.

ta ta ta

Educational reform in the social studies, much like reform of education in general, hinges upon community awareness and especially community involvement.

Community involvement goes far beyond P.T.A. memberships, attending Christmas concerts, or occasional tutoring. Most P.T.A.'s have limited the meaning of community involvement with education to fund-raising activities for such items as band uniforms or athletic equipment. Except for an occasional "Drugs in the School" seminar, the P.T.A. infrequently promotes parental or community involvement in the educational process. This must change. With education being held in such low regard at this point in American educational history, it is imperative that schools promote community involvement.

For 150 years, educators have been telling parents that, in effect, "we will take care of the education of your children." Far too often, this resulted in the presumption (mostly by educators) that education was a commodity one could receive only in school and only by trained professionals. (The message of "stay away" has not been missed by parents, as witnessed by the disruptions caused by any unexpected cancellation of school.) The attitude that education takes place only in school by teachers must be discarded. Fortunately, some school districts have begun to correct this attitude and have started to draw parents back into the shaping of their children's education.

Source: Staley, George, and Joe Kincheloe. "Community Involvement in the Social Studies." *USA Today,* May 1988, p. 84.

ঌ ঌ ঌ

For all the attention American students are getting, they still lack something that most Japanese students have: a kyoiku mama, or education mother. "The single biggest influence on a kid's ability to learn is parental involvement," says Jerome Rosow, president of the Work in America Institute. "Research shows that the home outweighs everything, including intelligence."

Constance Barkley puts it best: "In the end, there is no substitute for active, individual involvement, whether it is going to a voting booth and pulling a lever, or going to a school and talking to teachers, or getting involved in a child's life." Barkley knows better than most how individual actions, added together, produce results. In New Orleans you don't see people trying to assign blame anymore. Now everyone is racing to be part of the solution.

Source: "Education Crisis: What Business Can Do." *Fortune,* July 4, 1988, p. 81.

Key Quotations

I am much afraid that schools will prove to be great gates of hell unless they diligently labor in explaining the Holy Scriptures, engraving them in the hearts of youth. I advise no one to place his child where the Scriptures do not reign paramount. Every institution in which men are not increasingly occupied with the Word of God must become corrupt.

Martin Luther

Our laws and our institutions must necessarily be based upon and embody the teachings of the Redeemer of mankind. It is impossible that it should be otherwise; and in this sense and to this extent our civilization and our institutions are emphatically Christian . . . This is a religious people. This is historically true. From the discovery of this continent to the present hour, there is a single voice making this affirmation . . . we find everywhere a clear recognition of the same truth . . . These, and many other matters which might be noticed, add a volume of unofficial declarations to the mass of organic utterances that this is a Christian nation.

Supreme Court Decision, 1892.
Church of the Holy Trinity v. United States

Hear, O Israel: The LORD our God, the LORD is one. Love the LORD your God with all your heart and with all your soul and with all your strength. These commandments that I give you today are to be upon your hearts. Impress them on your children. Talk about them when you sit at home and when you walk along the road, when you lie down and when you get up. Tie them as symbols on your hands and bind them on your foreheads. Write them on the doorframes of your houses and on your gates.

Deuteronomy 6:4–9

THE EVOLUTION MYTH

Key Question: Isn't evolution the only reasonable explanation for how the world came into existence?

Setting: David Sheffield debates the creation/evolution issue on television.

S o, this must be the Christian. He even looks like a Christian," said Joe Goldman as he was about to be introduced to David Sheffield in a television studio in downtown Chicago. David had been contacted with this opportunity just the day before by the program director for a local talk show. The topic of the day was to be "Creation versus Evolution." David was meeting Joe for the first time, though he knew Mr. Goldman's reputation as a fierce opponent of Christianity.

As they shook hands, David was impressed by Joe's relaxed attitude and warm smile. He had visualized a vicious, confrontational person but Joe Goldman proved him wrong. "So, what does a Christian look like?" he responded to Joe's comment. He was eager to correct any other misconceptions he might have of his debate opponent.

"Maybe we can cover that another time," said Joe. "Right now I need some makeup before we go on the set."

Shortly, the program director rounded them up and guided them to the stage. David was amazed at how adamant Joe was about the seating arrangements he desired. He was obviously a veteran debater and even understood the importance in our television age of effectively using lighting, makeup, and position to his best advantage. He insisted on being seated right next to the moderator. This meant he was almost always on the screen. David told the director he had no problem with Mr. Goldman's requests.

The host and moderator was a popular news anchorman at the station, known for his subtle, yet relentless attacks against anything even slightly resembling Christianity. Following brief introductions, the host announced that he wanted to set the stage for the debate by showing a video of a recent presentation made by Pastor Sheffield on scientific creationism. The studio was darkened and the tape rolled. The clip highlighted several statements David had made emphasizing the fairness of giving equal exposure to creationism alongside evolution in the school classroom. The clips had been carefully edited, splicing together the comments to make them so nonsensical that even David had to laugh. Judging from the laughter in the studio audience, no one else agreed with the taped version of David's statements either.

When the lights came up and the cameras moved in, the moderator turned to Mr. Goldman and asked him to comment on the minister's views. Joe didn't hesitate. "Mr. Sheffield obviously needs to enter the twentieth century in his thinking. We are no longer living in the dark ages when Christianity with its suppressive views kept people in mental bondage. I don't think people are willing to live in fantasy land any longer about such notions as a God, or for that matter, a creation. And as for being scientific, I believe the claim to be so ludicrous as to not even warrant further comment. Our public schools are teaching the fact of evolution and the sooner we can eradicate these ridiculous notions, which are nothing less than religious superstition, the better."

The moderator turned to David, confidently expecting to find an intimidated spokesman. David said, "Mr. Goldman has certainly made a bold statement about the 'fact' of evolution. Did I hear you correctly, Joe?"

"Yes, David. How could anyone in their right mind dispute that evolution is a fact?" responded Joe.

Although he suddenly wasn't sure where this was going, the moderator was glad this debate was off and running.

David continued, "Tell me, Joe, exactly which theory of origins do you adhere to?"

Joe looked puzzled. "I'm sorry, I don't understand what you mean. I thought I made it clear that I am convinced that evolution is the correct explanation for our present existence."

"What I am getting at," said David, "is that you have just made the audacious claim for the 'fact' of evolution. I am sure you are just as well aware as I am that there are at least thirty-two major competing theories of origins and I was interested in your sharing with the audience which one you believe in."

A few seconds passed which, in front of television cameras seemed like a lifetime, before David continued. "You seem somewhat perplexed. I'll mention some of the main theories. Which one makes the most sense to you, Joe? First, there is the oscillating universe theory. Then there is the expanding universe theory, which is also known as the big bang theory —"

At this, Joe interrupted to say eagerly, "Of course, everyone believes in the big bang theory."

"On the contrary, Joe," said David. "Your answer reveals that you are a child of the sixties. Scientifically, the big bang theory is considered an archaic view. The view in vogue today is the oscillating universe theory based on the evidence that there are red galaxies which are moving away from the Milky Way and blue galaxies which are moving toward the Milky Way. This definitely indicates the universe is in an oscillating pattern. If the big bang theory were correct, the one you state as fact, then all the galaxies would be red galaxies, since they would be moving away from us. That is required by a theory which pictures a large mass exploding at some point in the distant past to move forever apart, but the theory doesn't fit the observable facts, so it cannot itself be called a fact. How were you able to confidently claim it was a fact, Joe?"

Joe had no immediate answer, so David continued, "Here is my direct challenge to you, Joe. Do some research on evolution and decide which one of those thirty-two theories really takes in all the facts, and then I will be glad to meet you here again. But I warn you. Whichever theory of evolution you choose, I will prove to you it is completely ludicrous by quoting non-Christian scientists out of non-Christian journals."

It was the moderator who now entered the discussion. "How would you propose to do that, Pastor Sheffield?"

"Well," said David, "the interesting thing about the theories of evolution is that scientists themselves are extremely divided and competitive over which theories they protect and advocate. You see, no group of scientists can conclusively prove their own theory, but they can disprove the other group's theory in the hopes of making theirs more appealing by comparison. So each group methodically exposes the weaknesses or mistakes of all the other theories, while others are doing the same to their theory. It is really a vicious cycle. Yet, in spite of all this confusion, one still finds people glibly claiming evolution as fact!"

As if prodded into action, Joe rejoined the conversation, attempting to change the subject. "David, on the video, you made the unbelievable claim that the earth cannot be over 12,000 years old. How can you possibly argue with geological evidence to the contrary?"

With this change, the moderator jumped back into the conversation and announced a commercial break. During the intermission the moderator asked David to supply him with any articles and other material which would substantiate what he was presenting on the show.

After the break, the moderator asked David to answer the question Mr. Goldman had raised before the commercials. David was ready. "Yes, it is indeed scientifically impossible for the earth to be over 12,000 years old. I will use four widely accepted basic facts of science to make a case for a young earth.

"First, let's consider, for example, that the earth could not possibly be over 10 million years old, because we know the sun shrinks approximately five feet per hour. At that rate, the sun would have been so large 10 million years ago that no life could have grown on this planet because of the sun's incredible heat!

"Let's also consider the fact that we know the magnetic intensity of the earth diminishes 50 percent every 1400 years. If the earth was over 16,000 years old, it would have competed at one time with the sun for gravitational pull. This is also impossible given the fact that a solid planet like ours doesn't have the right kind of core to have had that kind of magnetic intensity.

"Also, we know, for example, that the earth's atmosphere is acquiring helium at a measurable rate. Since we know that helium does not escape the earth's atmosphere, we can measure the existing amount of helium, divide it by the rate of helium being added to the atmosphere, and come up with a time frame of less than 12,000 years. Using the ages often given to the earth, the amount of helium produced by now would have insured not only that we could not breathe, but that even if we could, we would all talk with squeaky voices!

"Moon dust is also a factual proof of a very young earth, and even for a young solar system. Remember when the Apollo space flight allowed Neil Armstrong to take that giant leap for mankind? Many scientists were expecting a depth of at least 100 feet of moon dust on the surface if the moon was 5 billion years old. After all, we can measure fairly accurately the amount of cosmic dust that falls on the earth's surface, and since that would be consistent with the moon's accumulation, that's the amount of dust we would expect to find there. The large figures for the age of these planets are pure guesses required by efforts to believe that all you need is time when you are waiting for primeval slime to evolve into you and me. But, back to the moon and what really happened. The whole world witnessed the disproving of many cherished scientific theories when Neil stepped off the ladder and stirred no more than a skiff of dust off the moon's rock hard surface."

The moderator couldn't hold back his question. "But what about all the scientists who still hold to evolution?"

"Actually," said David, "more and more scientists are abandoning the theory of evolution and embracing creation or at least some other explanation simply because evolution requires too much faith to believe. After all, Einstein himself claimed we certainly live in a universe of order and design which would logically require a Designer. A universe created by time and chance is a great fairy tale for those who just don't want to face the reality that there is a Being who is their Creator and to whom one day they will have to give an account for their lives. One group, the Creation Institute, now has over 600 scientists who hold to a literal twenty-four hour, six day creation having occurred some 6,000 to 10,000 years ago. I think that group will continue to grow as other scientists bail out of the evolution ship that is sinking from the damage of so much contradictory scientific data."

After the program, Joe and David happened to take the same elevator downstairs. David was again impressed with how cordial Joe had been. In spite of their differences, David found himself liking the man. When in the course of their conversation it became apparent that Joe would be taking a taxi home, David offered to drive him. He knew that an opponent defeated in debate is not usually convinced, but a person truly cared for will often be open to change. Besides, offering a ride was what Jesus would want him to do. They ended up having a delightful conversation. David discovered Joe was Jewish, and sincerely hoped that this man would meet the God who had chosen His people. David was delighted to hear not long after this that Joe had become a pro-life champion, even though many of his other views had remained unchanged.

Comment

Debates, like most competitive situations, can make enemies out of opponents. For the Christian, the words of Jesus about the treatment of those who see themselves as our enemies must be our guide. To disagree with another's ideas while loving him or her as a person is a task for which we need God's help. But we can't afford to forget that it is the error or the evil behind ideas that is our real enemy, not the people representing those ideas. They are also humans for whom Jesus died.

The theory of evolution is a good example of the fact that people who may resist our objections to the theory based on its contradiction of Scripture may be willing to question the theory themselves if given the chance to see its own internal weaknesses. Also, what may seem like a powerful idea under one name (evolution) may turn out to be fairly insignificant when seen as a group of diametrically opposed theories.

In the News

The fossils that decorate our family tree are so scarce that there are still more scientists than specimens. The remarkable fact is that all the physical evidence we have for human evolution can still be placed with room to spare, inside a single coffin!

There are gaping holes in the evolutionary record, some of them extending for 4 to 6 million years. Modern apes, for instance, seem to have sprung out of nowhere. They have no yesterday, no fossil record. And the true origin of modern humans—of upright, naked, toolmaking, big-brained beings—is, if we are to be honest with ourselves, an equally mysterious matter.

[One] theory is that of British marine biologist Sir Alister Hardy. In the light of the black hole in human history, it is an appealing idea, one well worth reviving.

In 1960, Hardy published a short paper in the British journal *New Scientist* in which he asked a simple question: "Was man more aquatic in the past?" He answered the question by suggesting that we might be the descendants not of an ancestor struggling to make good and stand on its own two feet in a dry and hostile environment, but of a successful aquatic ape. Sir Alister speculated that the "black hole" was, in effect, a "water hole" in which we not only learned to swim but became truly human.

In support of his hypothesis, Hardy pointed out that humans are unique among primates in having naked skin, something appropriate to an aquatic animal in a warm climate. Further, the areas of tiny residual hairs that still remain on the skin (and are clearly visible on a human fetus) are arranged in such a way that they offer least resistance to water flowing past the body during swimming.

Source: Watson, Lyall. "Speculations: The Water People." *Science Digest,* May 1982, p. 44.

ɪ ɪ ɪ

Life on earth may have been born in a thick, protein-rich stew rather than in a thin consommé of amino acids, says Clifford N. Matthews of the University of Illinois in Chicago. His controversial hypothesis suggests that first hydrogen cyanide was created from methane and ammonia found in the earth's primordial atmosphere. Clouds of hydrogen cyanide then rapidly polymerized to produce a complex mixture of long-chain molecules that settled into the earth's oceans and reacted with water to form proteins. This scenario differs markedly from other, more widely accepted theories that propose the formation initially of amino acids from which proteins were later built (SN: 1/31/81, p. 72).

Source: "In the beginning, perhaps cyanide." *Science News,* April 21, 1984, p. 247.

ια ια ια

When the Earth was very young, it rumbled with active volcanoes, and the skies swarmed with heavy clouds from which rain poured. Then, within half a million years, the conditions necessary for the development of life were met. Trying to unravel just how life came to exist on this planet has been one of science's most fundamental and perplexing problems. Working scientists, 4 billion years after the fact, have come to believe that the elemental building blocks of life — the amino acids, the purines and pyrimidines, the sugars and fats — arose in the Earth's primordial broth through the action of lightning and sunlight on simple atmospheric molecules. For the past three decades they have assumed that the recipe for this soup of life contained ammonia, methane, hydrogen and water. But recently they seem to have come to a new consensus about the probable composition of the early atmosphere; the cosmic cookbook is being rewritten.

"The overwhelming majority of chemical-evolution experiments since the first one, done thirty years ago, may have been conducted with the wrong atmospheric mixture," he says [Dr. Joel Levine, a 40-year-old atmospheric scientist at NASA's Langley Research Center in Hampton, Virginia]. "None of the experiments included oxygen, which we believe was present in at least small quantities. And until recently no one was aware of the high levels of ultraviolet radiation that the young sun most probably emitted. These levels are lethal to living systems as we know them. How could life have formed and evolved in such a hostile environment?"

Source: Huyghe, Patrick. "New Recipe for Cosmic Soup." *Science Digest,* May 1983, p. 42.

🌺 🌺 🌺

In This History of the Earth according to many college students, cave-men fought marauding dinosaurs and fossils are the remains of animals that didn't make it onto Noah's ark. These and other opinions contrary to established science are drawn from a survey of 2,100 students at 41 campuses around the country and are reported in this month's issue of Current Anthropology.

More striking than this is how many students adhere to Biblical ac-counts — 38 percent agreed that human life began in Eden.

Source: "Caveman Smarts." *Newsweek,* May 30, 1988, p. 59.

🌺 🌺 🌺

In the 1970's . . . the fundamentalists developed a new strategy: to es-tablish the Biblical account of creation as a respectable scientific theory and demand equal time for its teaching. By one count there are some 700 scientists with respectable academic credentials who give credence to creation-science, the general theory that complex life forms did not evolve but appeared "abruptly."

Justice Antonin Scalia, in a dissent joined by Chief Justice William H. Rehnquist, argued that the citizens of Louisiana were entitled to pro-vide their students "whatever scientific evidence there may be against evolution."

Source: "Keeping God Out of the Classroom: A New High Court Ruling." *Newsweek,* June 29, 1987.

🌺 🌺 🌺

It was only seven years ago when Ronald Reagan, on a campaign swing through Texas, was asked what he thought about the teaching of evolu-tion. He replied, "It is a scientific theory only, and it is not believed in the scientific community to be as infallible as it once was believed. But if it is going to be taught in the schools, then I think the Biblical story of creation should also be taught."

Newspaper polls, over the years, have consistently shown that one-half to three-fourths of the public believe that both evolution and creationism should be taught in public schools.

Source: Donaldson, Ken. "The Creationism Controversy: It's Only the Beginning." *School Library Journal,* March 1988, p. 107.

ва ва ва

Earth's Magnetic Field: The needle of the compass points to the North Magnetic Pole. Like all forces of nature, the energy in this dipole magnetic field is decaying (decreasing in strength) due in part to the 2nd Law of Thermodynamics. The strength has dropped 6 percent since measurements began in 1835.

The physicist who has studied this in greatest detail is Dr. Thomas Barnes. His conclusion is that the half-life of this magnetic field is approximately 830 to 1400-years.

This means that 830 to 1400-years ago the magnetic field would have been twice as strong as it is today. Another 830 to 1400-years before that, it would have been 4-times as strong and so on. According to Dr. Barnes:

"If we went back about 10-thousand years, the Earth's magnetic field would have been as strong as the field in a magnetic star. A magnetic star is like our Sun; it has a nuclear power source. Surely our Earth never had a nuclear source like the Sun. Surely our Earth never had a magnetic field stronger than that of a star. That would limit the age of the Earth to 10-thousand years."

Helium in Earth's Atmosphere: Former Nobel-prize nominee Dr. Melvin Cook has studied Earth's natural helium supplies extensively. Eventually, he became convinced that the reason there is so little of this gas in the atmosphere is that the planet is relatively young.

Uranium and thorium deposits throughout the world are steadily producing helium. More helium enters our atmosphere from the Sun and from helium leaking from the Earth's core through the crust. If Earth was actually billions of years old, Dr. Cook believes the atmosphere should now contain a much larger amount of helium, up to a million times more than now exists.

Where is the helium? Very little of it can escape into space. Dr. Cook and other physicists believe the atmospheric helium indicates Earth's age is no more than 10-to 15-thousand years.

Population Growth: The rapid growth of Earth's human population has been an important topic of concern for a number of years. This study has produced information which has been interpreted as evidence of Earth's young age. If people have been living here for a million years or more (as Evolutionists claim), some Creationists wonder: why has there been no global overpopulation problem long before now?

Some say the average world population growth over the centuries has been about 2 percent per year. One can be generous to the Evolutionists and assume that the growth rate was actually much smaller, perhaps ½ percent per year.

Even at that rate, it would take only 4,000-years to produce today's population beginning from a single original couple.

Is the Sun Shrinking? Even at very conservative rates there is still a problem for those who believe in a billions-of-years-old Earth and Sun.

It can be shown that for 99.8 percent of Earth's supposed Evolutionary age it could have been too hot for life to exist due to the Sun's greater size. These conservative figures also indicate the Sun could have been twice its present radius only 1-million years ago. 210-million years ago the Sun could have been large enough to touch Earth. Even only 10-million years ago, the Sun could have been too large for life on the planet.

Meteorites: Meteorite: Fallen meteor; a mass of metal or stone from a meteor that has fallen upon Earth, the Moon, or any other body in space.

Every year, many meteorites pierce Earth's atmosphere and are deposited on the ground. Thus, if Earth's strata have indeed been building up over billions of years, it would seem that finding pieces of "fossil" meteorites in the strata should not be too uncommon. Yet, it is—extremely so. Meteorites are almost never found in the strata (some say never).

This makes good sense if Creationists are right. They believe the majority of Earth's strata were laid down rapidly, mostly during the year of Noah's Flood.

Space Dust: When astronauts first landed on the Moon, many Evolutionists expected a very thick layer of loose dust. Depth estimates ranged from 50 to 180 feet—and even much higher. Sinking deep into this dust was at least one astronaut's greatest fear about landing on the Moon. Thus, large, saucer-shaped feet were provided on the Lunar Lander.

What did astronauts actually discover? The loose dust layer was quite minor. Dr. Slusher and others interpreted this as evidence that the Moon is not billions of years old, and have also pointed to low loose meteoritic dust measurements on planets and the rarity of meteoritic material in Earth's oceans.

[Author's note: In our opinion, this company has produced the best video series on the evolution/creation debate currently in existence.]

Source: "The Earth, A Young Planet." *The Illustrated Origins Answer Book,* pp. 14, 16–17.

Key Quotations

Atheism is so senseless. When I look at the solar system, I see the earth at the right distance from the sun to receive the proper amounts of heat and light. This did not happen by chance. The motions of the planets require a Divine Arm to impress them.

Isaac Newton

I don't believe there are any new objections to be discovered to the truth of Christianity. Men may argue ingeniously against our faith, but what can they say in defense of their own?

Francis Scott Key

The wrath of God is being revealed from heaven against all the godlessness and wickedness of men who suppress the truth by their wickedness, since what may be known about God is plain to them, because God has made it plain to them. For since the creation of the world God's invisible qualities—his eternal power and divine nature—have been clearly seen, being understood from what has been made, so that men are without excuse.

For although they knew God, they neither glorified him as God nor gave thanks to him, but their thinking became futile and their foolish hearts were darkened. Although they claimed to be wise, they became fools and exchanged the glory of the immortal God for images made to look like mortal man and birds and animals and reptiles.

Therefore God gave them over in the sinful desires of their hearts to sexual impurity for the degrading of their bodies with one another. They exchanged the truth of God for a lie, and worshiped and served created things rather than the Creator — who is forever praised. Amen.

Romans 1:21–25

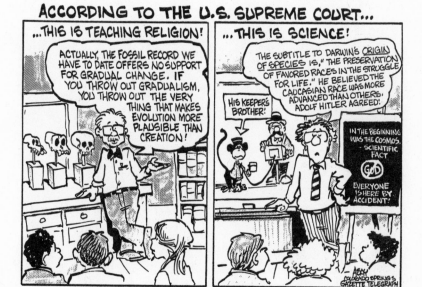

THE SPIRITUAL ESCAPE MYTH

Key Question: What may happen in our future if Christ doesn't return
soon to take us out of this mess?

Setting: Christian young people develop a play to explore potential future consequences of today's actions (Act I).

G etting calls from the Jenkins family had recently become one of
the highlights of David's life. He could see specific ways in
which each of the members of that family were growing in their desire
to be consistent with their faith in Jesus Christ. So, David was more
delighted than surprised by Mike's latest call. He and several other high
school students had come up with an idea to communicate, through
drama, what might happen in our society in the next twenty years if
things continued as they were. As they talked, David noticed that Mike
had obviously gotten his organized mind from his mother. The plan was
well along already. Mike was asking David to meet with the group and
give his input.

After meeting with Mike and the other students from the youth
group, David concluded that he finally understood why they call a wide
open, no-holds-barred, creative session, brainstorming! From the start,

the kids owned the idea. It was to be their play. David felt like he had another front row seat to something new God was doing.

David, used to leading, found himself in the follower's seat. For once it felt good. As the students planned, they occasionally glanced a question his way, but they were doing so well that his only responses were smiles and approving nods. These young people had been listening after all. Now they had something to say. Roles and duties were snatched up as the script began to take shape. By the end of that first meeting, the students had a story outline, several main characters described, and many technical decisions made. Almost everyone left the session with specific duties to accomplish. It turned out they even had a role for David to play. The kids laughingly told him they had tried hard not to typecast him, so they had given him the role of pastor in the play.

The next two months were a whirlwind of re-writes, twice-a-week rehearsals, and prop-building parties. Repeatedly, students commented that never before had they worked so hard, yet had so much fun. Along the way, what began as a simple play for the church family mushroomed into a sold-out extravaganza for the entire community. The youth group decided to use the proceeds to help underwrite a trip to Washington, D.C. for the March for Life, held every January 22 to remember the infamous 1973 Roe vs. Wade decision that made abortion an epidemic in America.

Finally, the night for the play arrived. The old gymnasium was packed with people as the lights dimmed and the curtains slowly opened.

Scene 1: Only one side of the stage was lit. Pastor David stood on some steps, leaning against a railing, while two high school boys sat on the steps. In deep discussion, the young men, Mike and Tony, looked husky in their school's sports jackets with large letters and other symbols of successful athletes.

Shaking his head, Mike said, "Pastor, I know the situation in our nation is getting bad—morally and spiritually—but I've always believed it has to get really bad before Christ can return anyway."

Tony chimed in, "Yeah, pastor. Aren't all these things just the signs of the times? Sometimes I even feel like the best thing to do would be for Christians to pray that things get worse so the Lord will return sooner."

Now David responded, "Listen, guys, why do we take it for granted that if America falls that will automatically mean Christ will return? I think Christians in America are being arrogant when we can't imagine the possibility of our children or grandchildren living in slave labor concentration camps. Let's keep in mind the Christians in places like Nicaragua didn't expect it could happen to them, or—"

He was interrupted by the office door opening as the church secretary walked in. She said to the pastor, "I'm sorry to disturb you, but a strange thing just happened. There was a knock on the office door, but when I went to answer, no one was there. These keys were on the ground just outside the door. They seem to belong to a wild-looking van parked out front. I don't know what to make of it."

At the words "wild-looking van," the two boys looked at each other and raised their eyebrows. Their interest was unmistakable.

"Thanks, Gloria," said David as he took the keys. "We'll check it out."

The pastor and the boys exited as the stage lights dimmed. In a few seconds, spotlights came on to show a van, parked in the corner of the gym. It was a brand new conversion van. The boys wasted no time admiring the van. Peering in the window, Mike exclaimed, "Wow, look at that instrument panel! I've never seen anything like it!"

They walked around the van with David, whose only comment was, "I think we'd better call the police. They'll be the ones to know if someone has misplaced this beauty."

As David turned to go to his office, Tony said, "Hey, leave us those keys so we can see if they fit, OK?"

He handed over the keys as he said, "Sure, but don't move it." With that, he left through a side door.

Tony unlocked the doors and both boys hopped in the van. They rolled the windows down so the audience could hear their conversation. Within moments the key had been tried in the ignition and found to fit. Then there was a brief discussion over whether starting the engine was a violation of the pastor's warning not to move the van. That issue being settled, the engine came to life. For a moment nothing could be heard in the gym except the sound of the revving motor. Then, suddenly strobe lights began to flash inside the van and a very loud sound of wind filled the air. All this lasted for a few seconds, then everything went dark and silent.

Moments later, as the lights came back on slowly, Tony and Mike could be seen still sitting in the van.

"What on earth happened?" asked Mike.

"I don't know," Tony started to say, but stopped mid-sentence. "Look, Mike, the clock here said 1990 when we climbed into the van, remember? Now it says 2010. This is weird. What's happening to us?"

"Beats me," answered Mike. "Let's go find out what's keeping Pastor David."

They both climbed out of the van, and, as the spotlights followed them toward the front, the lights came up on the stage. They revealed a line of women with small children standing in front of the door to the church. They were wearing unusual clothing. A number of three- and four-year-olds stood fearfully among the women.

Mike and Tony burst onto the stage and stopped, obviously stunned. Mike was the first to speak, "Hey, what has happened? The church looks different! Where did all these people come from? What is going on?"

Tony spoke to a woman passing who was about to join the line of women. "Excuse me, what's going on here at the church?"

She looked at him strangely, shook her head and continued toward the line. It was Mike's turn. "Could you tell us why everyone is waiting in line?"

Another woman from the line looked up impatiently from her magazine and answered, "You dense or somethin'? We're the lucky ones chosen by Planned Population to bring our kids here for donation to the organ bank so we can meet the population reduction quotas for our zone." Her attention went back to the magazine. She seemed oblivious to the consequences of what was about to happen.

Just as Mike was about to ask another question, a large window in the old church building opened and a garbage bag was thrown out, landing with a thud on top of similar bags in a half-filled dumpster. Almost immediately, a young woman came walking slowly out of the building, head down, and shuffled away. The audience thought they could hear her weeping.

"Wait a minute," Mike choked, "I don't understand! What's going on inside the church?"

"That hasn't been a church for years now, denso," the impatient woman answered. "Planned Population had that group kicked out because they were resistin' progress. Why, if that group had their way, the world would be crawlin' with billions of people standin' on top of each other by now. Our new target goal of 2 billion people will be reached through the reduction of these 'privileged' ones," she said with a bite of sarcasm.

The boys noted with shock that she had been referring to the three-year-old whose hand she was holding. She seemed indifferent to what was happening.

Then, as if having an afterthought, she said, "You know, Jimmy here has actually been a pretty good little boy. For a while, I really thought about asking for one of those exemptions for him. But then he threw a temper tantrum the other day, and I decided that was it." She was talking as if she couldn't believe someone actually wanted to listen to her. Then she shrugged her shoulders and continued, "No more inconveniences for me. I volunteered my older daughter a couple years ago when Planned Population had their big 'Save the Wombat Campaign.' They actually gave me a nice plaque I have at home. It says, 'Proud parent of a volunteer to save the Wombats.' Volunteers, you know, that's what they call those who donate their organs for the survival of the animals."

Mike was incredulous. "You mean you gave your daughter's life to help save a wombat, whatever that is?"

"Well, sure," said the woman, somewhat surprised by his question. "They're almost extinct. Just a couple thousand left in the whole world. We do have to keep our priorities straight, right?"

A young woman had approached the back of the line with a newborn baby in her arms during the conversation. Suddenly, she blurted out, "I think it's just horrible!" She began to cry in great, heaving sobs. After a few moments, she struggled to continue, "I can understand if you have to do it, but only if you have to." With that she turned and began to walk quickly off the stage.

The other woman who had been talking shouted after her, "You'd better come back and take care of it today, or they'll be after both of you tomorrow." Then she added for the boys and the rest of the line, "After all, they do have their quotas to meet, right?"

Mike and Tony looked at each other. As if having the same thought, they ran offstage in pursuit of the fleeing mother. Their voices could be heard calling her to wait for them.

On stage, the line continued its gruesome wait. The impatient woman reopened a magazine she had been holding under her arm. Moments later, another garbage bag was tossed through the window. A loud voice was heard from the darkness in the building, "Next!" The lights dimmed and the curtain closed.

Scene 2: When the curtain opened again, the scene was a crude park, decorated with graffiti on everything from sidewalks to trees. The young mother had just sat down on a park bench as Mike and Tony caught up with her. She was still sobbing and clutching the baby in her arms.

Mike began, "Excuse me, but I hope you can help us figure some things out. Like, what year is this?"

The young woman looked at him, obviously questioning his sanity. She wiped her tears, but said nothing.

Mike tried again. "Look, I know it may sound strange, but we were at church talking to our pastor, and then we decided to check out a van, and then things started to get really strange. When we climbed out, we were here."

The young woman stopped him with a question of her own. "Did you say you were talking to a pastor?"

"Yes," they both answered in unison.

"When I was a little girl," said the woman thoughtfully, "I used to attend church where the clinic is now. They used to have buses that would go all over town and pick up kids for Sunday school." She paused, looking puzzled. "You said you were talking to the pastor? Wait a minute! That building hasn't been a church for over eight years now. I don't know what's wrong with you guys. Why don't you leave me alone?"

"But listen," said Mike. "We still need your help. My name is Mike and this is Tony. What's yours?"

She hesitatingly responded to their outstretched hands, but only after looking around to make sure no one was watching. Almost in a whisper she said, "My name is Lisa."

Now Tony spoke up. "Believe us, Lisa, we don't know what's wrong with us either. You said the church hasn't been in that building for years? What happened? Did they build a new church on the edge of town?" At this there was a ripple of laughter in the audience. A current hotly debated issue in the church had just been put neatly into perspective by these young people.

Lisa shook her head sadly as she said, "The church is gone. Planned Population sure had a hard time shutting it down, though. I think that's why they turned it into a clinic instead of a warehouse or museum like they have with most of the other former churches."

Mike and Tony looked at each other, stunned. "You mean there aren't any churches open anymore?" asked Mike.

"No," said Lisa, "this church was one of the last around here to keep its doors open. When churches were heavily taxed and then outlawed about ten or eleven years ago, most of them shut down right away. But there were a few churches that stuck it out to the bitter end. The pastor here was a guy named Sheffield, I think."

"So you knew Pastor David?" asked Tony.

"Not really," answered Lisa. "But his daughter, Katherine, and I went to public school together, and she invited me to church many times. She even asked me if I wanted to be a Christian. But I got scared when I found out that the Christians were all being volunteered."

Mike was urgent with his question, "What do you mean when you say, 'volunteered'?"

Tony added, "Yeah, that other lady said something about volunteering her daughter to help meet a quota or something."

"Well," answered Lisa, "it actually means two very different things. Because the population was out of control, Planned Population convinced people that radical measures were necessary in order to allow the global community to survive. So, at first, they asked people who were older, or infirm, to 'volunteer their lives for the betterment of humanity.' It all sounded so good and honorable when it first started. Then one thing led to another. Pretty soon a person could be volunteered by someone else, as long as they were related. They only had to sign a paper saying they knew the old or sick person would want to volunteer if they were in their right mind. But it wasn't long before anyone could volunteer anyone else. That's what happened to Pastor Sheffield and his family. The reasons always sounded right. Some had to die so more could live. The ones who could really make a contribution to the future of the world must be allowed to survive, whatever the cost."

Mike was staring at her in unbelief. "You believe that?" he asked.

"Well, it does make sense, doesn't it? They wouldn't lie to us, would they?" answered Lisa in a voice that betrayed her uncertainty.

Now Mike was getting angry. "No, it doesn't make sense! And, yes, they have lied to you!" he said vehemently.

Lisa looked around them in fear. People didn't dare raise their voices. She whispered back as if to compensate for Mike's loudness, "I guess I kinda believed until my little Ruth was born. Now I don't know what to think. I only know I love my baby!" With that she hugged the baby and began to weep again.

"So, what happened back there," asked Tony with amazement in his voice, "was that you have been told to volunteer your baby?"

Lisa nodded.

Mike and Tony looked at each other and shook their heads in disbelief. A stern voice was heard offstage. "Hey you, over there! Are you Lisa Simmons?"

With stark terror on her face, Lisa looked past the boys. They whirled around to face the direction of the voice. Four uniformed men burst onto the stage. Mike and Tony leaped in their way and began grappling with them. Mike shouted to Lisa to run. She dashed away. The struggle continued as the lights dimmed, the curtain closed, and the sounds faded.

Comment

One of the effective ways to test our understanding of a principle or truth is to put it in our own words, or apply it in a new setting. In authoring this play, the young people are learning the important skill of predicting possible consequences. The students are realizing that today's decisions and actions are not carried out in a vacuum. They are a preview of the future. If the students were even partly correct in their predictions, it should be enough to significantly change present attitudes.

In the News

The year is 2010. America is a very different place from what it was in 1989. The population is healthier and happier. No one suffers from severe handicap or debilitating disease.

There are no babies with Down's Syndrome. No broken, drooling patients in nursing homes. No quadriplegics.

They have all been killed.

Doctors decided their lives were not worth living, so they quietly, politely put them out of their misery—by lethal injection, of course, the most humane method.

In Cruzan vs. Missouri Department of Health, the high court will consider for the first time the so-called right to die. Many believe this ruling on the issue of euthanasia may prove as significant as Roe v. Wade, the 1973 case that legalized abortion.

"The Supreme Court could decide that the state has an interest in deciding quality of life, and if they allow that, it's time to move out of the country," said John Whitehead, president of The Rutherford Institute. "It's a very important ruling."

Institute attorneys argue that the Constitution does not sanction the denial of food and water to severely handicapped persons by their guardians. In short, it does not contain a right to kill.

In taking the position, The Rutherford Institute faces formidable opposition. Many other groups—including the American Medical Association—are arguing in favor of allowing the death.

Source: "Is There a Constitutional Right to Die?" *ACTION,* A Monthly Publication of the Rutherford Institute, October 1989.

ख़ ख़ ख़

Biomedical researchers have experimented with tissue from aborted and anencephalic babies (those born without most of the brain) in the treatment of disease.

Fetal cells are especially attractive because they are less likely to trigger an immune response within a recipient. They multiply rapidly—enabling them to survive in almost any environment.

Says neurosurgeon Barth Green of the University of Miami, "These properties make fetal cells a very exciting glue to tie together injured or diseased areas of the body" ("Help from the Unborn," *Time,* January 12, 1987).

Such uses of fetal tissue raise a number of moral and ethical questions, not the least of which is the right of a physician to determine the definition of life and death.

After they are born, many anencephalic babies are placed on respirators to keep their organs fresh for use in transplantation. Doctors frequently do not know when death has legally occurred because conventional methods of measuring brain death are useless in the case of anencephalics. Therefore, many doctors are removing organs while the anencephalic infants are still alive.

The prospect of farming human tissue has raised the possibility of women aborting their babies for the purpose of "healing" themselves or others. As Arthur Caplan, director of the Center for Biomedical Ethics at the University of Minnesota, remarks, "Somehow reproduction has shifted away from an act that creates a family into an arena in which money, profit and benefits for others start to enter" ("A Balancing Act of Life and Death," *Time,* February 1, 1988).

Source: "Farming Human Tissue." *The Plain Truth,* March 1989.

ﻩ ﻩ ﻩ

Researchers at the University of Colorado Health Sciences Center believe transplanting pancreatic cells from aborted fetuses to diabetic patients could reduce their need for insulin.

But the use of fetal tissue for research is causing unrest in the anti-abortion movement, where it is believed medical acceptance of the research would effectively sanction abortions.

Supporters argue that the traditional insulin therapy doesn't cure diabetes, and many Type I diabetics suffer complications that sometimes result in death, including blindness, kidney disease and hardening of the arteries.

Since the study began two years ago, Lafferty has found that fetal tissue does grow, develop and produce insulin in humans when the immune system is blocked.

Opponents of fetal tissue research argue that using the tissue implies moral approval of abortion and that social acceptance of such a procedure will lead to more abortions. Others say they fear the research will lead to "custom pregnancies," where women become pregnant and abort fetuses to help ailing relatives, or for profit.

Another researcher at the Health Sciences Center, Dr. Kurt Freed, performed the nation's first fetal brain cell transplant on a Parkinson's disease patient in November.

Source: "CU Fetal Cell Research Questioned." *The Coloradoan* (Fort Collins, Colorado), April 9, 1989.

ᔑ ᔑ ᔑ

A leading American medical center has concluded it is ethical to use tissue from aborted fetuses for research as long as guidelines are in place to avoid encouraging more abortions, it was reported April 19.

The decision by the Stanford University Medical Center marks the first time a major U.S. medical facility has published a position on the controversial use of fetal tissue for research.

The center's Committee on Ethics, in a report in *The New England Journal of Medicine,* said that "subject to certain important conditions, ethical considerations allow the appropriate medical use of human fetal tissue."

Source: "Stanford: Fetal Tissue Use 'Ethical' Within Guidelines." *Daily Herald* (Suburban Chicago), April 20, 1989.

ᔑ ᔑ ᔑ

The world's population, currently 5.2 billion, is likely to nearly double to 10 billion by 2025 and to reach 14 billion before the end of the next century unless birth control use increases dramatically around the world within the next few decades, according to a report released yesterday by the United Nations Population Fund.

The report revises an estimate that the agency made a decade ago and that has been widely quoted since. The earlier prediction was that the world's population would stabilize at about 10 billion late in the 21st century. That estimate assumed a greater increase in the worldwide use of family planning than has occurred.

"There has been a failure to address the problem on the scale that it should be addressed," said Stirling D. Scruggs, deputy director of the agency's division of external affairs.

Source: Washington Post. "Population Could Double by 2025." *The Pantagraph,* May 27, 1989.

ﻬ ﻬ ﻬ

Diana Ray, a junior at Pius XI High School [Milwaukee] said, "I don't think I could ever bring stuff" from Planned Parenthood to her Catholic school. Some friends are interested in her work and some aren't, she said.

McBride, Hentz, Ray and 47 other area teens took the $50 course, which covers everything from anatomy, sexuality and contraception to values awareness, communications skills and decision-making techniques. "We picked the best of the bunch" to be paid agency staffers, Caballero said.

Using skits and games that involve their audiences, peer educators help classmates determine answers, and the consequences of acting on them, to questions like:

Am I ready for sex? How do I avoid pregnancy? Am I pregnant? Should I have and keep the baby? Do I have a sexually transmitted disease?

[Author's note: If Planned Parenthood can recruit and train students to propagate their message of death, why can't the church encourage young people to promote the message of life?]

Source: "Teenagers Help Educate Peers About Sex." *Milwaukee Sentinel,* June 12, 1987.

ખ ખ ખ

After 18 years in hiding, John E. List, 64, is on trial in Elizabeth, N.J., for the 1971 murders of his wife, three children and 84-year-old mother. Last week the judge released a five-page-letter List left behind for his pastor. Excerpts:

> I know that what has been done is wrong from all that I have been taught and that any reasons that I might give will not make it right. But you . . . will at least possibly understand why I felt I had to do this.
>
> 1. I wasn't earning anywhere near enough to support us. Everything I tried seemed to fall to pieces. True we could have gone bankrupt and maybe gone on welfare.
>
> 2. But . . . knowing the type of location that one would have to live in plus the environment for the children plus the effect on them knowing they were on welfare was just more than I thought they could and should endure. . . .
>
> 3. With Pat [daughter, 16] being so determined to get into acting I was also fearful as to what that might do to her continuing to be a Christian. . . .
>
> 4. Also, with Helen [wife] not going to church I knew that this would harm the children eventually. . . .
>
> At least I'm certain that all have gone to heaven now. If things had gone on who knows if this would be the case. . . . I'm sure many will say "How could anyone do such a horrible thing" — My only answer is it isn't easy. . . .
>
> I'm only concerned with making my peace with God and of this I am assured because of Christ dying even for me.
>
> P.S. Mother is in the hallway in the attic — 3rd floor. She was too heavy to move.

Source: "Memorandum on a Mass Murder." *Newsweek,* April 9, 1990, p. 25.

Key Quotations

We have been the recipients of the choicest bounties of heaven. We have been preserved, these many years, in peace and prosperity. We have grown in numbers, wealth and power, as no other nation has ever grown. But we have forgotten God. We have forgotten the gracious hand which preserved us in peace, and multiplied and enriched and strengthened us; and we have vainly imagined, in the deceitfulness of our hearts, that all these blessings were produced by some superior wisdom and virtue of our own. Intoxicated with unbroken success, we have become too self-sufficient to feel the necessity of redeeming and preserving grace, too proud to pray to the God that made us! It behooves us, then to humble ourselves before the offended Power, to confess our national sins, and to pray for clemency and forgiveness.

President Abraham Lincoln's Proclamation
for a National Day of Fasting, Humiliation and Prayer
April 30, 1863

"O God, I cannot see my way. Give me light. I am ignorant, give me wisdom. Teach me what to do and help me to do it. . . . O thou God who heard Solomon in the night when he prayed for wisdom, hear me. I cannot lead this people, I cannot guide the affairs of this nation without Thy help."

Abraham Lincoln's prayer

As Jesus was sitting on the Mount of Olives, the disciples came to him privately. "Tell us," they said, "when will this happen, and what will be the sign of your coming and of the end of the age?"

Jesus answered: "Watch out that no one deceives you. For many will come in my name, claiming, 'I am the Christ,' and will deceive many. You will hear of wars and rumors of wars, but see to it that you are not alarmed. Such things must happen, but the end is still to come."

Matthew 24:3–6

THE MASTER RACE MYTH

Key Question: What are the consequences of living life as if there is no God and we are masters of our own destiny?

Setting: The play continues with the young men in jail discussing their predicament with their cell mates (Act II).

B etween acts, there was considerable noise behind the curtains. When the curtain opened again, there was only one harsh, hooded light on the stage. It hung over what was obviously a prison cell in which there were four bunks. The only other furnishings were a bare sink and toilet in the center. Mike and Tony were seated on a bunk facing the audience with their backs against the wall. Above them, just visible in the light, was a barred window. Two of the other bunks were occupied by men who were lying down. The boys' clothes were torn and there were bruises on their faces.

Scene 1: Mike turned to Tony and said, "Can you figure out what's going on? We must be in some kind of time warp. Or, maybe this is a dream? What do you think?"

"I don't know," said Tony, gently touching the back of his head. "This doesn't feel like dream blood to me. I didn't think you could get concussions in dreams."

"Yeah," said Mike, "if this lump on my head is what I get for dreaming, I'd hate to have a nightmare!"

The prisoner lying to their left swung his feet down to the floor and sat up. He had been listening. Now he gave a low whistle and said, "I haven't seen many guys lately who will tangle with the security boys. You guys must have a big operation going to fight for it. What's your racket?"

Mike thought for a moment and then answered, "We don't have any racket. We were just trying to help a young mother keep from having to, I think you call it, 'volunteer' her baby."

The man was startled. "You what?"

"Well," explained Mike, "we met this young woman who didn't want to give up her baby for body parts or whatever they use them for."

The man shook his head as he said, "No wonder they beat you up. The Fed's don't like competition with that market, and the P.P. crusaders don't like any interference in their plans to produce a master race."

"What do you mean by P.P.?" asked Tony.

The man seemed proud to be initiating these novices. "P.P. stands for Planned Population."

Tony continued, "Oh, yeah. I remember we heard several speakers from Planned Population at our high school. But, what do you mean, 'competition'? And what 'master race'?"

Now the cell mate was curious. "Where did you boys come from? You been hiding out in Northern Canada or somethin'? The religious leaders in Planned Population are hell bent on producing a master race and for keeping the population explosion under control. So volunteering the children gets both jobs done. They get good body parts for the 'special' people and animals they want to save, and they also reduce the human population. Nice neat package."

He considered for a moment before going on, then lowered his voice a little. "You see, I'm in here because I was givin' 'em competition myself."

Tony looked as if he was still trying hard to believe this was really happening. He asked, "How did you give them competition?"

"Simple. I'd find desperate people or those who were scheduled for being volunteered, and I'd buy their kids. We've got a nice body shop set up out in the boondocks. I hired a foreign doctor who does a real nice job salvaging the choice body parts. He doesn't give me any trouble because he's one of the 'undesirables' that the P.P. boys have tagged for eliminating." The man noticed the expression on the boys' faces and became defensive. "Hey, don't look so shocked! This is just good old free enterprise competing for market share. I mean, the kids are going to be done in anyhow, so they might as well help feather my nest, if you know what I mean."

Seeing the grimaces on both their faces, the man realized these boys were not his type, so he stretched out on his bunk, yawned, and went to sleep. After a while, the other cell mate, silent up until then, raised his head and said, "You guys obviously don't like that kind of business, do you?"

Mike answered, "You can say that again. It goes against the Bible and everything I believe."

At the mention of the Bible, this formerly silent prisoner jumped up, came over, and sat on the bunk with the boys.

He spoke softly, "You guys know the Bible? You'd better talk soft like because if they hear you, you'll really be in trouble. I mean, it's bad enough being accused of helping someone escape the quota, but knowing the Bible is even worse." He paused, walked to the barred door of the cell and checked the hall both ways, as far as he could. Then he moved back to the bunk.

His voice changed to an excited whisper. "Are you guys real believers, I mean in the Bible and Jesus and like that?"

Both boys nodded their heads in agreement. The man's face lit up with a happy smile as he extended his hand.

"I'm Garrett, and I've been trying to find out about God with a few other people in my zone. We weren't sure there were any real believers left."

Mike and Tony introduced themselves, assuring him they were followers of Jesus Christ. The young Christians shared again how shocked they were with what was happening in the world. They asked Garrett to tell them how it had all come to pass.

"Well, you know, back at the end of the '80s and early '90s, it looked like legalized abortion would be overturned. But then, when the economic downturn became severe, and the AIDS epidemic got so bad, and unrest in the Soviet Union and other countries threatened to spill over into the rest of the world, well, saving little preborn babies got lost in the shuffle of concerns. But the real clincher was the drought in the Midwest U.S. When food became short in this country, then came the talk about quality of life and the need to do something about those who had caused the AIDS epidemic."

Tony broke in, "You mean homosexuals were exterminated?"

Garrett looked surprised, "Oh, no. When it came down to it, the minorities took the blame for AIDS — mostly Blacks, Hispanics, and Orientals. The media made a convincing case that it was the poor, uneducated people in the slums who were the breeding grounds for disease. So, when there was rioting and burning in the cities, nobody lifted a finger when thousands were rounded up by the army and shipped to who knows where. Word was, when you were shipped out, you never came back. Food shortages got worse, there were more old people than the government could take care of with Medicare and social security, and the defense budget kept getting larger . . . something had to give. Eliminating unwanted elements in society really seemed like the right thing to do."

Mike turned to Tony and said, "That's what Lisa said, too."

Tony was deeply puzzled. He asked, "But were you a Christian? Couldn't you see what was really happening?"

Shrugging, Garrett answered, "Well, I had gone to church as a child. But the media and the government were putting so much pressure on the churches that I didn't want to get involved. After all, you don't have to go to church to be a Christian. But I have to admit that it has gone too far. I kept waiting for the Rapture to happen. I didn't know a lot about the Bible, but I had heard about the Rapture. I was told it was about to happen so many different times that after a while I started questioning Christianity in general." Then, looking down at the floor, he continued, "But, when I saw them taking little children in to be volunteered for body parts, and mothers being paid to kill their pre-born babies, I just couldn't take it anymore. I found a Bible in my grandmother's house and started to read it for myself. It didn't matter anymore if Christ was going to come back right away or not. I just wanted to know Him if I could. I began to look for others who could help me understand what it was saying. Then I met a man at work who was part of this group that I mentioned, and I started meeting with them at night. It turned out there was an informer in the group, and that's how I ended up here. What really bothers me is that even though I'm in jail, I still don't know what to believe."

Mike reached over and put his hand on Garrett's shoulder. Their eyes met, and the young man said softly, "Garrett, it's not what you believe. It's who you believe in. The Lord Jesus Christ died on the cross and rose from the dead to pay for your sin and to give you eternal life. Do you believe in Him?"

Garrett responded with real intensity, "As you were explaining it just now, it finally made sense. I thought there had to be something else, like maybe I needed to change something in me before I could believe. But I see it now. I do believe Jesus died for me!"

At this, the other cell mate spoke up. "Oh brother, I didn't know I'd gotten into a cell with some religious nuts. I thought the folks at Planned Population were the only religious crazies left in our society."

Mike turned to him and said, "Jesus died for you, too. He'll give you the same forgiveness Garrett just discovered if you'll only believe in Him."

"Ha!" said the man in rejection. "I've found there is only one person I can trust in this world, and that's me. If you guys are so weak that you need a god to prop you up, then go right ahead. But go without me!" He rolled over on the bed with his back to them.

Mike's attention focused back on Garrett. "Now that you've told me you believe in Jesus, don't you think it would be a great idea to tell Him?"

"I can't remember the last time I prayed out loud," said Garrett.

"Well," said Mike, "let's get down on our knees together, and you tell Jesus you realize you're a sinner, that He died for you, and that you want to accept His forgiveness and invite Him to become Lord of your life."

Garrett said, "All right, but what if a guard sees us?"

Mike didn't hesitate, "The Bible tells us if we are afraid to admit to others that we know and trust Jesus, then He will not be willing to admit that He knows us when we stand before God. We can't let fear of others keep us from Jesus."

That was enough for Garrett. Without further delay, the two men knelt together and the older one prayed in simple words, "Jesus, I do believe You are the Son of God, and I want eternal life. I know I don't deserve it because I am a sinner. But I realize that You died for me, so I'm asking You to forgive me. Please give me peace and the strength to be faithful to You."

Mike, Tony, and several voices in the audience said, "Amen!"

Mike and Garrett stood and spontaneously hugged each other. Tony, who had been standing by the cell bars, anxiously signaled them that a guard was coming. A man in uniform walked on stage and approached the cell.

"Hey, you two!" he yelled through the bars. "Your prints don't show up on any of our records! We need some more identification. Those driver's licenses and other junk you gave us are real antiques. Where did you find that stuff, and where did you get your pictures on them?"

Instead of answering, Tony decided to try an idea. "We would like to see an attorney," he said.

The officer gave a coarse laugh. "Who do you think you are? We don't have money to pay an attorney to see some scum that wanders in from the hills! You had better start cooperating with us or you're going to be in even deeper trouble than you already are."

Mike spoke up this time. "We know our rights and . . ."

The officer cut him off mid-sentence. "Rights? You must be kidding! That's a good one, don't you think, Georgie boy?" He was addressing the sullen prisoner still lying on the bunk. "Do you know these punks, George? Are they working for you?"

George kept his back turned to all of them. But he snarled his answer. "I don't work with saints and crusaders and I want nothing to do with these. . . ."

"Well," the officer continued, "our young crusaders might enjoy a little report on how successful they have been. That young lady you tried to help this morning? You know, the one who got you in here? You'll be happy to know she turned both herself and her little bundle of joy over to the P.P. center."

He paused, seeming to enjoy the moment. Then he went on, "Surely this shouldn't surprise you. We don't spend all those billions on public conditioning, I mean education, for nothing!" He was smiling.

Mike blurted out, "You mean she actually had her baby killed?"

"I keep forgetting, you boys are from the hills," the officer said. "We don't use that word. She volunteered her baby for higher purposes. You need to learn that we now believe that, even though she gave birth to the child, it was not hers. She and the baby both belong to the state, and it is the duty of the government to be concerned about the greater good of the entire global community. So, what happens to one child is of little consequence when compared to the greater good of mankind. You see, boys, in just a few more years The Scientific Solution will become a reality."

"What's that?" inquired Mike.

"You mean you guys haven't even heard of The Scientific Solution?"

Tony came to Mike's rescue with a touch of sarcasm, "Sounds like us country boys need a little further education."

Missing the humor, the guard continued, "The Scientific Solution was the logical next step to the 'final solution.'"

Mike interrupted, "You mean what Hitler did to the Jews?"

"Listen," responded the officer, "Hitler was just misunderstood, that's all. He just went about it in the wrong way at the wrong time. But his basic idea was good. You see, you have to be a little more subtle and clever than Adolph was. Take Margaret Sanger for example. Now there was one sharp broad. She was just as much an apostle of the Master Race concept as Adolph. It's real simple — no God, survival of the fittest, man in a constant state of evolution — it all adds up to man eventually finding the solution to his own problems. Man will figure out how to make himself perfect.

"After that, the only frontier will be to solve the problem of death. It's only a matter of time with evolution before we live forever."

Garrett asked, "So, do you think you are going to live forever as you are?"

The guard sneered his response. "You're a pretty bright boy there. Too bad you're not one of those 'chosen' to benefit from the new finding about blood containing the secret to ongoing evolutionary development. Scientifically processed blood—that's the key to The Scientific Solution. We're on the brink of eternal life right here in River City. That's why the P.P. boys have stepped up the elimination of the less desirables. Only the best get to last forever . . . right, George?"

George rolled over and growled, "I couldn't have said it better myself. The only trouble is that the money goes to those clowns at P.P. and into the government bank accounts instead of into my pockets." Then he grinned and added, "And I think I could have found more fun things to do with it. And if you weren't such a deadbeat, you'd let me out of here, and I'd be happy to share some of my profits with you and your fellow officers."

"Please, George," the officer mocked, as he walked away. "We wouldn't want to give the impression that the noble servants of the state, the very ideal specimens of the master race, could be corrupted from our great calling by such filthy and mundane things as money, would we?" He laughed as he left the stage.

"Ha!" snorted George. "Master race, my foot. They are just a bunch of master swindlers and deceivers. They make honest crooks like me look like saints."

"Does that mean you'll get out of here by bribing the guards?" asked Tony.

"Hey kid!" said George laughing sarcastically, "The more things change, the more they just stay the same, right? I think that some of the crusaders down at P.P. believe in what they are doing. Probably. But the rest of the bureaucrats who run the system . . . hey, they're no different. They go where there is the least resistance and the best pay—just like the rest of us. You guys and your outdated church religion. Looks to me like you just got beat out by some other religious nuts."

Tony asked, "What do you mean, we got beat out?"

"I'm no dummy," replied George. "I remember when church people believed they had to save everybody before the world could become a better place. But when all the big troubles hit, the religious people suffered with the rest of us. That's when the people from Planned Population moved in and said they could save the world if everyone would let them run the show." Then he added, almost as if he were sorry, "No disrespect, fellows, but they cleaned your clocks. The churches in this country never really knew what hit them!"

Mike turned to Tony and shook his head in amazement. "These are just the kind of things we've been talking about in church. Pastor David keeps telling us if we're not ready, we may fail to be what God wants us to be as individuals and as a church."

Tony said, "Yeah. I hope we get a chance to tell him he was right."

The curtain closed. There would be an intermission before the final act. The house lights came on and there was scattered applause. The message was hitting close to home.

Comment

Faith that relies on external circumstances for its strength will fail. If our view of God rises and falls with our feelings or experiences, we will not have, nor be able to share, the solid, unchanging presence of God who is at the heart of every person's quest. The students are asking Christians to be serious in their examination of the vitality of their faith. They are also clearly demonstrating what can happen when a basic Biblical truth, like the sinfulness of man, is forgotten.

The Master Race theory is a dominant theme repeated throughout history as man continues to attempt to solve life's problems apart from God. The understanding that humans are on their own and in control of their own destiny is a basic component to human nature in rebellion against God. It saturates every area of life from sophisticated philosophy to beer commercials. But, apart from God, every solution to the problems and challenges of life is human centered, and bound to fail. Humans who remain blind to their separation from God are destined to enter eternity apart from Him.

In the News

Last January, *MediaWatch* reported the results of a study on abortion labeling. The results of the study showed that network reporters used the preferred "pro-choice" for abortion advocates, but used "anti-abortion" for abortion foes instead of the preferred "pro-life."

A recent study by the Center for Media and Public Affairs (CMPA) has confirmed *MediaWatch*'s findings. CMPA reported between last

January 1 and August 31, ABC, CBS, and NBC television reporters preferred "pro-choice" over "abortion rights" labels by a nearly three to one
margin. But they rarely used "pro-life" or "right to life" to describe the
other usage of "anti-abortion."

Source: "Media shows bias toward abortion." *MediaWatch,* 1/90.

ta ta ta

Access to abortion has been expanding steadily around the world in the
past decade as nations have stepped up efforts to limit population
growth. In India and China, for example, the number of "pregnancy ter-
minations" has increased sharply with the support of both governments.
Some 450 million legal abortions are now performed worldwide each
year, with three quarters of the world's population living in countries
where abortion is legal. Last week, the worldwide movement toward
protecting women's right to terminate their pregnancies suffered a sudden, dramatic setback, followed just two days later by a dramatic rever-
sal that put the pro-choice forces back in control.

The French company Roussel Uclaf, citing anti-abortion pressure
and harassment of its top officials, announced that it would cease manufacturing a new abortion pill that just a month before had been approved
for marketing in France and China.

Source: "The Great Pill Flip-Flop." *U.S. News and World Report,*
November 7, 1988, p. 12.

ta ta ta

Many black leaders have been ambivalent about abortion over the past
two decades. Strong opposition has come from the pulpits of largely
conservative black churches, and from black-power activists who
equated abortion with genocide. Before his 1984 presidential bid, Jesse
Jackson was an ally of the right-to-life movement. Polls have been confusing: different surveys show blacks both favoring and opposing abortion rights. For many poor women, even though they may be in favor of
abortion, the issue is not a high priority. "Women [talk] about how

drugs are tearing apart their neighborhoods or how husbands have been laid off from work," says Georgia state legislator Mable Thomas. "As an issue, abortion just does not click."

A small number of blacks still preach abortion as genocide. Trimelda McDaniels, 35, a former Black Panther and now a member of Feminists for Life of America in Peoria, Ill., says some doctors practice a kind of economic genocide by persuading poor women to have abortions. "The message these women get constantly is: if you don't have the bread, you don't deserve the kid."

Source: Baker, James N. with Daniel Glick, Tony Clifton, Patricia King, Howard Manly and Frank Washington. "Blacks Agonize Over Abortion." *Newsweek,* December 4, 1989, p. 63.

ठ ठ ठ

While passive (voluntary, abandoning lifesaving efforts, living will) euthanasia has been used to urge the sick and elderly that they have a "duty to die and get out of the way," a group of active euthanasia advocates has formed. They want to legalize hastening death by administering increased dosages of drugs or by lethal injections.

Under the guidance of the Council for Democratic and Secular Humanism, 20 scientists, philosophers, doctors, and lawyers have signed a statement entitled "The Case for Active Voluntary Euthanasia" which also clearly acknowledges the potential for abuse of active euthanasia. The signers are predominately secular humanists or members of the euthanasia lobby.

Source: "Active Euthanasia Advocated." *Scoreboard Alert Newsletter,* April 1989.

ठ ठ ठ

"In order to get Roe v. Wade passed, the number of back-alley abortion deaths had to be exaggerated by a hundredfold," Surgeon General C. Everett Koop said January 19 in Washington, D.C. "The greatest number of deaths ever in one year was 373. That's a terrible number, but it wasn't 10,000. And I think that with the techniques that are being used by abortionists now, those same techniques will be used in the future, and they are safer."

Source: "Koop Exposes Back-Alley Abortion Myth." *The New York Times,* January 20, 1989.

ta. ta. ta.

For every 100 births in the Soviet Union there are 106 abortions, a medical newspaper said November 19. It said Soviet abortions in 1988 totalled nearly seven million.

"These monstrous statistics are difficult to believe," *Meditsinskaya Gazeta* said. It added that they were not complete because they did not include illegal abortions performed outside hospitals.

The figures on abortions released by the Health Ministry showed the Soviet Union's abortion rate was higher than that of all developed countries in the world, *Meditsinskaya Gazeta* said.

"For 100 births we have 106 barbaric operations. And what are the consequences? Mass complications, infertility and deaths because of poor treatment afterwards."

The weekly *Moscow News* reported in January that 90 percent of all first pregnancies in the Soviet Union end in abortion and hundreds of women die each year as a result of the operation.

The trade union newspaper *TRUD* said that 10 million Soviet women were infertile, but it did not say whether this was the result of abortions or other causes.

Source: "Soviet Journal: 7 Million Abortions in '88." *Daily Herald* (Suburban Chicago), November 20, 1989.

ta. ta. ta.

In projecting the slowest rate of population growth in our history after 1995, and a declining population after 2038, the Census Bureau has merely confirmed that the demographic trends of the past thirty years are not likely to be reversed. Since 1973, American women have been having babies at less than the 2.1-per-lifetime rate needed to keep population constant. The current fertility rate — 1.8 births per woman — is 50 per cent below the baby-boom peak reached in 1957, and is unlikely to change in the foreseeable future.

A number of factors argue against our becoming alarmed at this, however. For one thing, these "best guesses" have in the past been notoriously wide of the mark. Both the baby boom and the baby bust were missed in previous Census Bureau prognostications, and many uncertainties surround the current forecast also. The spread of AIDS to the heterosexual population, for example, could produce an earlier and sharper population decline than currently anticipated.

Source: "The Birth Dearth Confirmed." *National Review,* May 5, 1989, p. 13.

Key Quotations

The moral principles and precepts contained in the Scriptures ought to form the basis of all our civil constitutions and laws. All the miseries and evils which men suffer from vice, crime, ambition, injustice, oppression, slavery, and war, proceed from their despising or neglecting the precepts contained in the Bible.

Noah Webster

If Christ is really king, exercising original and immediate jurisdiction over the State as really as he does over the church, it follows necessarily that the general denial or neglect of His rightful lordship, any prevalaent refusal to obey that Bible which is the open law-book of His Kingdom, must be followed by political and social as well as moral and religious ruin. If professing Christians are unfaithful to the authority of their Lord in their capacity as citizens of the State, they cannot expect to be blessed by the indwelling of the Holy Ghost in their capacity as members of the Church. The Kingdom of Christ is one, and cannot be divided in life or in death. If the Church languishes, the State cannot be in health; and if the State rebels against its Lord and King, the Church cannot enjoy his favour. If the Holy Ghost is withdrawn from the Church, he is not present in the State; and if he, the only 'Lord, the Giver of life,' be absent, then all order is impossible, and the elements of society lapse backward to primeval night and chaos . . . I charge you, citizens of the United States, afloat on your wide sea of politics, there is another King, one Jesus; the safety of the State can be secured only in the way of humble and whole-souled loyalty to His person and of obedience to His law.

A.A. Hodge

Then they said, "Come, let us build ourselves a city, with a tower that reaches to the heavens, so that we may make a name for ourselves and not be scattered over the face of the whole earth."

But the Lord came down to see the city and the tower that the men were building. The Lord said, "If as one people speaking the same language they have begun to do this, then nothing they plan to do will be impossible for them."

Genesis 11:4–6

THE DEIFICATION
OF MAN MYTH

Key Question: What happens when man insists on being God?

Setting: The play continues as Mike and Tony discover the ultimate driving belief behind the changes they have encountered (Act III).

W hen the curtain opened following the intermission, Mike and Tony could be seen sitting in front of a large desk. On the office door behind them was stenciled the name of its occupant: Commissioner Mark Hansen. Behind the desk was an older man whose tailored uniform and shining boots spoke of rank and authority.

Scene 1: Looking at a computer screen, the Commissioner said, "This doesn't happen very often, but we do occasionally have someone show up who has somehow escaped our screening and recording. However, to have two fine specimens like yourselves show up at the same time, well, this is very unusual."

With that, he sat back and looked at Mike and Tony, weighing his options.

"I can understand why you want to keep silent about where you came from and how you got these false records, but it is puzzling to me that you thought you could get very far with such out-of-date identification papers. You obviously come from the country because you don't have a birth tattoo or electronic implant. I didn't realize there were still areas on this continent that had not been completely registered and monitored. As hard as we try, there are always some slip-ups.

"You realize, of course, that we can't allow strays, such as yourselves, to simply run loose. You could get into all kinds of trouble, not to mention the problems you have already caused in our carefully orchestrated system."

Then, as if talking to himself, the Commissioner said, "We still have trouble with a certain percentage of the population not wanting to conform to our noble aspirations. I suppose it will take a couple of generations to breed this rebellion out of them."

Focusing his attention on Mike and Tony, he raised his voice, "But we will bring this all under control! You can be sure of that!

"Now young men, before we go to all the expense of medical and psychological therapy to get to the truth, I've been asked to spend some time with you to see if we can reason with you and find a suitable solution to your situation. Isn't that reasonable? All our evaluation, up to this point, shows an amazing degree of independent thinking ability on your part, so I'm hopeful that we can proceed without a lot of difficulties.

"Michael," began the Commissioner.

Mike interrupted him, "You can just call me Mike."

"Very good, Mike. What made you come, from wherever you were, to this city?"

After hesitating, Mike said, "I guess we came to find out what it was like here."

"Well, of course! It's natural to be curious about what the progressive side of the world is like," said the Commissioner, genuinely pleased.

Mike responded sharply, "I'm not so sure it's all that progressive. It seems to me that society has taken a big turn for the worse — back to the Dark Ages, with a modern twist, I'd say."

The Commissioner smiled in a condescending way. "Well, we do have some serious problems to deal with. We certainly do not have our population growth and resource production where we'd like them, but our centers of higher learning are truly a marvel. You young men seem to have been taught to read and such, but the young people in our environmental centers are not only learning the rudiments of what used to be considered an adequate education, they are exploring the higher reaches of the mind and achieving levels of consciousness that previous generations could not even imagine."

Tony spoke up, "If people are getting so smart, why do they still kill the pre-born, and why does society have to murder little children? I haven't seen many older people around either. Where are they, anyway?"

"Oh, my goodness!" groaned the Commissioner. "I was warned about your crude, backward ways, but I must admit that I'm a little shocked to be confronted with them in person. I'm sure you've already been told that we don't kill people. We did away with the death penalty years ago."

Now Tony was clearly frustrated. "What the heck do you call what you're doing to those children?"

"Now, now, Tony. No need to be so emotional," said the Commissioner smoothly, "I'll explain that fully if you will allow me. You see, you have obviously been conditioned under some primitive notions about reality. Somehow you have not been exposed to the higher ways of understanding the ultimate. All life is one — a part of the higher consciousness of the universe. Different words and concepts can be used to explain it, but in reference to your concern about the children, you have to understand that life is not something that begins or ends. Neither is one part of reality more important than other parts. We exchange the bodies of some for others. Some do not reach their full potential in the life form in which you see them. But, never fear, they will have other chances, in other life forms until they are able to achieve the higher good that we all seek. What is important is that the global community, or universal consciousness, be restored to the harmony that it once had before all the wars and pollution of the last century."

The Commissioner stopped in acknowledgment of Mike's and Tony's agitation and vigorous headshaking in disbelief at what they were hearing.

"I guess I'm going to have to start your indoctrination a little farther back in history. We now know that early religious leaders in the Far East knew of the higher consciousness and ability within man, but this knowledge was suppressed by the naive beliefs of Christianity and the greed and corruption of capitalism. Those two belief systems almost destroyed this planet. By the end of the twentieth century, the environmental pollution alone would have made life impossible on earth had we not begun cutting back on man's needs so that the entire natural order, so painstakingly evolved over eons, could be preserved.

"Margaret Sanger was one who saw the need for eugenics, the need to do with humans what man had learned to do with animals — and that was, simply through selective breeding, to eliminate the weak and build up the strong. Of course, she didn't know of half the advances in science that came in the latter part of the 20th century. With manipulation of the DNA molecule and gene structure, we could eliminate diseases and weak characteristics that held back man's advancement. Since we have coupled this new technology with advances in the science of the mind, will, and spirit, man has risen to heights that before were reserved for the gods."

Mike pointedly interrupted, "I thought from what our guard said earlier that you didn't believe in God."

"Oh yes, but you are perceptive, aren't you?" responded the commissioner. He lowered his voice to a near whisper and continued. "You see, even in our own enlightened age there are still those who refuse to see the spiritual dimension of all things. Unfortunately, there are many who are content to just improve those things that one can experience with the five senses. But the true intellectuals of every age have always known there is a sixth sense, a spiritual dimension if you will. A force that drives us all in our quest for infinite knowledge, power, and pleasure. This presence has directed us in its agenda toward its goal and promised us its essence. One day it will swallow us all and harmonic convergence will be achieved in an eternal state of nirvana."

Tony commented, "This force you describe sounds an awful lot like the one the Bible calls Satan."

The commissioner chuckled, "The Bible? A book of legends and confusion. Satan is a mere Christian superstition. The force I am referring to does not want to be God, but has promised to make us gods."

"That's exactly what Tony means," said Mike. "The Bible tells us that Satan tempted Eve with the promise she could become like God if she only disobeyed God's command."

The commissioner realized he was no match for the boys in questioning the Bible, so he shifted his comments to more familiar ground. "Can't you see that in order to achieve the advancements that were necessary to save the environment, to preserve the full range of life on earth, some sacrifices were necessary, and some methods had to be used that we wish we didn't have to? But of course, the noble ends do justify the means, do they not? All those poor and wretched elderly, languishing in nursing homes and the crippled ones who had no real possibility of ever being of any use to society did in fact perform a great service by allowing themselves to be terminated. They naturally had to be willing to stop being such burdens on an overburdened world. And now we have virtually eliminated a number of inferior races of humans, which has enabled us to transfer huge sums for welfare to education, thus stamping out old superstitions."

"Such as Christianity?" Mike asked.

"Yes, as a matter of fact, that is one superstition which, I must say, I'm glad has been nearly wiped out. Strange though, most of the Christians didn't resist in any way, with their intellects or their strength. I mean they had a history of non-violence, but you would have thought that some would have resisted, at least with ideas. They weren't at all like those Islamic peoples. Just when it appears that we have finally silenced the Muslims, another prophet arises to lead them and they're off to the hills. We could decrease our military budget by half if we could solve the Islamic problem. Christianity has splintered into small, quietly devoted groups that crop up here and there. It's hard to believe that any intelligent person would want to hang on to such naive and outdated beliefs. I suppose we will eventually wear them down to final extinction sometime soon."

The Commissioner stopped for a moment. A new idea had just dawned on him.

"That's it isn't it? You are two of them. You have both been infected with those dangerous beliefs, haven't you? That's why you wanted to help that poor, confused girl who was scheduled to volunteer her child."

He sighed out loud.

"Well, I'm afraid this does complicate matters a great deal. And you are such fine specimens, so healthy and strong. I was thinking that with some drug therapy you might be useful for introduction into our controlled breeding program. But even with drugs and surgery, I'm not sure you could be salvaged."

He stopped to punch some keys on the computer keyboard as Mike and Tony looked at each other, still shaking their heads in disbelief.

Then he continued, "I'm going to do some checking on this, but I want you boys to consider going into the military training program. We can create files on you, and you look like you're in good enough shape to be useful in Asia or Eastern Europe where the army is still mopping up the nationalistic movements which occasionally create headaches for us. As Christians, this may not appeal to you, but you may like the other options open to you even less."

With that, he pushed a button on his desk and shifted his full attention to the keyboard. A guard entered and somewhat roughly ushered the boys out of the office and off stage. The lights dimmed and the curtain closed.

Scene 2: The next scene opened with Mike and Tony back in their cell. Garrett was gone, but George was still there, looking completely at ease.

As Mike sat on his bunk, he said, "Is that Commissioner dude crazy or does he really think that he has become some kind of god?"

Tony thought for a moment, then said, "Most of what he said sounded like the stuff Pastor David told us is part of the New Age movement. Seems to me like a real handy way to justify doing whatever you want to do."

Mike changed the subject to their immediate concerns. "What is going to happen to us? I wonder where Garrett is?"

"They sent him out on work therapy," said George as he rolled over and propped his head up with his hand.

"Work therapy!" exclaimed Mike. "Is that what they call it? I'll bet we would have called it slave labor in the old days, but then, that kind of terminology just doesn't fit in with this enlightened age!"

Tony asked, "So what do they do with their slave labor?"

George looked at them in wonder. "You boys are either dumb as stumps, or you've just come from the Stone Age. Since the government took over everything and takes practically all of everyone's wages in taxes, most of the incentive to work has disappeared. And then, with the population reduced so much, there are lots of jobs that no one really wants to do. So they have resorted to that age-old solution. They take those who don't fit into their mold or ideal, and make slaves out of them. Work them 'til they drop dead. It's a pretty efficient system, really."

"I couldn't have imagined this is what America would become," said Mike sadly.

"You boys can't be old enough to remember what America was really like, but I do. Man, it was a great place back in the old days. People just didn't realize how good they had it," said George.

"Well, if you and others can remember the way it was, why did you let it get like this?" asked Mike in consternation. "And why have you let yourself do the kinds of things you're doing now?"

George answered, "You're right, kid, I should have known better. But when things go bad, you do what you have to do to survive. I was a lab technician back then, but my job got too dangerous because of AIDS. I ended up not being very picky about my work. The black market was the only system that still functioned. It seemed like the more we heard about the advancement of society and the bright tomorrow, the darker it got around us and the worse conditions grew. It's amazing what people will pay just to stay alive a little longer—and what they'll kid themselves into believing to justify doing what they do. At first, replacement parts came from people killed in accidents. But the demand was so much greater than the supply. People smelled incredible profits. The next logical step seemed irresistible. A society which had already accepted the killing of babies in the womb didn't have much argument against the killing of children a few years old."

"Now we know what was happening at the old church building," said Tony grimly.

"George, what would have been in those garbage sacks they kept throwing into the dumpster?" asked Mike.

"Those were what they call 'surplus parts' in the human parts business," answered George. "It's kind of wasteful, not using everything, but that's the way it goes."

"How can you be so casual about people being butchered like animals?" asked Mike, whose anger was about to erupt.

"I guess it happened with me like it did with society in general," said George, sounding suddenly distant. "Remember, we didn't start here. First, as I recall there were abortions to save the mother's life. Then in 1973, abortion was legalized at any stage of the pre-born's development. Maybe you don't know it, but over 30 million babies were killed that way. That was almost stopped in the early nineties, but people loved their convenience more than doing what it took to make it illegal."

George paused and Mike asked, "So, when things got hard economically and internationally, people's attention went to survival instead of worrying about saving babies?"

"Yeah," George admitted. "That's about it. I recall that some groups kept on fighting. But with the economy so bad, it was easy to 'move on' to killing the old people, the handicapped, and others. Eventually even suicide among teenagers was encouraged, since it fit with the 'survival of the fittest' idea. Children received values clarification in school that emphasized what an honor it was to volunteer to die, just like the kamikazes of Japan during the Second World War. Funny thing, though. Somehow, the Planned Population's crusaders never seemed to get around to volunteering themselves. In fact, what it came down to was that those in power actually killed off anyone they didn't happen to like. All the while they were talking about their goal to build a master race of gods. Personally, I decided they could all go to Hades, and I was going to look out for number one. That's exactly what I've been doing."

Again, both boys were struggling to take all this in. Mike seemed on the verge of tears of frustration as he said, "It makes sense, but it is hard to believe it could happen. . . ."

Meanwhile, George began to act like a plan was about to go into motion. He went to the cell door and checked for guards. Then he turned and said to the boys, "Look, guys, they have been treating you nice up 'til now because they're trying to find out as much as they can from you. They're also trying to figure out what to do with you. But let me warn you, they don't treat kindly those who don't fit their mold. In fact, if you stay here I can guarantee you will regret they caught you.

"But, I've got a deal for you. I could use a couple of guys like you in my business. I realize you don't like much of what I do, but I think I could keep you busy doing stuff that wouldn't involve the 'spare parts' end of things. If you're interested, I can get you out of here."

Mike was skeptical. "How are you going to get us out of here? This place looks pretty escape-proof to me."

"Oh, it is, all right," said George with a big smile, rubbing his fingers together to signify money, "unless you have the right kind of grease. And I've got some stored away just for this purpose. I've also made some friends in the computer control department, so stick with me. I'll get you out of here, and then, you owe me."

Just then there were loud noises, and the guard approached and opened the cell door. "Hello again, Georgie boy. We got things fixed up. Here are the bank codes you'll need to transfer the money. Let me warn you, though. You'd better get these country hicks out of town and keep them there because they have already caused a big mess with the religious freaks at Planned Population. They don't like any religious competition. And the next time you come to market, check things out a little better. We've got to keep things looking like we've got control. . . ."

George hung his head in mock shame and responded, "Hey, to err is human! Maybe I'll sign up with the Commissioner's group to raise my consciousness to such a high level that I won't make such stupid mistakes, right?"

The two men laughed like old friends who have just pulled off a mean practical joke and walked off stage, with Mike and Tony at their heels. The curtain closed.

Scene 3: The final scene began with George, Mike, and Tony standing on a dimly lit street corner.

Tony was curious and asked, "How can they just let us go like that and not get in trouble with their bosses?"

George kept looking around as he explained, "Happens all the time. The computer age does have some advantages, ya know. They keep track of just about everything and everyone, but the computer is only as honest and accurate as the person who enters the info. That's where my special kind of grease comes in.

"So, tomorrow someone will discover a big foul-up in the prison records, and no one will seem to know how it got there. Unfortunately, the names of several prisoners will have been lost in the shuffle. But, fortunately for us, we'll be those cons.

"One thing about bureaucrats is they don't want to take risks or accept responsibility. So, while some will be mad, instead of making a stink over it, they will conveniently forget that the incident happened and will go on their merry way. I'm sure the Commissioner will realize someone got paid off, and he won't like it. But he'll chalk it up to some lesser human down the line who needs to develop that higher consciousness he likes to talk about so much."

During the conversation, Tony was looking around too. Now he blurted out, "Mike, I recognize this spot. We're only a block from the old church. Do you think the van might still be there? I got the keys back from the guard along with my other stuff."

Mike immediately turned to George and said, "Listen, thanks for getting us out. I guess we'll have to work for you if that's the way it is. But right now we've got to check something out down the street."

"This is probably not a good idea," said George, "but if it's gotta be done, let's get it done quick."

The stage curtain closed as the men came down from the stage on to the gymnasium floor. A spotlight followed them back to where the van was still parked.

Halfway there, Tony shouted, "There it is! The van is still here!" He ran ahead of the other two, pulling the keys out of his pocket. He had just begun to unlock the doors when another light shined on them and a loud voice commanded them to stay where they were. Two men walked out of the shadows. One had a gun pointed at Tony, while his partner held the flashlight and spoke into a small radio, calling for a squad car.

The one with the radio said, "We've been watching this vehicle for a couple of days to see who owned it. We have some questions to ask you down at the control center."

As the men got nearer, George calmly announced, "Good work men. I'm Captain Fox with Intelligence. We just came from the control center over on Main. Commander Pierce asked us to come by and check this situation out. We confiscated some keys from a suspect and decided to try them out."

He reached into his coat as if to pull out an ID card, but instead out came a small object which gave off a bright electrical spark, immediately knocking the officer with the gun to the ground. In a split second, the other man also dropped without a sound.

In a shocked tone, Mike asked, "Did you kill them?"

"Of course not," said George laughing. "Haven't you guys ever heard of stun-guns?"

A siren began to wail in the background.

"Hey, we've got to get out of here!" yelled Mike as he went to the passenger door of the van. Tony was already climbing into the driver's seat.

"Where do I get in?" asked George.

Halfway in the van, Mike turned and said, "Look George, we'd better see if it will start up first." Then, just before he closed the door he added, "I don't think you would want to come with us."

Tony turned the keys and lights began to flash brightly. A moment later, the gym was in total silence and darkness.

When the lights came back on seconds later, George and the officers were gone. Mike and Tony jumped out of the van and looked around. Realizing they were home, they ran around and gave each other a bear hug.

"We're back! We made it!" yelled Tony.

"I wonder what happened to George?" asked Mike as they celebrated.

Tony chuckled as he said, "I don't know, but I think he'll figure some way out of the situation."

Then, as if the shock of returning was wearing off, Tony asked, "How are we ever going to tell what we've just . . . do you think anyone will ever believe us?"

"I don't know," said Mike. "We'd better think about that! Let's go find Pastor David and tell him what happened. Boy, is he going to be surprised!"

As they ran toward the stage, the curtains opened to reveal Pastor Sheffield seated at his desk, talking on the phone. The boys burst into his office and David ended his phone conversation. He looked at the boys for a moment, his finger drumming on the desk.

"I thought I told you guys not to take the van for a drive," he began.

Mike and Tony flopped into chairs, each interrupting the other as they tried to tell their experience. Finally, Tony signalled Mike to go ahead.

"Pastor, remember how you were saying that you thought the abortion issue could lead to worse things in our society if the church didn't wake up and turn things around?"

David nodded his head in agreement, with a puzzled look on his face.

"Well," Mike went on, "now we know you're right. We're also convinced that we need to challenge people to do everything they can, while we still have time, to get things turned around in this nation."

David still looked puzzled as he said, "That's great! But what on earth happened to you guys in the last few minutes that made you change your minds?"

The curtains began to close, and the lights began to dim as Mike answered, "Pastor, you'd better hang on to your seat. . . ."

The lights in the gym stayed low. A subdued applause broke out as David stepped from behind the curtain. Holding a small candle in his hand, he waited as the student actors and actresses filled the space in front of the stage. Each one also held a lighted candle and a box of candles to distribute.

David began, "You have witnessed a grim but logical projection of what could happen in our society. While we want you to think seriously about the possibilities, we do not want to leave the impression that we have no hope."

He paused to allow his words to sink in.

"When you came into this auditorium," he continued, "it was well lit. Now it is dark except for our small candles. This nation was once full of the light of Christ and bursting with life. However, now America is full of darkness, and our society is characterized by death.

"We would like you to participate in a simple illustration which will demonstrate to all of us what is necessary if we are to return our nation to a condition in which life really is respected and God's truth is allowed to speak. These young people are going to offer you each a candle. Please light your candles from theirs, and then light your neighbor's candles until everyone in your row and section has a lighted candle."

The young people moved up the aisles, giving candles to everyone, lighting them along the way.

David continued, "Notice how the room fills with light. Listen carefully to what I'm about to share with you.

"The prophet Jeremiah lived in a time when the nation of Israel was on the verge of God's judgment because of the terrible sins of its leaders and people. Jeremiah warned his nation of the coming judgment. He was also instructed by God to tell them that, just as a potter could take a lump of clay and change it from one type of jar to another, if the people would turn from their evil ways, God would not send judgment but would return their nation to life. We know that the people of Israel did not repent, and were later killed or carried away into slavery into foreign lands.

"In modern history, about 250 years ago, the nation of England was in a similar situation. Historians believe England was ripe for a bloody and destructive revolution similar to what the French had experienced. But instead, the British responded to the preaching of John Wesley and others, turning to God. There was not only a revival which brought many people to faith in Christ, but their new-found faith spilled over to touch all of society. Child labor laws were passed. Slavery was abolished by an act of parliament, not by a destructive war. Thousands of missionaries were sent around the world. In numerous ways, that nation was spared God's judgment of civil revolution."

By this time, almost everyone in the gym had a candle.

"Look at how this room is again full of light!" exclaimed David. "By the simple use of individual candles, by the simple act of giving and receiving, together we have transformed this place from gloomy darkness to the warmth of joy and life!

"Now, carefully lower your candles in front of you to muffle the light. See how much darker it immediately gets? Now, slowly lift your candles up over your heads. Notice how the room bursts into light.

"Jesus said, 'You are the salt of the earth, the light of the world. Let your light shine.'

"God does not want darkness to settle over this great nation of ours. He does not want precious pre-born babies to die and their mothers' hearts to bear scars for the rest of their lives. God wants healing in our land. He wants light to go to those who are in darkness. And it can go out to them, if you will be one who determines to open your life to God's light and then simply let it shine wherever you are. Will you give your life to Christ for that purpose?"

With that question, David asked them all to bow their heads. He led them in a passionate prayer thanking God for His presence and asking

Him to help each person live in a way that would count for the message of real life. He prayed that God would have mercy on the nation and stop the unholy holocaust against innocent children. He expressed the hope that our nation might return to a celebration of life in its fullness.

Following the prayer, David thanked the people for coming and announced that there would be a number of opportunities in the near future to become better informed on the abortion issue.

The evening ended as the somber, quiet audience left the gymnasium. People spoke in whispers as they drifted into the night. There was a keen sense that God's Spirit had been with them in a powerful way that night. Many realized they had been confronted with the need to take action or perhaps live to see the shameful results of a society that has completely drifted from God's way.

Comment

Christianity is not for spectators. God does not limit His work to a few special people while expecting the rest to look on as spectators. The real wonder is that He has a place and work for everyone. Our "candles" may not seem all that significant, but we have been asked by God to place them in His hands. How He uses them is His business. The part we play may not attract attention from others, but that is not really our purpose. Our purpose is to make ourselves available to God for big or little assignments. What we do is important not because other people notice, but rather because it is what God has directed us to do.

We begin by consciously asking Him to use us. Usually, we won't know what His specific plan is for us, but we start with what we do know: that we should read and obey His Word, that we should encourage others who are also letting their "candles" burn for Him, and that we should ask for and depend on His guidance each day.

In the News

Harmonic Convergence is roughly as important to followers of the post-hippie New Age movement as Yom Kippur is to Jews. Maybe more so. If Harmonic Convergence fails, a 25-year period of increasing earthly catastrophe will ensue, and by 2012 we will all die. But it's OK. All you have to do to forestall Armageddon is, and we can't stress this too strongly, get together with some friends and hold hands and hum, and everything will be fine.

December 4, 1983. That's the day the idea for Harmonic Convergence came to Arguelles, a 48-year-old art historian. He was driving along Wilshire Boulevard at the time. First, he says, the Aztec calendar, with its 13 cycles of Heaven and nine cycles of Hell, comes to an end on August 16, 1987; the Aztecs believed that the end of the ninth Hell cycle would mark the second coming of Quetzalcoatl, the god of peace. Second, Arguelles says, Hopi Indian legend has it that on August 16, 1987, "144,000 Sun Dance enlightened teachers will help awaken the rest of humanity."

Hostility toward earthbound miseries like disease and war and drug addiction, or any one of a million kinds of human problems can't be solved by standing around in a circle and smiling. Making yourself feel good about the world is not the same thing as improving the world. Want to think a good thought? Think about 144,000 people volunteering an hour a week to work in shelters for the homeless. That would be something to hum about.

Source: Baron, Bill with Pamela Abramson. "The End of the World (Again)." *Newsweek,* August 17, 1987.

ॠ ॠ ॠ

As for the prophetic planetary lineup, Dr. William Gooch of Hayden Planetarium in Manhattan affirms that Mars, Venus and Mercury will pass behind the sun during the last week of August. But, he adds, "as far as science is concerned, there is absolutely nothing unusual about the day. Events like this happen quite regularly. It just depends on which group of planets you choose to pick. The only cycle I see is that a lot of people want to get back to hippie days."

Source: Smilgis, Martha. "A New Age Dawning." *Time,* August 31, 1987, p. 63.

ta ta ta

Crystal gazing, channeling, witchcraft, and other subjects of the New Age movement were included in workshops sponsored by the Women's Center at Red Rocks Community College (Colorado). The workshops were part of a Learning Fair held at the college on September 17. All the presenters were practitioners of New Age skills and religion, although for fear of public scorn, organizers denied advocating any particular religion or cult.

Source: "New Age Goes to College." *The Eagle Forum* (Colorado), Winter 1988.

ta ta ta

Still: the word contains a whole philosophy of history. . . . There is a canker in the fruit, a cancer in the marrow. It will have its way in due course. Believers ask, Can one still pray? Can faith still survive? When they ask it that way, they betray a sense of futility. It's only a matter of time.

Since *still* is usually used against causes I cherish, I got compensatory delight from a big headline in *Publishers Weekly* (December 16) announcing the zillion New Age books published in the past six months: "NEW AGE: STILL GLOWING," it cried. My opinion of the New Age fad should make me appalled by endless fine-print lists of books on the topic. But the word *still* cheers me. The editors, publishers and readers are letting a metaphorical cat out of the bag: the days of unchecked growth for the New Age market are limited.

Yet the New Age is not coming; it is only "still glowing." And I am letting New Year optimism run away with me. Because after the New Age, many well-off, highly educated disdainers of everyone else's faith and practice will still constitute a market for fads and foolishness. So someone will invent a new name for a new set of market items and find a new market. "A glut appears inevitable." Still.

Source: Marty, Martin E. "Still the New Age." *The Christian Century,* January 4–11, 1989, p. 31.

☙ ☙ ☙

Shirley MacLaine must be in seventh heaven. In 1983, when she published *Out on a Limb,* the book that detailed her faith in reincarnation, she worried that people would think she was crazy. Some did, but millions bought the book.

Since 1983 MacLaine has shepherded into the American mainstream a host of ideas and practices known as the New Age movement. Gallup Polls show that from 20 percent to 35 percent of the American public believe they have had a past-life experience. And according to a study by SRI International, some five percent to ten percent of the population have adopted other New Age beliefs. One is "channeling," a kind of psychic talk show in which human mediums call forth the voices of long-dead spirits. Another involves crystals, which are quartz rocks. Thousands of people believe that crystals have the power to cure diseases and transmit human thoughts.

The New Age movement began in California in the 1960s with the spread of Eastern philosophy, particularly Buddhist and Hindu, among a small number of mostly white, mostly young Americans.

To their utopianism they added a modern twist: the idea that devoting oneself to self-improvement was personally valuable and socially beneficial. They dubbed their cause the "human potential movement." Social pundits dubbed them the "Me Generation." Perhaps most indicative of the era was Werner Erhard's emotionally manipulative (and immensely profitable) est program, featuring weekend seminars at which you couldn't use the bathroom until you learned to love yourself.

Source: Blow, Richard. "Moronic Convergence." *The New Republic,* January 25, 1988, p. 24.

☙ ☙ ☙

It started with a terrible backache. That's when I realized how pervasive the new-age mentality has become. When I read that Shirley MacLaine, its leading practitioner, had convinced her devotees that people create their own reality—"You are God," she said—I assumed she meant nothing more by it than inspirational motivation.

Then I discovered the flip side of MacLaine's argument: if I'm sick, it must be my fault. If my life is a mess, I've failed to fulfill my potential. Real life isn't always perfect. Extrapolate from that to such realities as poverty and pestilence and you have what I view as a contemporary madness: for every misfortune in life, we seem too ready to blame the victim.

Friends are now Freudians; everyone is "into" psychology. And when I shared the news that I have a herniated disc, all-knowing laymen looked at me and repeatedly asked: "Why are you letting stress get to you that much? Why are you doing this to yourself?"

Believe it or not, wear and tear, age and time, can actually cause damage to bodily parts and functions.

Feelings can foster health. Attitude may mean the difference between life and death. But—and here is the crucial cautionary *but* that's often lost in the upbeat literature of our day—disease is still a cruel killer. Cancer victims who truly want to live do nevertheless die. Wishing doesn't necessarily alter dreadful conditions.

Source: Blech, Benjamin. "Don't Blame the Victim." *Newsweek,*
September 19, 1988, p. 10.

ta ta ta

By now it should be clear to even the most casual observer that the New Age is more than a passing fad—it is a deep cultural trend attracting thousands of people from all walks of life. It has galvanized a host of disparate organizations, events, individuals, and ideas around its self-deifying themes. Celebrity evangelists such as Shirley MacLaine and John Denver, scientific sages such a Fritjof Capra, and entrepreneurs such as Werner Erhard tout a burgeoning market of books and magazines, magical crystals, exotic therapies, and mind-expanding seminars.

One area of culture after another is being touched—if not consumed—by a New Age orientation. Christians, while initially slow to respond to the New Age's growing cultural clout, have now rushed to analyze, expose, debate, and debunk the movement. Unfortunately, many of these recent responses are superficial. Their examination of the

New Age probes only skin deep. They expound sensational conspiracy theories that alarm the ignorant instead of equipping the saints.

At least three scriptural themes address our interaction with culture — separation, transformation, and conservation. They are foundation to a solid response to the New Age, and without holding them in proper balance we fall into error.

Source: Groothuis, Douglas. "Confronting the New Age." *Christianity Today,* January 13, 1989, p. 36.

Key Quotations

Men may be induced to abandon their old religion and to adopt a new one; but they never can remain long free from all religion. Take away one object of worship and they will soon attach themselves to another. If unhappily they lose the knowledge of the true God, they will set up gods of their own invention or receive them from others.

Archibald Alexander

How you have fallen from heaven, O morning star,
    son of the dawn!
You have been cast down to the earth, you who
    once laid low the nations!
You said in your heart, "I will ascend to heaven;
I will raise my throne above the stars of God;
I will sit enthroned on the mount of assembly, on
    the utmost heights of the sacred mountain.
I will ascend above the tops of the clouds;
    I will make myself like the Most High."

Isaiah 14:12–14

T H I R T E E N

A PERSONAL START

Key Question: What is a Christian's appropriate response to God's command to have an impact in the world?

Setting: Businessman/father discovers that life itself limits the choice to *how* we will be involved, not *if* we will be involved.

B ill Jenkins gripped the steering wheel a little tighter. Being stuck in rush hour traffic wasn't a new experience. But lately, he had come to dread the unavoidable delays. He watched his own knuckles turn white, then, as if suddenly seeing himself in a new way, he burst out laughing. An outside observer, familiar with rush hour behavior, might have assumed Bill was approaching the borders of sanity. Still chuckling, he began to talk to himself.

"Never have been able to figure out why they called this rush hour. Should have called it 'slow hour', or 'stop and go hour.' You used to get upset at what the traffic was doing around you. Now you're upset at the traffic inside your head."

Like a sluggish millipede, the cars in front of him came to life and surged forward a few feet. Bill interrupted his conversation with himself as he took his appointed turn to close up the ranks. His actions were mechanical. Traffic jams were so familiar that at times he felt as if he could have gone to sleep downtown and his body, operating on auto-pilot, would have gotten him home. He wasn't tired, and he knew that sleep would have probably brought on dreams that covered the same thoughts that seemed to hound him every moment he wasn't occupied with something else. That was what had been so hard about rush hour lately. There was too much time to think about things he hadn't thought about for years.

Random thoughts and a familiar uneasiness had taken on a definite pattern in his mind shortly after he had seen the play which had so deeply involved his son Mike. As a father, he had experienced the play in at least three different ways. He had been fiercely proud of his son's part in such a dramatic statement. He had also been challenged by the significance of the message in the play. But he knew from his response to similar events that these two levels had only touched his life without really troubling him. There had been a deeper, surprising shock to his system as he had watched his son on stage. He had seen himself. Vivid flashes of his own life crowded his mind during the performance. Several times, the corners of his eyes glistened as the memories became almost too real to keep inside.

Like the frame around a captivating painting, the surrounding details had been lost in his mind, but the central memories remained. He saw a boy about Mike's age, in single-track pursuit of fun at a Christian summer camp. He could still recall the startling derailment of that pursuit by a simple message one evening. In the middle of the distracting sun, fun, and romance of that rustic setting he had suddenly been overwhelmed by his own emptiness. Without knowing how at the time, he had realized that many of the frantic efforts in his life had been unconscious attempts to avoid or fill that emptiness. It had swallowed everything he offered. But then, through the words of someone whose name he had forgotten, had come the news that one person, Jesus Christ, could fill that emptiness. It was an offer he couldn't refuse. Following the meeting, the speaker had helped Bill understand that the emptiness he felt was created by the sinful difference between himself and God. That difference wasn't something he could change. It was something he had to allow God to change as Christ entered his life. He explained to Bill that

Jesus Christ had come to offer God's love and forgiveness, and had guaranteed it by dying on the cross in his place. He had died in his place to offer him His life. Much of this wasn't new to Bill. He had been raised in a church where the gospel was preached. But this was the first time all these facts had fit together like a jigsaw puzzle with his name on it. Bill had prayed a simple, personal prayer that night, admitting his sinfulness, and inviting Jesus Christ to be his Lord and Savior.

As Bill watched Mike on stage, the growing commitment of his son to Jesus Christ as Lord was obvious. Bill realized he had been the same way. Christ's presence in his life had made an immediate impact. His priorities had changed. He realized that Barb, the vivacious girl who had become his wife, had been attracted to him partly because she had sensed Jesus in him. But even as these memories passed through his mind at the play, and almost daily on the freeway, a haunting question kept intruding. What had happened to that committed young man in the past twenty years? He had left the play knowing the question would pursue him until he answered it. Ever since then, the traffic in his mind had been more difficult to deal with than the traffic on the road.

On that particular drive home, something new did happen. Bill made a decision. He decided to talk to Mike about his question. It seemed like such a simple plan, he wondered why it had taken him so long to come up with it. Then he realized what it would mean to his pride as a father to ask for his son's advice. It would mean admitting to his son that, in spite of their shared faith, Mike's life had a quality his father wanted to have again in his own life. It would mean switching roles as teacher-student. (Except he had to admit with shame that he couldn't remember the last time he had consciously tried to teach his son anything in the spiritual area.) But the decision was made. As he steered his car toward the welcome emptiness of his exit ramp he murmured to himself, "I guess dads still have a lot to learn, even if their children have to teach them."

During supper that night, Bill tried to be casual about his desire to talk to his son later. "Mike, I need to talk to you for a few minutes after we eat," he said between bites of roast beef and other conversation. But the awkward silence that followed reminded him that formal requests for an audience with one's children always carry an ominous tone even when expressed with a mouth full of food. He felt compelled to add,

"No problems, just need to check with you about something." That seemed to get the conversation flowing around the table again.

Bill was sitting in his favorite chair with the unread paper on his lap when Mike stuck his head around the corner. "You wanted to see me, Dad?" he asked tentatively.

"Yes, Mike," answered Bill, still unsure of where or how to start this conversation. He remembered some of the same feelings from years ago when he had tried to talk to Mike about sex. But he pushed those thoughts aside and began, "Look, I've had some things on my mind, and I just thought I'd maybe talk them over with you."

Mike seemed to sense that this conversation would revolve around his father and not one of his own shortcomings. He relaxed. "Sure, Dad. Shoot."

"Well, I wanted to tell you again how proud I was with the work you did on the play at church. It meant more to me than I can say. And I've noticed how you've treated Wendy Peterson and it's made me proud in yet another way. It's like you've learned to express what you believe, but you've also learned how to treat people with Christlike love. She's nice and I think you've helped her. And I've just been watching you in general, and what I've seen has really made me feel honored to be your father." He realized he was having a hard time coming to the point, but he also knew these were important things that needed to be communicated to his son.

Mike gave his dad one of those looks that says, "You can stop saying all those nice things about me in the next half-hour or so," and then added out loud, "Thanks, Dad."

"You know," continued Bill, "a lot of what has happened to you reminds me of part of my life. There was a time when Christ was an important part of each day that I lived. I think that's what I'm really seeing in you, and I don't want you to lose that."

He stopped for a moment and his son said with feeling, "I don't want to lose it either, Dad. But sometimes I get scared."

"You do?" asked Bill, surprised by the sudden turn in the conversation.

"Yeah. I think it's fantastic to be a little part of what God is doing right now, but I think about how long life can be and I wonder if I'll ever settle down and . . ." Mike trailed off as he realized he had been about to finish the sentence with words that related to his parents' lives.

Bill felt a twinge of pain, but knew his son would have been speaking the truth. Mike's reluctance had been a gesture of honor and an expression of his unwillingness to pass judgment on his parents. Bill was thankful. He also wanted in the worst way to have Mike be just as proud of his father as he was of his son.

"Hey, thanks for sparing your Mom and me," Bill said with a smile. "But I want you to know that both of us feel bad about settling down in such a way that our faith has stopped growing. We want to change that. With all the stuff going on with PTA, I'm sure you realize your Mom isn't settled at all anymore, is she?"

"Boy," said Mike, "you can say that again! You really should have seen her at that meeting. And I only thought she got upset when I broke things around the house. I've even had kids at school say what neat parents I have."

"Mike, I should have been at that PTA meeting, business or no business. I feel like I let her down, and you and your brother. What you guys are learning ought to be my most important business. What I've really got to do is find a way to let Jesus be just as real in my life as I see Him being in your life."

Mike was genuinely puzzled. "What do you mean, Dad? I know you're a Christian."

Bill was now intense, "Thanks, son, but let me tell you something. My family and the people at church are probably the only people who know it. I don't think anyone where I work has any idea what I believe other than I happen to be a person who doesn't smoke or use bad language. When I first became a Christian I couldn't imagine keeping it a secret. Christ made a difference in my life and I could see others needed Him. I got embarrassed sometimes, but that hardly slowed me down. What happened to me? I keep asking that question."

"I don't know, Dad," said Mike. "But I hope you can find out, because I'm afraid it might happen to me. I do want the people in every part of my life to know that I'm a Christian, even if they don't choose to be one themselves."

As his son was speaking, Bill had a significant insight. "I just realized one of our differences, Mike," he said. "Each of our lives is like a school building, with many different rooms, connecting halls, and special areas. By inviting Jesus into our lives, we give Him the freedom to roam through our halls. Right now, there doesn't seem to be anywhere in your life where the door is locked for Jesus. But there are some big areas in my life that are shut off to His presence. And when He isn't allowed to go everywhere, it sometimes seems like He isn't anywhere in the building at all. Does that make sense?"

Mike could hardly believe this conversation was happening with his dad. He felt like it was he who was being allowed into locked places in his father's life. He couldn't remember feeling as close to his dad ever before. He answered, "Yeah, Dad. I can see your point. But how do the areas get locked?"

Bill thought for a moment, then said, "I guess what happened is that, as I had new experiences in life — as new additions were constructed on the building — I never actually invited Christ to be part of them. He doesn't seem to force Himself where He hasn't been invited. So, as I began my career in business, I never really asked Him to come along. I hate to say this, but Christ is not a part of my life at work. That is going to change."

"How will you do that?" asked Mike, genuinely interested.

"Well," said his dad, "I don't think I can figure out exactly how things got the way they are, but Jesus understands it all in detail. I think what I want to do is tell Him He now has my specific permission to take over any areas of my life that have been closed to him. I don't know what that will mean, but it is what I want. Then I want to also ask Him to remind me when new doors open and new opportunities come to me, that I'll include Him from the start."

Mike made a quick application to his own situation. "So, what you're saying means that I have to watch out that I keep my relationship with Christ up to date. It's like the future isn't a problem as long as I make sure that Jesus is involved in each day I live."

"Right, Mike," said Bill, "and what I realize is happening in your life right now is that Christ's presence is allowing you to see many opportunities to be useful to Him that I've been missing. I'm sure there are people at work who need to hear about life from God's point of view. I want them to see Christ in me the way the people you go to school with see Christ in you."What I'm finally realizing is how the things you and Pastor David have been involved in really do fit the Christian life. My avoiding issues like abortion doesn't mean I'm not involved; it means I'm involved in the wrong way. I've never really gotten hold of the fact that Jesus doesn't offer me a choice of whether or not to be involved. The choice is only how I'll be involved. I see now that Jesus wants me to be involved for Him, in all of life. I know that if I set out to be obedient to Him, I can't predict where that will take me, but I can expect I will be involved in real life issues. I also know I need to be better informed and prepared. I guess avoiding action means that we also avoid Jesus, because He always demonstrated by His life His involvement in real issues that impact real people in real life."

"Dad," said Mike, "you're sounding a little like Pastor David. But it sure is neat coming from you."

Each of them felt the forging of a new bond between them. They realized they were allowing each other to know their intentions before God. They also felt that in a strange way, each of them owed the other a faithfulness to what they said they were going to do. It was a moment they would never forget.

Bill did something that even surprised him. He suggested to his son that they pray together. He wondered how prayer in Christian homes gets relegated to those brief moments before the meals. As he and his son prayed for each other, he realized they had certainly been missing out on an important part of spiritual life. He was determined that would change also.

The next day, the drive to work was a completely different experience for Bill. The traffic was still there; the stalls and stops were still there; but one driver was elsewhere. Dreaded delays became opportunities for brief prayers. Driving and praying reminded Bill of a fragment of God's Word he had memorized years ago. "With eyes wide open to the mercies of God . . . ," he said to himself several times. He wondered if work itself would be different now that Christ was a welcomed companion.

Comment

Considering a change is often more difficult than the change itself. In these events, a father discovers the gift of growing in his walk with

Christ by humbling himself with his own son. After the first step he is amazed to find that God provides direction a step at a time. The presence of Jesus is affirmed as a necessary part of every area of life for those claiming to be Christians.

In the News

Mother Teresa vows that her work with the sick and poor in Calcutta, India, will continue, even though she resigned Wednesday as head of the religious order she founded.

"To me, the work and the cause of my mission is more important than any individual," Mother Teresa, 79, said after saying ill health forced her to step down.

The frail but dynamic Catholic nun was born in Yugoslavia to Albanian parents. She founded Missionaries of Charity in 1950 in Calcutta's squalid slums. She received the Nobel Peace Prize in 1979.

The order now maintains orphanages, clinics, hospices and homes for the poor in 87 countries, including the USA.

Asked who would take over, Mother Teresa raised her hand toward the heavens. "We will act the way he leads us."

Mother Teresa received a pacemaker last year. She rarely leaves the second floor of her Calcutta home.

Of her future, she said only that she plans to pray and "thank God for giving me a chance to serve his cause."

Source: Moss, Desda. "Mother Teresa passes along her 'cause.'" *USA Today,* April 12, 1990.

ها ها ها

The Beethoven project—formally called the Center for Successful Childhood Development—was inspired by Irving Harris, a Chicago philanthropist who has spent $1 million on the experiment. (Harris, 77, made his fortune developing home-permanent products for Toni Co. and now runs Standard Shares, a holding company.) His idea is intriguing: He wants to identify all the approximately 125 children who will enter

Beethoven Elementary in 1993 — some of whom have not even been born yet — and provide them and their mothers with special services over the next five years. Mothers will receive prenatal care, counseling, and classes in parenting. Children will get pediatric care and be enrolled in preschool.

To find participants, nine family advocates from the community roam the dingy corridors, knocking on doors. Women who are pregnant or who have recently delivered babies — 120 as of May — are asked to join. The typical mother is black, single, and 20 years old, and has at least two other children.

Gaining the trust of the Robert Taylor residents has not been easy. To show its commitment, the center's 43-member staff — mostly social workers — took over the second floor of one of the housing project's 16-story buildings. Gang wars and frequent gunfire did not deter them from moving in last fall; faulty plumbing almost did. "There were no toilets. The place was bombed out," says Harris. "By herculean effort we got it renovated."

Source: "How One Man Makes a Difference." *Fortune,* July 4, 1988, p. 76.

ᴥ ᴥ ᴥ

Our institutions of family, religion, education, business, labor, and community are attempting to keep afloat while wrestling with both internal and external combatants. Each group's purpose or *raison d'etre* is challenged constantly while it seeks acceptable canons in which to function in a modern society.

Perhaps it is time for our institutions to answer the age-old question Lewis Carroll implored in *Alice's Adventures in Wonderland.* "Cheshire Puss," Alice began, "would you please tell me which way I ought to go from here?" "That depends on where you want to get to," said the cat. As an answer to the question, an appropriate quality of life, one with values, would not elicit too many complaints from the varied constituencies of our institutions.

Source: Rauch, Richard A. "A Quality Life Should Be Full of Values." *USA Today,* January 1990, pp. 73–74.

ಏ ಏ ಏ

A Decree of the 101st Congress:

Whereas the Bible has made a unique contribution in shaping the United States as a distinctive and blessed Nation and people;

Whereas deeply held values springing from the Bible led to the early settlement of our Nation;

Whereas many of our great national leaders, such as Presidents Washington, Jackson, Lincoln, and Wilson, paid tribute to the important influence the Bible has had in the development of our Nation;

Whereas President Jackson called the Bible "the rock on which our Republic rests";

Whereas the history of our Nation illustrates the value of voluntarily applying the teaching of the Bible in the lives of individuals and of families; and

Whereas numerous individuals and organizations around the world are joining hands to encourage international Bible reading in 1990: Now, therefore, be it

Resolved by the Senate and House of Representatives of the United States of America in Congress assembled, that 1990 is designated as the "International Year of Bible Reading." The president is authorized and requested to issue a proclamation recognizing both the formative influence the Bible has had on many societies of the world and the value of the study of the Bible.

Source: Public Law 101–209, 101st Congress, December 7, 1989.

ಏ ಏ ಏ

Turner's "Voluntary Initiatives" [on family planning, and ecology] include:

- I promise to have not more than two children, or no more than my nation suggests.

- I support the United Nations and its efforts to collectively improve the condition of the planet.

Now Turner has created "Captain Planet," an animated action-adventure series featuring the first ecologically minded cartoon hero. Blessed with the power of nature itself, and serving the earth spirit Gaia, Captain Planet and his five multiracial Planeteers combat not the standard monsters of the present substandard children's fare but, rather, such planetary evils as overpopulation, global warming, acid rain, and the depletion of endangered species. TNT has also embarked on a television anti-nuke parable, the *Butter Battle Book.*

Explaining his programming philosophy, Turner told *People* magazine: "I'm putting on the full-court press now—to stop the arms race, control the population, and protect the environment. I want to be successful with business so I can communicate with people. It's true that everything I do is a war."

Source: Lanham, Julie. "The Greening of Ted Turner." *The Humanist,* November/December 1989, pp. 6–7.

ﻌ ﻌ ﻌ

Ted Turner, self-proclaimed "News King": "We're living with outmoded rules. The rules we're living under is [sic] the Ten Commandments, and I bet nobody here even pays much attention to 'em, because they are too old. When Moses went up on the mountain, there were no nuclear weapons, there was no poverty. Today, the commandments wouldn't go over. Nobody around likes to be commanded."

Ted Koppel, host of Nightline: "What Moses brought down from Mt. Sinai were not the Ten Suggestions. They are commandments. Are, not were. The sheer brilliance of the Ten Commandments is that they codify in a handful of words acceptable human behavior, not just for then or now, but for all time. Language evolves. Power shifts from one nation to another. Messages are transmitted with the speed of light. Man erases one frontier after another. And yet we and our behavior and the commandments governing that behavior remain the same."

Source: T.V. news quotes from CNN and ABC.

≈ ≈ ≈

Protestants of all major groups have generally agreed in their doctrine of Biblical authority. Lutherans, Reformed, Anglicans, Wesleyans, and charismatics have historically stood for the complete truth of the Bible as God's inerrant Word to guide human beings. And the Roman and Greek Orthodox traditions have stood with evangelicals in defending the inerrancy and infallibility of Scripture.

Of course, the doctrine of the infallible authority of Holy Scripture has not been without opposition. But until modern times that opposition largely came from outside the organized church. In the last century, however, it welled up within the structures of the church itself.

Source: Kantzer, Kenneth S. "Why I Still Believe the Bible is True." *Christianity Today,* October 7, 1988, p. 22.

Key Quotations

I am only one, but I am one. I cannot do everything, but I can do something. What I can do, I should do and, with the help of God, I will do!

Everett Hale

[To the church in Laodicea:] "I know your deeds, that you are neither cold nor hot. I wish you were either one or the other! So, because you are lukewarm — neither hot nor cold — I am about to spit you out of my mouth."

Revelation 3:15–16

A PUBLIC STAND

Key Question: What opportunities do Christians have to speak out for life?

Setting: At work, Bill Jenkins discovers a multitude of questions he hadn't even been aware were being asked.

When Bill Jenkins drove to work with Jesus the morning after his long talk with Mike, he expected great changes. Actually, work was still work. His fellow employees had always known Bill as easygoing and friendly. They really didn't notice anything unusual in his greeting. He didn't float through the halls. The intercom failed to take the initiative and announce to everyone that Bill Jenkins had brought an important guest to work with him. No one saw Jesus in Bill that whole first day. At least, not in a conscious way.

In fact, a week went by without any apparent change in Bill. Then, someone mentioned in passing that Bill seemed to be arriving late for all the coffee breaks. His secretary said she had opened his office door to say good night at the end of the day and caught him with his eyes closed. "Almost looked like he had a headache, except he was smiling," she added, "and I think he was talking to himself." Actually, Bill had developed a little habit of committing his coffee breaks to God. It was the only time during the day when he had opportunity to mix with others. Mostly, his work kept him in his office. He had been asking God to help him really listen to those he worked with. He had also been ending each day with a brief prayer of thanks to Jesus for being with him that day. On his way to the coffee break that particular morning he really didn't expect it would be the first time at work someone would notice Jesus was with him.

The coffee break area was a conference room with a large table. Bill found his office-mates already in their favorite seats. Conversations around the table were usually pretty informal. There were four women and three men at the table when Bill took his place. The group seemed a little somber. Bill asked, "What's happened to you guys?"

His secretary, Molly, answered, "We just heard that Betty from accounting was rushed to an emergency room by ambulance a while ago."

Bill remembered Betty although he had never met her personally. He had heard she was part of the outspoken feminist group in the company. He felt genuine concern for her. He asked, "Does anyone know how she got hurt?"

"Story is," said one of the other secretaries, "that she had an abortion yesterday and something went wrong. She showed up for work this morning and passed out at her desk. She was bleeding badly." Then she added as an afterthought, "We're collecting for some flowers. She's not married, and I don't think she's got any family here in the city."

Bill was searching his pockets for some money when Molly spoke up again.

"Listen, I just have to say something. I really don't know how they do it. I mean, I really feel bad for Betty. And I hope she's all right. But I've raised four kids and I can't see how anyone could deliberately and knowingly kill an innocent little baby while it's safely in its mother's womb." Bill was startled by the directness of Molly's comment. So was everyone else.

She paused as if realizing she had gone too far to back out, then went on. "I think I know something about how scary an unexpected pregnancy can be to a young teenager, or the anguish of a mother of more children than she can feed who finds herself pregnant again. I can even identify with women who don't want to deal with postponing professional plans like I had to in order to have my family. I realize these people feel in some way or another that they have to have an abortion. But they don't do abortions. That's who I really wonder about. How can doctors and nurses who perform them day in and day out, who have to make sure all the pieces of the little child are out of the womb, who throw them in garbage cans and plastic bags, how can they sleep at night?"

One of the men broke the heavy silence which followed. "Molly, you sound like one of those radical pro-lifers," he said chidingly. "I'm not so sure they are in fact 'babies.' I think it's merely a blob of tissue and it's no big deal. As far as I'm concerned, they're not babies until they're born."

"Now that's another issue with me," said Molly hotly. "Who has proven that they're not babies? When I was pregnant I never dreamed of calling what was growing inside me anything but a baby! And I'll tell you something else, too. Sometimes I feel like becoming a radical pro-lifer. I get tired of all the fancy words that people use to hide the fact that a pre-born child has been killed. And I don't like the fact that I'm hearing more and more stories like Betty's involving complications for the mother, like bleeding and sometimes an inability to have children later on. But what really gets me wondering about those doctors and nurses is the number of women I've run into who carry deep guilt and sorrow over the abortions they've had. How do the medical people handle the guilt? With thousands of abortions going on, there's got to be a lot of guilt. . . ."

Before he realized it, Bill found himself gently correcting his secretary. "It's millions, Molly. Millions of babies being aborted. And I think you're right, there is a lot of guilt. I guess I would say that people are handling guilt like they always have. Doctors and nurses are humans, too."

"What do you mean?" asked Charlie, the man who had just chided Molly.

"Well, I'm finally realizing something very basic that all humans share. It's the way we tend to handle guilt. We tend to either excuse, blame, or deny," answered Bill.

The other man, Pete, chimed in, "Wait a minute, Bill. You were talking about the doctors and nurses. Why did you change the word to *we?*"

"Yeah," said Charlie, "and I still don't understand what you mean by excuse, blame, or deny."

"Well, let me put it this way," said Bill. "When I do something that makes me feel guilty, I instinctively resist admitting I've done something wrong. Instead, I will try to excuse what I've done by appealing to some special reason, or I will blame someone else for influencing or 'making' me do it, or I may just deny that the action was wrong. I think doctors and nurses use all three ways to justify what they are doing. Humans have had thousands of years of practice at avoiding guilt. We haven't been able to get rid of it, though."

"Oh, oh," said Charlie, "this is suddenly sounding like a religious discussion."

"I don't really care what you call it, Charlie," said Bill with a smile. "The point is, is it the truth? I mean, in order to solve a problem, and I think guilt is a big problem, you have to know what the cause is. A fact doesn't stop being the truth just because someone put the label 'religious' on it."

Charlie wasn't ready to back down. He continued, "Well, I resent it when I run into people who want to force their beliefs down other people's throats."

"I have to agree with you in a way, Charlie," said Bill. "But I've also noticed something recently. Both medicine and poison can be hard to swallow. I think people sometimes resist the truth by calling it poison instead of admitting that they just don't want to change.

"And as for forcing beliefs on others, I keep running into people who believe others should be silent about what they believe. But, forcing them into silence by intimidation is just another way of forcing a belief down somebody's throat, wouldn't you agree?"

"So, I suppose that next you'll be saying that we're all sinners, right?" said Charlie with some defensiveness.

"It's not what I say," responded Bill in as friendly a tone as he could. "It's what the Bible says. It is just as direct as you just were, Charlie. It says, 'All have sinned.' And I'm definitely included."

"Well, I can see it's time to excuse myself and get back to work," mumbled Charlie as he got up and put his coffee mug away. He was gone in a moment.

Molly chuckled and said, "Well, Bill, I think that hit close to home with Charlie. I do have a couple of quick questions for you, though. In saying we're all sinners, it sounds like you're the one letting the doctors off the hook by blaming everyone for what's going on with abortions. How do you answer that? You also said something about a solution to the problem. What is it?"

Bill laughed out loud and said, "Those are wonderful questions—but they're definitely not quick. Besides, I want to think about them for a while. Can I try to answer them this afternoon?"

"O.K.," said Molly as she and the others got up from their chairs. "The rest of you guys interested?" There was a general murmur of agreement. As they went through the door Molly added thoughtfully, "I think something has gotten into you, Bill Jenkins."

"Well, not exactly something," he said smiling. "It's Someone." And for the first time in years he sensed the almost physical presence of Christ by his side.

Comment

God's work is immediate; it's our ability to see the results that takes time. Discussions in settings like work and school are never predictable or controllable. More often than not, everything that could be said can't be said. People who decide to represent Christ through the various outlets in their lives must be content with His scheduling, giving as much of the message as they're allowed to give. Social issues are the hottest topics on people's minds. The right comment by a Christian can open the door for the gospel. The two most important preparations are a growing awareness of basic answers and a willingness to let God create and show us opportunities. We don't have to know everything before we are usable to God!

In the News

Can you imagine, in this day and age, anyone in business refusing service to someone because he or she is Jewish or black? Even more incomprehensible, can you imagine a company employing high-level executives who admit they are discriminating against customers for those very reasons? Not only would it be an extremely bad business practice, it would be downright illegal and immoral.

Where, you ask, is such a backward and bigoted policy tolerated? Is it some neo-Nazi or skinhead organization? Is it in some isolated, unenlightened, backwater klan community?

No, the kind of discrimination described is taking place today in that bastion of tolerance and pluralistic liberalism, Hollywood USA. Except those targeted in this particular incident are not black or Jewish, they are Bible-believing Christians.

Strange that an industry still shuddering from a political blacklist 40 years ago would condone another kind of blacklist — one admittedly based on politics and religion.

Source: "Hollywood's Ugly Anti-Christian Bigotry." *New York City Tribune,* September 18, 1989.

☙ ☙ ☙

What would happen if a Hollywood studio made a film about blacks taking over a fictional country, turning it into a police state and persecuting whites?

First of all, we all know such a film could never be made. The premise is outrageously racist and inciting. But, if some maverick filmmaker did manage to produce such a movie, surely it would be roundly and deservedly condemned by critics and shunned by major distributors.

Let's see what happens with a slight twist in the plot.

It is called *The Handmaid's Tale,* and, while it doesn't suggest blacks have a proclivity toward repression, authoritarianism and brutality, it does portray fundamentalist Christians as leaning toward such fascist ruling tendencies.

The Handmaid's Tale is set in the future in the land of Gilead, a country that, according to a prologue, just plain "went wrong."

A coup, of sorts, has taken place in the country. Blacks are being trucked off to God-knows-where. Homosexuals are being persecuted. Women are reduced to servile roles. Catholic nuns are hanged for not giving up their vows. Books have been burned. And white men claim to rule with the Old Testament as their literal and only constitution.

The movie suggests that the Hebrew Bible—the document that inspired great nations and great systems of government—is really a blueprint for a form of neo-Nazism. In this sense, the movie is not only anti-Christian, it is anti-Jewish, as well.

Source: Farah, Joseph, ed. "Hollywood's latest anti-Christian slur." *AFA Journal,* April 1990, p. 18.

ↆ ↆ ↆ

The *Milwaukee Journal* has admitted it erred in firing newsroom secretary Diane Dew for her off-hours pro-life activism.

Dew lost her job after she was seen participating in a pro-life rally. Both her supervisor, Editor Sig Gissler, and the *Journal* financially support Planned Parenthood.

The Rutherford Institute, a Christian legal service, negotiated a settlement in which the newspaper confessed its actions infringed on Dew's freedom of expression.

"The settlement signals a clear vindication of [Dew's] First Amendment rights. The settlement also sends a message as clear as any teletype: No organization or institution, no matter how powerful, may freely trample under foot the sincere religious beliefs of its pro-life employees," said a Rutherford press release.

Dew accepted a cash award rather than reinstatement as a *Journal* secretary, and is attending college to study journalism.

Source: "Pro-Life Secretary Wins Fight with Newspaper." *Focus on the Family Citizen,* 1/90.

ɜ. ɜ. ɜ.

It should be pointed out that on March 4, 1987, U.S. District Judge W. Brevard Hand, in Smith v. Board of School Commissioners of Mobile County, Ala., ruled that secular humanism is a religion. The 172-page ruling defines religion and concludes, after reviewing the relevant aspects of humanism, that "For purposes of the First Amendment, secular humanism is a religious belief system, entitled to the protections of, and subject to the prohibitions of, the religion clauses."

Judge Hand wrote: "The entire body of thought has three key documents that furnish the text upon which the belief system rests as a platform: *Humanist Manifesto I, Humanist Manifesto II,* and the *Secular Humanist Declaration.*

"These factors . . . demonstrate the institutional character of secular humanism. They are evidence that this belief system is similar to groups traditionally afforded protection by the First Amendment religion clauses."

Source: "Is Humanism a Religion?" *The Blumenfeld Education Letter,* July 1989.

ɜ. ɜ. ɜ.

Dr. George Gallup, Jr., whose famous polling results on religion in American have done more to awaken Christians to their opportunity to influence society than any other person, has done it again.

At a time when the "TV scandals" have rocked the credibility of many Christian leaders, Mr. Gallup is now using his considerable Christian influence to put a whole new face on the Christian Church. He portrays the Church as the most humanitarian organization in the country by a factor of two or more. That is, churches in this country, according to Mr. Gallup, gave over $19 billion last year to "community services such as religion-affiliated schools, nursing homes, and day care centers," while the totality of all U.S. foundations and American corporations gave only $10.1 billion to these programs.

The reason this is so important to publicize at this time is because all over this country there are secularizers who want to do away with the tax deductions of churches — as though this is unfair, preferential treatment of the religious people in the nation. In truth, it is an excellent way to encourage generosity and help needy individuals who would otherwise not be helped.

As George Gallup said, "Our religious bodies are some of the most cost-effective institutions in society." That news needs to be spread everywhere.

Source: "Churches Far Exceed All Other Groups in Charitable Giving."
Capital Report with Tim LaHaye, January 1989.

❧ ❧ ❧

Samaritan's Purse, a Christian mission organization headed by Franklin Graham [Billy Graham's son] and based in Boone, N.C., has announced a drip-irrigation and greenhouse construction venture with the Kale Heywet Church of Ethiopia. Plans call for the construction of three large greenhouses and for inexpensive drip-irrigation kits to be distributed to farmers and families to help increase the food production and reforestation programs. Drip-irrigation uses 30 to 50 percent less water than other systems. One kit can help a family grow all the food it needs. By working with Heywet Church, the largest evangelical church in Ethiopia, Samaritan's Purse will be able to help destitute people as well as introduce them to Christ.

Source: "Greenhouses and Drip Irrigation Help Evangelism." *The Church Around the World,* June 1989.

❧ ❧ ❧

The Browns and the Smiths received the same letter today. Each family sponsors a child in a program of a large, evangelical relief and development organization. Each had been contributing regularly toward the support of a particular child in the Third World. Now, says the letter, the project is finished. Contributions from these two families and thousands of others like them have been applied within the communities of the two children. Conditions have improved significantly, and the children's families have become economically self-sufficient.

In the short time since 1970, relief organizations have established a new science, recorded a history, and presented a literature. The science is called "development." The work that was centered in relief in 1970 is now dedicated to development.

What does this mean? Development is the science of encouraging economic and social progress that is self-sustaining. The credo of development carefully defines its three key terms:

Relief brings to an end the suffering and other effects of a disaster or crisis.

Rehabilitation returns the community to the stable circumstances prevailing before the crisis.

Development enables the community to better itself and attain a new self-sufficiency.

The development credo says that relief, rehabilitation, and development are a progression. Workers should always move from one to the next. This is because relief, if prolonged, makes the recipient dependent on the practitioner. A sustained relief effort leads easily to the loss of a good reputation in the community of development specialists.

Source: Youngblood, J. Alan. "The Shell Game Donors Love to Lose."
Christianity Today, June 18, 1982, pp. 39–40.

Key Quotations

Amongst other strange things said of me, I hear it is said by the deists that I am one of the number; and indeed, that some good people think I am no Christian. This thought gives me much more pain than the appellation of Tory: because I think religion of infinitely higher importance than politics; and I find much cause to reproach myself that I have lived so long, and have given no decided and public proof of my being a Christian. But, indeed, my dear child, this is a character which I prize far above all this world has, or can boast.

Patrick Henry, from a letter to his daughter

Therefore go and make disciples of all nations, baptizing them in the name of the Father and of the Son and of the Holy Spirit, and teaching them to obey everything I have commanded you. And surely I will be with you always, to the very end of the age.

Matthew 28:19–20

SHARING THE LIFE

Key Question: How do people who realize they are guilty before God deal with the problem of sin?

Setting: Before the afternoon office coffee break, Bill has an unexpected chance to apply the truth of the morning's conversation.

As thrilled as he was about what had happened in the morning coffee break, Bill tried his best to focus on his work until the lunch hour came. In his briefcase he had a stack of articles he had gotten from Pastor David which he hoped would help him give a clear answer to Molly's questions. When he had asked the pastor for some material with a Christian perspective on current issues in society he hadn't anticipated he would need it quite so desperately.

Noontime found Bill with a sandwich in one hand, pouring over one of the articles on the abortion issue. He wanted to use every moment of the hour to prepare. He was still amazed at how God had seemed to provide the answers he needed in the morning, but now, thinking about this next opportunity, he wasn't sure what he would say. He was starting to jot down some notes when he heard a soft knock on the door. His first thought was disappointment. How would he prepare for later? But he felt he needed to at least find out what the person wanted. He called out, "Come in." The door opened and Jean slipped into his office and shut the door behind her. She seemed agitated but said quietly, "I . . . I was wondering if I could talk to you about something . . . privately."

Bill remembered she had been in the conference room that morning, but had remained silent during the discussion. "Sure, Jean," he said in what he hoped was an encouraging tone. "What's on your mind?"

"You said some things about guilt this morning," Jean began. She stopped, visibly struggling to keep control. "Sometimes I feel like I'm carrying all of it." She paused, blinked, and a large tear rolled down her cheek. She looked up at the ceiling, took a deep breath, then continued, "I had an abortion two years ago on the fifteenth of next month. I don't know if I can bear another anniversary of the worst day in my life. . . ." She trailed off as she lowered her head and began weeping softly. Jean sat down in one of the chairs facing the desk and tried to compose herself.

Bill was surprised to realize how close to tears he was himself. His heart went out to this woman he hardly knew. He got up, went around his desk and sat down in the other chair beside Jean. "I'm so sorry," he began, and then ended because there didn't seem to be anything else to say.

After a few moments, she wiped her tears, sighed and said, "I just didn't know if I could sit through the coffee break this afternoon. It's like I think I need to hear what you have to say, but I'm afraid it might make me feel even worse than I already do, though I don't know how."

Bill was at a loss for words. Later, he realized this was fortunate, since she needed to talk at that point more than listen.

Jean continued, "I guess in a way, this morning really helped me. I was trying so hard to not feel responsible for what happened to my baby that I wasn't able to admit that I did have a part. I mean it was like I was convinced that the only solution was to find some way of saying I was completely innocent. And deep down I knew that wasn't true. I knew I chose to listen to certain people and opinions and not to listen to others. There were certain options I didn't consider at the time. Admitting my own guilt has actually helped me see things better. I never realized before that even the abortion itself was a desperate way to handle guilt I was already experiencing. As soon as he found out I was pregnant my boyfriend treated me like someone with a disease. There was a whole bundle of guilt wrapped up in that relationship. I allowed myself to be convinced that I wasn't having my baby aborted, I was having all my problems, guilt, and mistakes aborted. In the recovery room I realized I hadn't lost anything except my baby. Everything else was still there, and worse. Now there was deep shame, more guilt, and a hopelessness that made even bright things in my life gray and empty. And almost two years later it doesn't seem to have gotten any better, except I don't cry myself to sleep as much anymore."

The man sitting next to her was still quiet. He was learning an important lesson about his renewed relationship with Christ. Bill had been thinking that his mission was to share a message with others. Now he was seeing that a big part of that mission was learning to really feel with others. He wondered how many women he had passed by carried the same crushing burden Jean was showing him. In that moment he silently prayed God would teach him how to speak the truth with genuine compassion. Almost instantly a word filled his mind that he knew he was understanding for the first time — compassion.

Jean had lapsed into a brief silence. Now she continued, "So, I came to tell you I know I'm guilty. Guilty of the murder of my own child." Each word was formed precisely, as if she wanted to make sure she meant what she was saying. She closed her eyes tightly against the pain. Her hands gripped the arms of the chair. Amazingly, after a moment, she relaxed, took several deep breaths, then went on. "This hurts more than I ever thought it would, and yet there's a rightness to it. I don't know where I'm going, but I feel somehow that I'm at least facing in the right direction. . . . What I need to know is if you can help me take the next step."

Frankly, Bill didn't know whether to weep or shout. This was life! Life that reaches down into the middle of a filthy world and wraps itself around a person who is all but lost and gives hope. Life that invites humans to confess their sinfulness. Life that tells a human being that the thing most resisted — admission of personal guilt — is a requirement for receiving what is most desired. And that is life itself.

Bill found himself saying, "I do want to help, Jean. Thanks for sharing all this with me. In spite of how much pain it has caused, I feel deeply honored that you have trusted me in this way. I can see that you have discovered in one of the most difficult ways possible that common disease of sin that infects every human. You've also tried hard to solve the problem, or cure the disease on your own. But things have just kept getting worse."

Jean was nodding her agreement to each of his statements. He went on, "The best help I can give you is to tell you how I got help. I mean, if we've all got the same sin problem, then real help has to come from someone other than another human being. The Bible tells us God is willing to help by forgiving us."

Jean's frown let him know she had a question. "Well, that may be true of your sins, Bill. But I can't forget what I did."

"Believe me," said Bill, "our specific sins may not be the same, but that isn't the point. God doesn't grade on the curve, Jean. With God all sin is as black as can be. His forgiveness doesn't depend on how bad we think we've sinned, it depends on our willingness to accept His forgiveness by faith. My pastor says God's forgiveness is a gift of grace I can't earn just by sinning less than my neighbor!"

"I guess it does make sense that you can't earn something that's a gift," Jean reflected. "I haven't been to church in years . . . maybe that's my problem," she continued.

"That may be part of the problem," said Bill, smiling. "But it's not the main problem. I can identify with the other side of the issue in my own life. I've been going to church regularly for years, but it hasn't been until recently that I've allowed Christ back into the center of my life. I know you've worked here several years. You probably had no idea I was a Christian, did you?"

"I guess I just thought of you as a nice guy who had a family and left the secretaries alone," she responded.

Bill wanted to get back on track, so he said, "Well, a faithful Christian is more than those things. If a person has accepted God's forgiveness and allowed Christ to move into his life, then Christ should be a part of everything he does — even his work.

"Going to church without knowing Christ is like being a stranger and sneaking into a family's Christmas celebration. That person will experience one of two reactions: he'll either wish he is a real part of what is happening, or he'll decide he made a mistake and dropped into a group that is wasting its time pretending to be happy. Knowing Christ personally makes church exciting and challenging. It's being together with others who also know Christ. It's also watching people who are strangers to God discover that they really can know Him. That they can actually be included in the family!"

"You make it all sound so simple," murmured Jean.

"It is simple," said Bill. "So simple that a child can understand. It isn't easy, though. Like I've been saying, we really don't naturally want to admit we need God's help or forgiveness. Both of us have had to go through some pretty tough times to get to the place where we're serious about our not being able to handle life on our own."

Bill reflected for a moment on what Mike had said about his first conversation with Wendy Peterson, and how things had just gone naturally from one topic to another. Mike said it was as if God really was in control. The same thing was happening now.

Jean interrupted his thoughts with a question, "So, Bill, how do I get to know Christ? I want to."

Bill wasn't sure how to respond. He was caught off guard by the decisiveness in her voice. He said, "Really? I mean, you do? That's great!"

She laughed at his obvious fumbling. "I didn't mean to surprise you, but what you've been saying is good news to me. I don't want to pass it by."

"Jean," Bill began, "the Bible describes getting to know Christ in several ways. Jesus Himself called it being 'born again.' In other places it is called 'receiving Christ' or 'believing in Him.' Basically, I've been telling you a little about Christ and what knowing Him can mean to you. Now it's time for you to meet Him. This is like any introduction, except you are meeting Someone you can't see. Now, that may seem like a limitation, because we have to meet Christ by faith, but it is actually an advantage. You see, when we meet Christ, the Holy Spirit comes to reside in us. We've recently been memorizing some verses as an entire church that explain what happens in a neat way. Listen: 'And I pray that Christ will be more and more at home in your hearts, living within you as you trust in him. May your roots go down deep into the soil of God's marvelous love; and may you be able to feel and understand, as all God's children should, how long, how wide, how deep, and how high his love really is; and to experience this love for yourselves, though it is so great that you will never see the end of it or fully know or understand it. And so at last you will be filled up with God himself' " (Ephesians 3:17–19 TLB).

"That's beautiful," responded Jean. "I've never heard that before, but it sure describes what I want in my life.

"There is one thing that really hit me in what you said, though. That phrase 'born again.' I've heard it many times, but I never thought it applied to me. Now I think it applies in a couple ways. First, I realize it's what I need. But second, it is amazing that I, who did not allow my own child to be born, am now asking God to let me be born again. I just can't begin to imagine His love. . . ." She trailed off as tears rolled down her cheeks again.

Bill said tenderly, "You're already experiencing what those verses describe. We can experience God's love, but we'll never get to the end of it, or fully know or understand it."

"So, what do I do now?" asked Jean through her sniffles.

"I think it's time for you to talk to Jesus and tell Him you're ready to let Him forgive you and move into your life. Invite Him to make Himself at home in you," responded Bill.

Jean seemed a little confused as she said, "You mean pray? How do I do that?"

"Well, remember that Christ is here with us. Talk to Him like you're talking to me. I usually close my eyes to eliminate distractions, but sometimes, like when I'm driving, I do talk to Him with my eyes open," explained Bill.

"All right. What do I say?"

"Well, cover the main points of our conversation. Tell Him you realize you're guilty as a sinner; that you believe He is offering forgiveness and love; thank Him for dying on the cross for you; and invite Him into your life."

Without hesitation, Jean closed her eyes, took a deep breath, and quietly turned her life over to Christ. Her words were simple and trusting. When she stopped, Bill also prayed and thanked God for the wonderful opportunity to be a part of what He was doing in Jean's life. As he opened his own eyes he noticed Jean was already staring out the window. After a while of silence, she smiled and turned back to Bill. "I feel clean," she said. "I feel like a huge weight has been lifted from my heart, and I'm tired, but happy. What am I supposed to do next?"

Bill continued to be amazed by her persistent progress. "There are several important things. If you don't mind, I'd like to have my wife, Barb, call you tonight and talk with you some. You also need to keep talking to God like you just did. Let Him know you're consciously including him in the details of your life. You also need to read the Bible so He can speak to you. And it will be important to find a church where you can worship," said Bill in an excited rapid-fire. Jean had reached over to his desk and grabbed the memo pad Molly always kept handy. Bill realized he had slipped into his dictating mode, but he saw that Jean had almost caught up with him by the time he stopped talking.

"O.K.," said Jean. "I'd enjoy talking to Barb. I've only met her a few times at office parties but I've always liked her. Let's see, oh, yes, where do I start reading?"

"Now that you've met Christ, it will be important to learn everything you can about Him. Find the gospel of Luke and start reading there. I'll bring you some other materials that I think will help you," Bill added.

Jean tore off the sheet and replaced the pad on the desk. She stood and then said, "Thank you, Bill. I really didn't know what to expect when I came in here. I know I'm leaving with something I've needed all my life. Thanks again!"

Bill felt drained. He couldn't get up. As she reached the door he said, "Jean, I can't tell you how much it has meant to me to be able to share these moments with you. If Christ can use me like this around here, I know my life is going to have new meaning. I'll make sure Barb gives you a call tonight."

"That would be great," said Jean over her shoulder as she walked out the door.

Bill got up slowly and walked back around his desk to his half-eaten sandwich and his barely-read article. Lunch was almost over. Molly stuck her head through the doorway and said, "Looks like our little coffee break seminar is going to have to be postponed. The health insurance people have claimed the time to talk to us about the new medical plan. Sorry. . . ."

He chuckled as he finished the remainder of his lunch. There would be other coffee breaks. He hoped there would also be many other lunch breaks like the one he had just enjoyed.

Comment

When Bill finally gets to have that coffee break seminar, he may find that the objections people have relate to overpopulation of the world (as in chapter 2), the shortage of food (chapter 3), distribution incapabilities (chapter 4), and the other "myths" exposed in the previous chapters.

For a believer representing Christ in society, the objective is not to prove to people they're wrong. The objective is to introduce others to Christ. Like Bill, the discovery must be made that we carry more than a message to deliver. We carry a personal relationship to share. The value we place on the lives of the pre-born is one example of the value God places on all human life. He loves even those who through intention, fear, or ignorance are involved in the killing of pre-born children. We must remember to temper our judgment with compassion. We all need Christ's forgiveness!

In the News

An analysis of Planned Parenthood's clinic visit records highlights that dismal truth. A random sample of nearly thirty-five thousand medical charts from fourteen affiliates coast-to-coast revealed that sixty-two percent of the girls receiving abortions identified themselves as Evangelical Christians. Another twenty percent professed to be either Catholic or Orthodox. Of those eighty-two percent, a full seventy-six percent not only specified their religious preference, they identified their local Church membership and pastor.

The notion that it is primarily "rank heathens" or "flaming liberals" who are aborting their future away simply doesn't hold up under the fact. The scandal of Planned Parenthood has become the scandal of the Church. Sowing the wind, it has reaped the whirlwind (Hosea 8:7).

Source: Grant, George. "Reaping the Whirlwind." *Grand Illusions: The Legacy of Planned Parenthood* (Brentwood, TN: Wolgemuth and Hyatt, Publishers, Inc., 1988).

⋅⋅⋅ ⋅⋅⋅ ⋅⋅⋅

At 22, Olivia Gans was an enthusiastic drama student at a New Jersey college. She had become involved with another student, an aspiring actor, but one day he told her he was thinking of ending the relationship. "You can't leave me now," she remembers saying. "I'm pregnant." Neither of them was ready for parenthood or marriage yet, the young man replied. Later on, perhaps. Gans figured she needed her lover more than a baby. And that simple calculus impelled her toward the act she has regretted ever since.

Looking back, she's resentful that she was never encouraged to consider alternatives. Nor was she warned about the physical and emotional pain involved.

The physical pain, she says, was excruciating. "It felt like every organ was being pulled out of me. . . ."

When her boyfriend left her three months later, however, the dam of her emotions finally broke. She stayed up night after night, weeping until there were no tears left, just a dry sobbing. "You know what this pain is from," she says. "Your body is empty of your own child." At a family reunion a few months later, surrounded by her cousins and their children, Gans felt isolated with her secret.

Now, she is against abortions on almost all grounds, except when it endangers the mother's life.

Source: Levine, Art. "'Your Body is Empty of Your Own Child.'" *U.S. News and World Report*, October 3, 1988, p. 27.

⋅⋅⋅ ⋅⋅⋅ ⋅⋅⋅

He was 24, she was 32, and he thought they had an open, loving relationship. But on a summer day in 1981, he came home from his job as a TV repairman and found his wife of nearly one year crying. "I've had an abortion," she said. For the first few moments, Gary Bell held his wife, because she was hurting. But he hurt, too. Bell says his wife didn't tell him then why she had the abortion. He still doesn't know, he says. She had an 8-year-old son from a first marriage, maybe she didn't want another child.

Rose Bell says she did tell her husband about the abortion beforehand. But without medical insurance, she says, there was no way they could care for a child. "We didn't have money to take care of a baby," she says. Rose Bell disputes virtually every point of her husband's story. Whatever the facts, Bell says the abortion devastated him. "It felt like a death to me," he says. He cried for hours.

"I felt as if I failed my child," Bell says. "I felt guilty and ashamed." In the weeks after, he says, their home, in Morgantown, W.Va., was filled with silent anger.

Source: Levine, Art. "I Felt as if I Failed My Child." *U.S. News and World Report*, October 3, 1989, p. 28.

᠉ ᠉ ᠉

A woman at odds with her husband over who should have control of their frozen embryos says the eggs represent life and the case should be looked at as a custody battle.

Her husband says the eggs represent his future and that he should be allowed to determine if he becomes a father or not.

The courts don't know what to say [because] there isn't much precedent concerning in-vitro fertilization and divorce.

"I consider them life," Mary Sue Davis, 28, said of the eggs that she and Junior Lewis Davis placed in frozen storage a few years ago as part of the in-vitro fertilization program at Fort Sanders Regional Medical Center in Knoxville.

"If I cannot have them, then I'd like to donate them to another person," she said in an interview March 4 at the couple's log home in the foothills of the Smoky Mountains.

Davis said his wife's ability to have the embryos implanted after the divorce violates his right to control his own future.

He did not ask that the embryos be destroyed.

It's unsettling "to know that . . . 10 years from now I could be walking down the street and bump into my child and not know it," he said.

Source: Umbreit, Kristi. "Couple Battle over Their Frozen Embryos." *Daily Courier-News* (Elgin, IL), March 7, 1989.

ta ta ta

Psychological and spiritual examination is essential to forgiveness. Too many counselors urge forgiveness as a hasty cure-all, instead of exploring what has happened and why. Worse, they urge "forgive and forget," which is impossible. Forgiveness works best when the hurt person has had time to face his anger, to recognize his own contributions to the debacle and to realize the consequences of a refusal to forgive.

Therapists point out that the inability to forgive can gnaw on us — depriving us of sleep, upsetting digestion, even causing high blood pressure. But when we forgive, we often experience a gigantic turnaround, a cleansing that could be called rebirth.

Source: Fleming, Thomas. "Forgiveness." *Reader's Digest,* June 1988, p. 100.

ta ta ta

I hated my father for the first 20 years of my life. I don't hate him anymore — today I understand some of the roots of his behavior. That he had an alcoholic father; that he grew up during the Depression; that he was a high-school dropout; that he served an 18-month stint in an Augusta, Ga., military prison for going AWOL to his mother's funeral. And that he had four children that he couldn't support. There are enough mitigating circumstances in my father's life to make me feel sorry for him and for others like him and to applaud their efforts to salvage something of their ruined lives. But *Tout comprendre c'est tout pardonner* is one maxim I don't buy.

I understand but I won't forgive. . . .

If you're genuinely sorry for whatever you've done and whomever you've harmed, tell them so. If feeling good about yourself is the only way to stay away from the bottle, feel free to feel good about yourself. Just don't think that a belated apology makes everything even-steven.

And don't go sticking your hand out waiting for someone to shake it. Keep it to yourself.

[Author's note: In contrast, the Bible says, "For if you forgive men when they sin against you, your heavenly Father will also forgive you. But if you do not forgive men their sins, your Father will not forgive your sins" (Matthew 6:14–15).]

Source: Queenan, Joseph M. "Too Late to Say, 'I'm Sorry.'" *Newsweek,* August 31, 1987, p. 7.

ہ ہ ہ

Washington (AP)—Legal, voluntary abortion in the first trimester of pregnancy does not threaten most women's mental health or cause them great emotional distress, a new study says.

Though some women may feel regret, sadness or guilt, "the weight of the evidence from scientific studies indicates that legal abortion of an unwanted pregnancy in the first trimester does not pose a psychological hazard for most women," said the study, to be published Friday in the journal *Science.*

Olivia Gans, director of American Victims of Abortion, called the study "a manipulation" of data from earlier studies.

"When you look at these studies, you can twist them any way you need to get whatever conclusion you want," she said.

The new study was commissioned by the American Psychological Association. Nancy Adler, a professor at the University of California at San Francisco and lead author on the report, said the committee looked at more than 200 studies and found only "about 19 or 20" that met solid scientific standards.

Once those studies were examined, she said, the conclusion "was really quite clear."

The psychological association convened the panel in 1988 after then-Surgeon General Everett Koop reported that studies were inadequate to draw final conclusions about the effects of abortion on women's mental health.

In the *Science* report, the authors said case studies have shown that some women do experience "severe distress . . . after abortion and require sympathetic care."

Source: "Panel Finds Abortion No Mental Risk." *Chicago Tribune,* April 6, 1990.

Key Quotations

The first and almost the only Book deserving of universal attention is the Bible.

John Quincy Adams

The Bible . . . is the one supreme source of revelation of the meaning of life, the nature of God and spiritual nature and need of men. It is the only guide of life which really leads the spirit in the way of peace and salvation.

Woodrow Wilson

Go to the Scriptures . . . the joyful promises it contains will be a balsam to all your troubles.

Andrew Jackson

Blessed is he whose transgressions are forgiven,
    whose sins are covered.
Blessed is the man
    whose sin the Lord does not count against him
    and in whose spirit is no deceit.
When I kept silent,
    my bones wasted away
    through my groaning all day long.
For day and night
    your hand was heavy upon me;
My strength was sapped
    as in the heat of summer.

Then I acknowledged my sin to you
        and did not cover up my iniquity.
I said, "I will confess
        my transgressions to the Lord" —
And you forgave
        the guilt of my sin.

Psalm 32:1–5

SHARING CONCERN

Key Question: What is the impact on their church and community
when a small group of Christians take Biblically-based
action?

Setting: A dinner discussion at the Jenkins' home opens the
door for the formation of a small group of Christians
to explore ways they can encourage one another to act
in accordance with what they believe.

W hen she asked Mike to set the dinner table with the fine china,
Barb Jenkins momentarily pictured herself handing a rare violin
to a gorilla. But the quiet ringing of the china being carefully placed
reminded her that she had another man in the house who was increasing
her motherly pride almost daily. Her eyes clouded when she realized the
significance of the evening's meal. Gathered in her home would be a
circle of people who, in a miraculous series of events, had had their
lives changed in the past few months. David and Julie Sheffield and
their children, Wendy Peterson and her parents, Jean Prosky from Bill's
office, and her own family would all be together.

Her thoughts were interrupted by Mike's voice, "Mom, what side do the forks go on?"

"Left side of the plate, just like last time," she shouted back in mock exasperation.

The house was filled with welcome smells by the time the guests began to arrive. Final preparations were a flurry of brief conversations, steaming bowls of food carried from the kitchen, children washing hands, and Bill's seating assignments. The adults, including Mike and Wendy circled the large dinner table. Ryan Jenkins was in charge of the kid's table with the Sheffield gang. In his prayer before the meal, Bill thanked God for these special friends and the food they would share. Barb received well-deserved compliments from everyone on her cooking. They all agreed that an observer would have known it was a great meal, since so little conversation actually got in the way of enjoying the food. But gradually, plates were cleared away, chairs were pushed back, and the conversation began to which they had all been looking forward.

Bill set his coffee cup down and cleared his throat. "Friends," he said, "if someone had told me a year ago that God would make a meal like this possible in my home, I don't think I would have believed them."

"Come on, Dad," said Mike with a mischievous smile, "Mom always cooks good meals . . . but I agree." He gave Wendy's hand, which he was holding between their chairs, a playful squeeze.

Bill appreciated his son's ability to take the edge off the moment. He had started a little too serious. Relaxing now, he continued, "Pastor David, I've been wanting to ask you about your thoughts on everything that's happened during the last few months."

"Well," began David, "I have to say that I'm just as amazed as the rest of you. I've looked forward to this evening because I think you are a key group God has chosen to have an impact on our church and this community. I have to confess that when the abortion issue finally got me upset enough to start taking action, my vision was pretty small. I just knew I had to do more than preach inside the safe walls of our church.

"First, I was shocked at how strong the attitude has become in our society that Christians should keep their opinions and beliefs inside the church. But it's disappointing to find out how many Christians agree with this attitude. The idea almost seems to be, 'If the world doesn't want to listen to us then we don't have to even try.' We've forgotten that Christians have always succeeded when they have challenged the forces of evil in their own strongholds. Real Christianity has always looked at life in unexpected ways: saving our lives by losing them; leading by serving; and keeping the faith by giving it away! When Jesus sent us into all the world, the only promise He gave us was that He would be with us. He never guaranteed the world would welcome us with open arms.

"But the fact is that each of us is here tonight because someone else stepped out of their world and into ours. God got the gospel to us through someone else. We've got to keep doing the same for others. It is so easy for us to forget how many in history have paid with their lives for the privileges we have."

There was a silence of agreement in the group. Heads were nodding as he made each point.

David continued, "One of the real turning points for me was when Mike took the risk of inviting me to come speak at the school. I saw that there were opportunities everywhere for Christians to speak out. We are actually being silenced by a group of people that is still relatively small. But if more Christians don't become involved in the issues, we may discover that even our churches are no longer a sanctuary in which we can hide."

"I guess I'm wondering if there isn't more we can do than we're already doing," Mike thought out loud.

Jean added, "I feel like I'm in the middle. I've only been a Christian a few weeks so I'm just learning about this whole new world. I'm also realizing that I really didn't understand the world I was living in. I've got a lot to learn."

"Believe me," added David, "every one of us has a lot to learn. One of the facts we have to realize and act on is that even if we only know a little, that small amount of the truth and light can do wonders for people who are lost in darkness. That illustration we used at the end of the play really makes that point clear. Each of us may only have a little light to offer, but in God's plan that can make all the difference. That's why it's such a privilege to be with you people. God has already used you to make a significant impact in my life. And I believe this might just be the beginning of a significant impact God wants to make through our working together."

"I guess one of the things that frustrates me at school," said Wendy, "is the response I get so often if I say anything about God, or right and wrong, or mention the Bible, that I'm trying to force my beliefs on others."

"The first time I heard your father say anything, he gave a pretty good answer to that problem," said David. "At that P.T.A. meeting, when they were jumping all over Barb for daring to speak up, he pointed out that we still have a legal right to say what we believe in this country. What we need to do more often is have confidence in the truth. After all, we have a Savior who called Himself Truth."

John Peterson added, "You know, it's hard for me to admit that God finally got through to me in a P.T.A. meeting, but that's how it was. I sat there listening to what was being said and I suddenly realized that I was uncomfortable because I had been on the wrong side of truth way too long. I went into law because I thought I loved truth, but I discovered that night that my idea of truth had gotten way off track somewhere along the way. It was Barb's simple courage that opened my eyes."

"That reminds me of something Dad said about getting that reaction you described, Wendy," said Mike. "The first time he took advantage of a chance to speak up at work, someone responded with the 'don't try to cram it down our throats' response. Dad reminded this guy that medicine which is good for us often tastes bad. The truth seems like that sometimes. People never get to the point of considering whether an idea is right or wrong. They just refuse to listen."

His dad added, "I realize what I said was a necessary response to my co-worker's attitude, but I sure hated offending him the way I did. . . ."

"Don't forget, Bill, I was there," said Jean. "I wasn't offended, and I don't really think he was either. It was just his way of avoiding the truth."

"Well, he sure has been avoiding me ever since that conversation," said Bill. "But I think you're right."

"I think so, too," said David. Then he added, "In fact, I'm convinced that most people who worry about offending someone else probably wouldn't. What we are really saying when we hesitate risking offense is that we may not care enough for others. If someone is about to step into a hole they can't see, I don't stop and ask myself if they will be offended by my warning. I also think that even people who disagree with us when we take a stand for Christ in public will find it difficult not to appreciate it if our words are soaked in real concern. Christ wants us to make sure they know we love them even if they don't agree with us."

"Pastor David?" asked Jean in the silence that followed. "I wanted to ask you about something you said in passing earlier. You referred to abortion as the issue that finally got you out from behind your pulpit. Why do you think it was that issue?"

"When I got out of Bible school I was convinced my calling was to preach the gospel. To tell people about Jesus Christ. I'm still convinced. The question I had never thought to ask during my training was, 'How do I get their attention?' It took me a while to realize that people wouldn't be willing to honestly consider the claims of Christ until their thinking in other areas had been challenged. In school, we talked more about expressing the faith than about defending the faith. I've learned since then that one of the best ways to find out if you really understand an idea is to defend it. Defending the Christian view of things has helped me preach better. I can help people to prepare for the attacks they will encounter, because I'm encountering the same attacks.

"I remembered reading somewhere in a book by C. S. Lewis that God wanted Christians to find the place where the battle line between good and evil was under fiercest attack and commit themselves right there to the struggle. So I asked God to show me where that was in our society. One of the first passages from the Bible I read after that prayer was Jesus' explanation of His purpose in coming to this world, 'I have come that they might have life, and have it more abundantly!' I realized that evil is completely anti-life. I'm sure you all realize the curious fact that these two opposites are mirror spellings; 'live' spelled backwards is 'evil.' This means that anywhere life is being devalued and destroyed, evil is accomplishing its purposes. When Jesus said those words I just quoted, He also described Satan as a thief who only comes to steal, kill, and destroy.

"I simply had to ask myself where Satan was most clearly at work, stealing, killing, and destroying. On the issue of abortion there was hardly a battle line left. The *Roe v. Wade* decision back in 1973 was like a devastating military offensive on the part of Satan that literally overwhelmed our defenses. It was like a spiritual 'Battle of the Bulge.' As a result, millions of unborn children have suffered and died. The church wasn't ready for the life and death issues it was suddenly confronted with. While we were arguing about whether or not to get involved, babies were dying. They still are, every day.

"I'm not saying that abortion is the only issue, or the only place in the battle line where we're weak, but I haven't found an issue with more wide-ranging implications than the issues surrounding the value of life in this society. I'm still ultimately committed to communicating the gospel of Jesus Christ, but I also realize that my involvement in the defense of life is one of the best ways to get people's attention."

David realized his tone had gotten very intense during the past moments, but these were deeply held convictions. He also realized that those who were with him were sharing those same growing convictions.

Bill said quietly, "Well, David, you've got our attention. What would you suggest we do next?"

"We've agreed we need to learn more. Let me suggest one opportunity coming soon. Next week I've been invited to the Community Church across town for two nights of meetings on the abortion issue. There will be some other leaders involved including at least one doctor. I think you would all be helped by those sessions. I sense there is a real commitment to action here. These sessions will also allow you to meet many other people with the same concerns. We need all the troops we can gather if we're going to be involved in an effective counterattack to re-awaken people to the high value of life!"

John Peterson spoke up next. "Pastor, I don't know how the others would feel about this, but I need strong fellowship like we've had tonight on a regular basis. Let me just ask everyone here if they would consider our getting together again. I want to be involved, but I need more information and training." Everyone nodded, also expressing the desire to get together regularly.

It also seemed that everyone would be able to participate in the meetings David suggested. He told them their presence would also be an encouragement to him. Conversation flowed back and forth for a while longer, then these growing friends parted company for the night.

Mike walked Wendy out to her parents' car as both their folks were saying their goodbyes. Mike said softly, "Couldn't help but think several times tonight how glad I am that we bumped into each other, books and all."

"Yeah," said Wendy chuckling, "I don't think I've had to carry a book or even open a door since then." After a moment, she added, "And you've helped open some doors in my life I never knew existed. Especially the one Christ was knocking behind. Thanks, Mike." They shared a tight hug of real friendship. Then as he opened the car door for her, they also shared a brief kiss that hinted at more than friendship.

Comment

The people in this chapter began to organize themselves to take positive action. There are many existing national and local pro-life groups that can help you, your church, or people from your community organize for effective action. Find out what groups are already working, and what resources are available in your area. See also the Addendum to this book for more information on how you can be involved.

As Christ was willing to clothe Himself in flesh and enter into a world of human issues and heartaches, those who follow Him will have to do the same. Jesus didn't separate body from soul, or physical life from spiritual life. He held them together, and valued them highly. He offered eternal life while He was healing mortal bodies. He loved broken humans and wanted to make them truly whole. He can teach us and help us to do the same.

In the News

Eastern European activists have a lot to tell us about how God rescues people from the depths of personal and political hell, but, somehow, much of the press has decided the public has no right to know this.

The Rev. Laszlo Tokes, the Hungarian pastor who sparked the Romanian revolution, told me of how the day before the hated Nicolae Ceausescu was overthrown, Tokes was being prepared for a show trial. He expected to be executed. Through "divine intervention," he and his pregnant wife can look forward to their baby — Esther or Joseph — being born in a freer Romania.

While Tokes put God at the head of Europe's liberation movement, the media are missing the message, he told me. "Eastern Europe is not just in a political revolution but a religious renaissance."

Another example: References to "Jesus," the "Christian spirit," and Czechoslovakia's role as the "spiritual crossroads of Europe" were omitted from excerpts of President Vaclav Havel's New Year's Day address. *The New York Times, The Washington Post,* and *Newsweek* were among the sinful censors.

What does the press have against Jesus? Is there a bias against Christianity?

Why are people who identify God—not politics or human endeavor—as responsible for changing world events not taken seriously by the media? In concluding that God isn't important, the press is trying to play God itself.

Source: Reynolds, Barbara. "Religion is Greatest Story Ever Missed." *USA Today,* March 16, 1990.

ະ ະ ະ

Abortion has engendered controversy in the United States since Connecticut first outlawed the practice in 1821. But a Supreme Court decision on July 3, strengthening the right of states to restrict abortion, has breathed fresh vigor into the debate. Pro-choice advocates say that the court's decision could lead to a major rollback of abortion rights. But anti-abortionists, encouraged by what they consider to be a newly sympathetic public, are campaigning for the tightest restrictions possible.

Until the July ruling, abortion rights had been virtually unrestricted in the United States for 16 years, ever since a landmark Supreme Court decision in 1973. In that ruling, Roe vs. Wade, the high court established that the right to privacy enshrined in the U.S. Constitution includes a pregnant woman's right to an abortion. Although the court permitted some limits on that right according to the stage of a woman's pregnancy, in effect the ruling gave women access to abortion on demand.

Source: Lowther, William, with Peter Lewis. "The Rights of the States." *Maclean's,* July 31, 1989, p. 21.

ია ია ია

Planned Parenthood Federation of America today released the results of a nationwide poll conducted by Louis Harris and Associates on teenagers' views on sex, pregnancy and birth control. The poll, titled "American Teens Speak: Sex, Myths, TV and Birth Control," revealed that more than half of all American teenagers are sexually active by their seventeenth year and only one-third of all sexually active teens use contraceptives consistently.

Teenagers rank television as the fourth (out of eleven choices) most important source of their information on both sex and birth control. And many teenagers believe that TV gives a realistic picture of such topics as sexually transmitted diseases (45 percent), pregnancy and the consequences of sex (41 percent), and family planning to prevent pregnancy (28 percent). The 1985 survey of adults, that Harris conducted for PPFA, however, found adults to be much more skeptical: a great majority believe that television presents either an exaggerated picture or fails outright to address these subjects. In fact, 85 percent responded that television should present messages about birth control as part of its programming.

According to the survey results, teenagers tend to begin sexual activity younger if they are from families of lower socio-economic status, have below average grades or do not go to school at all, are unemployed, live with only one parent or have parents who are not college graduates. These same groups are also the least likely to use contraceptives.

Source: "Planned Parenthood/Harris Poll Finds Teens Sexually Active, Sexually Illiterate." *Planned Parenthood Federation of America, Inc. News Release,* December 16, 1986.

ია ია ია

There was more than a little irony at work. Here was Fred Silverman, the legendary television executive of the '70s, sitting in his West L.A. office, shaking his head in dismay as he reflected on the dominant TV trend of the late '80s: trash TV.

"These trash television shows are popping up on every station, and there are three or four more ready to go," said Silverman, a disgusted look on his face. "This kind of tabloid garbage is even starting to creep into more traditional shows like '20/20' and 'West 57th Street.' "

With 1989 newly arrived, Silverman had some serious concerns about the state of broadcasting. He even categorized the situation as "dangerous" and called on broadcasters and producers alike to begin "exercising some restraint."

"The people out there can only take so many Geraldos. There are only a finite number of variations on a theme, and what most of the press seems to forget is that the television audience is not a single audience. They write for the liberal, free-thinking yuppies, but there is another, sizable constituency out there.

"Call it what you want, the moral majority or whatever, but they represent the majority of the population, and they're very vocal. They wield an enormous amount of clout, and they've had it with trash television."

Source: "Talking Trash: Fred Silverman Warns that TV is Flirting with Danger." *Chicago Tribune*, January 4, 1989.

ta ta ta

In a recent poll of their readership, *Glamour* magazine found that their readers are fed-up with television trash. Eighty percent said TV has become too trashy for their tastes. Eighty-four percent say they're less inclined to watch a TV program if they know it is going to contain a lot of violence. Fifty percent said graphic violence offends them the most, while 23 percent said explicit or "kinky" sexual activity did and 16 percent said foul or sexually explicit language did.

Eighty-one percent say networks are not justified in programming anything that brings in high ratings. Sixty-four percent said they would approve of television instituting a movie-style ratings system.

And 80 percent said if trash TV continues, they feel Americans will become more tolerant of violent or bizarre behavior in real life.

Source: "*Glamour* Poll: Women Fed up with TV Trash." *Glamour*, May 1989.

≥a ≥a ≥a

New York: Two-thirds of adults in a survey believe television programs that ridicule religion, home and motherhood should be censored, regardless of their popularity, *Parents Magazine* reported March 19.

The survey of 1,004 people nationwide also showed:

- 72 percent said there should be a ban on ridiculing religion.

- 62 percent said there should be a ban on ridiculing traditional values, such as marriage or motherhood.

- 55 percent said scenes that even suggest homosexual activity should be cut.

- 50 percent said scenes suggesting sexual activity between adults, or including graphic violence, were acceptable, so long as the programs were restricted to late night.

Only 3 percent of those polled rated television programming as excellent, with 46 percent saying it was fair. Nine percent said it was "terrible."

Source: "TV Watchers Favor Some Censorship." *The Detroit News,* March 20, 1990.

≥a ≥a ≥a

I am often asked by pastors and other Christians about how to "redeem" the media because many Christians believe the media is responsible for the dissolution of fundamental American values.

First, I do not totally accept the idea that "the media" (a phrase that I hate) is responsible for the gutting of values in America. Videotape, microphones, ink and paper, and cameras are morally neutral agents. They carry only what people decide they will carry. The problem has been that most of us who are followers of Christ and have listened to God's voice through His Word have not seen the press and entertainment industries as part of our mission field. We would rather curse the darkness than light candles. Of course, we have abandoned other professions as well, such as education and the law. We seem to take an "on-hold-for-the-next-life" view of things so we spend more of our energies complaining about the way things are instead of plotting strategies to change them. Thus, the only contact that many Christians have with journalists is when they write and call them secular humanists or communists. Is it any wonder, then, that members of the media perceive followers of Christ as being judgmental, hypocritical, uneducated, and basically humorless?

The ultimate problem in America is not the media. It's the church. It is the followers of Christ who have been conformed to this world and not transformed by the renewing of their minds. For example, I actually receive letters from Christians who are looking for Biblical justification for putting their children in public schools where they are taught that they evolved from slime or that it's okay to have sex before you are married as long as you use a condom. Christians have lost their power because they have lost their mandate. They've lost their vision. We are more interested in the praise of men than the approval of God. Our basic task as Christians when relating to the media is to stop looking at the big picture and focus on particulars. We must begin to see people in the media as individuals. Once we do, we are better able to plot strategies for effecting them.

Source: Thomas, Cal. "The Media or the Church . . . Which Needs
Redemption Most?" *Table Talk* (Ligonier Ministries), February 1990.

Key Quotations

He knows not how to rule a kingdome, that cannot manage a Province; nor can he wield a Province, that cannot order a City; nor he order a City, that knows not how to regulate a Village; nor he a Village, that cannot guide a Family; nor can that man Govern well a Family that knows not how to Govern himselfe; neither can any Govern himselfe unless his reason be Lord, Will and Appetite her Vassals: nor can Reason rule unlesse herselfe be ruled by God, and (wholy) be obedient to Him.

Hugo Grotius (1583–1645)

I tell you the truth, whatever you bind on earth will be bound in heaven, and whatever you loose on earth will be loosed in heaven.

Again, I tell you that if two of you on earth agree about anything you ask for, it will be done for you by my Father in heaven. For where two or three come together in my name, there am I with them.

Matthew 18:18–20

"WELL, I SAY TV VIOLENCE WON'T HAVE A DETRIMENTAL EFFECT ON ANYBODY!"

EQUIPPING OTHERS

Key Question: What are the realities hiding behind so much of the language being used to refer to abortion practices?

Setting: A seminar at Community Church seeks to clarify some of the underlying issues.

W hen David arrived at the Harrington Community Church that night, he was delighted to find the parking lot almost full. Apparently, abortion awareness was a significant concern in this local church. Mike and Wendy had asked to ride with him so all three had a chance to meet Dr. Mortenson who happened to park next to them. He was the physician who would be helping with technical questions, and David had already spoken with him several times on the phone.

In their plans for the evening, they had kept in mind that their audience would be mostly new to the battle for life. The announcements about the meeting had stressed that those who had questions about abortion, the pro-life movement, and the medical perspective on life issues would be welcomed.

David was introduced to the large crowd by the local pastor and began by inviting all present to join him in prayer. He asked God to be part of their time together, to help make the words clear, and to use people from this gathering to save the lives of those not yet born. He thanked God for loving the human race enough to share our entire experience, from conception to death, and for offering the free gift of eternal life through Jesus Christ. He closed his prayer to a chorus of heartfelt "amens" from his audience.

David looked out hopefully on the sea of expectant faces and began, "When I asked in my prayer just now that God would make the words clear, I meant that in two different ways. First, I want the answers and terms we give tonight to be the truth, and to be clearly understood. Second, I hope you will leave here understanding that words are often used to hide the truth. This practice of using words to distort or cover the truth is in constant use anytime the subject of abortion is discussed in public.

"My friends, we've been listening to soothing, seemingly harmless words instead of seeing the horrors those words are covering up. When we understand what is really happening, we will be compelled to do something or admit that we have abandoned what we say we believe.

"The statements and descriptions you will hear tonight are not intended to hurt or shock you, but they probably will. We simply cannot imagine, without detailed description, what is happening to unborn children across our land and around the world. If what you learn makes you angry, offended, or hurt, bring those experiences under the compassionate truth of Christ and let Him use your life to make a difference.

"Our first question tonight will be, 'What is actually aborted?'"

After pausing for a moment to let the question take hold, David continued, "Babies are aborted, not tissue! In fact, the word 'fetus' means 'small child.' Those who participate in abortion want to make themselves believe they are simply removing what they describe as 'mere tissue similar to an appendix or tonsils.' The term 'fetal tissue' certainly sounds like it might be some kind of disposable growth. But is that the truth? What do we actually see when we look at what is called 'fetal tissue?' "

David held up a large poster of a hand in a surgical glove. The fingers were closed in such a way that nothing could be seen except two tiny, perfect human feet. Two words were printed at the bottom of the poster: Ten Weeks. He then proceeded to show other pictures of children aborted at various stages of development. Several times he asked the question, "When you look at this, is your first thought, human baby or a blob of tissue?" There were audible sounds of dismay and horror from the audience.

"My friends," David continued, "one of the strictest rules at abortion clinics is never to allow the woman to see what is being aborted. They know the sight would be unbearably sickening.

"A crucial question which continues to be debated is, 'When does life begin?' Given the fanatical interest in personal rights in our society right now, the most widely accepted answer has become, 'Life begins when the mother, or her advisers, say it begins.' Few people realize that it is legally permissible to abort a child the day before it is born.

"The beginning of life is a fundamental question that won't go away. It is impossible to honestly deny that the fetus looks like a human being. But, is it truly alive and human? Its heart may begin to beat at three weeks, but does that mean it's a living human being? Let me read you what a doctor wrote:

"'Years ago, while giving an anesthetic for an operation on a ruptured tubal pregnancy in the second month, I was handed what I believed to be the smallest human being ever seen. The embryo sac was intact and transparent. Within the sac was a tiny, one-third inch, human male swimming extremely vigorously in the amniotic fluid, while attached to the wall by the umbilical cord. This tiny human was perfectly developed with long, tapering fingers, feet and toes. It was almost transparent as regards the skin. The delicate arteries and veins were prominent to the ends of the fingers. The baby was extremely alive and did not look at all like the photos and drawings of "embryos" which I have seen. When the sac was opened, the tiny human immediately lost its life and took on the appearance of what is accepted as the appearance of an embryo at this stage, blunt extremities, etc.' (Paul E. Rockwell, M.D., "When You Were Formed in Secret," *Intercessors of America Newsletter,* 1980).

"The Bible makes some startling and comforting statements about the beginning of life. Let me tell you some of them. When God spoke to Jeremiah in Jeremiah 1:5a about the prophet's life, He said this, 'Before I formed you in the womb I knew you, before you were born I set you apart'. In Ephesians 1:4 we are told that God 'chose us in him before the creation of the world to be holy and blameless in his sight.' In the Psalms, David included several references to his understanding of the origin of his life. He told God, 'For you created my inmost being; you knit me together in my mother's womb . . . your eyes saw my unformed body. All the days ordained for me were written in your book before one of them came to be' (Psalm 139:13, 16). He also said, 'Surely I was sinful at birth, sinful from the time my mother conceived me' (Psalm 51:5).

"If you believe in the Lord God and the truth of his Word, then there is no denying his intimate involvement in our formation. There are no 'accidents' in God's creation. God never refers to us as blobs of tissue.

"But the church is not the only place where belief in life beginning at conception is accepted. At the First International Conference on Abortion, held in Washington, D.C., in October, 1987, approximately sixty major scientific authorities from the fields of medicine, ethics, law, and social sciences participated as consultants. They were carefully chosen for their scientific knowledge and integrity. They represented a cross-section of race, religion, culture, and geographic backgrounds. After several days of discussions, they came to the conclusion that the majority of their group could find no point in time between the union of sperm and egg and the birth of the infant that was not a human life. The changes occurring between implantation, the six-weeks embryo, six-months fetus, a one-week-old child, or a mature adult are merely stages of development and maturation.

"When Mary went to see her cousin Elizabeth, who was pregnant with John the Baptist, the baby (notice that it doesn't say the 'tissue') in Elizabeth's womb leaped for joy when she heard Mary's greeting (Luke 1:44). Here is a powerful example of God's care for the pre-born and how He works in their lives even before they are born.

"The November 1989 issue of *Reader's Digest* has an article entitled, 'The Fascinating World of the Unborn,' by Henri Goer. He used material taken from the book, *The World of the Unborn,* by Daphne and Charles Maurer, which reports on research done on babies in the womb using ultrasound scanning and fiber optic pictures and sound recordings. This research shows the babies in very close, intimate contact with their mothers and the events in the outside world. With this evidence it is inconceivable that anyone could honestly question that inside a woman's womb is a living, pre-born human being.

"An abortionist in Sweden vowed never to kill another pre-born baby after a ten-week-old baby he was aborting screamed. Air bubbles can occur during an abortion, and a baby even at that stage has functional vocal chords. All that was needed was for an air bubble to form over the baby's mouth during the act of murder. Dr. Mats Waktel declared, 'I won't perform another abortion as long as I live. And I'll never forget that scream'" (*ALL*, June-July, 1989).

Most of the audience was clearly stunned by the information many of them were hearing for the first time. David introduced Dr. Mortenson and invited him to come and briefly explain, in laymen's terms, the specific methods used in performing abortions.

Dr. Mortenson came forward and spoke with intensity. "What I'm about to tell you is a brief summary of surgical methods used in abortion. Before I begin, let me warn you that these methods are currently in use and have already been used at least 25 million times in America since 1973. One use would have been too many in my view. I'd like to be sensitive in these descriptions, but it is difficult to be delicate in talking about ways tiny children are being killed.

"Let me begin by informing you that you do not have to be a licensed medical doctor to be an abortionist. To remove your daughter's tonsils, she has to see a licensed doctor; but to have an abortion, she does not. Also, abortionists are paid on commission and are looked upon by most legitimate doctors as a disgrace to the profession. Because they are paid by commission, as are most of their attendants and even the 'counselors' (who woo the unsuspecting girls into having the abortion in the first place), abortion clinics have a tendency to be run like factories. This is why they are often referred to as 'abortion mills.'

"As unbelievable as this may sound, a veterinary clinic has higher health regulations governing it than does an abortion clinic. So much for the noble claims of the pro-abortionists that their primary concern is the health and safety of the woman. All that they have accomplished in legalizing abortion is moving it from the back alley to Main Street.

"There are five primary surgical/medical methods used in abortions. The first is the suction method. In early pregnancies the abortionist may choose to use a suction apparatus similar to what is used to clean your carpets. Only this tube is inserted into the womb. The vacuum is so powerful that the baby is crushed into a fluid mass of blood, tissue, and cartilage. It passes through the tube and into a bottle. Sometimes, parts of the womb are destroyed in the process.

"Secondly, abortionists use a forceps or currette. Again these devices are actually inserted into the womb. Working by touch alone, the abortionist uses these instruments to remove the body of the baby a piece at a time. He normally has to cut the baby apart to get it out. In order to remove the baby's head, he uses forceps to crush it and pull it through the birth channel, often in several large fragments. Then he has to scrape the womb to make sure each of the body parts is removed. The nurses assisting are usually given the duty of re-assembling the baby in order to account for all the body parts. Following this check, the remains of the child are disposed of, often in plastic sacks dumped into disposal units for garbage pickup.

"Thirdly, in babies who are more developed, right up to full term, a saline solution may be used. In this procedure, the doctor inserts a needle through the mother's belly and into the womb. A strong saltwater solution is injected into the amniotic fluid that surrounds the baby. It immediately scalds and burns the child's skin. In effect, the baby is pickled alive. The child may thrash about for hours before dying. In about twenty-four hours labor will start and a dead baby will be delivered. Unfortunately, some babies have been known to survive this torture and be born alive, though terribly burned.

"A fourth procedure involves the use of drug-induced labor. A drug called *prostaglandin* will induce labor and delivery at whatever stage of pregnancy it is given. The drug forces the uterus to go into labor and the mother delivers vaginally whatever size baby she is carrying. If the baby is old enough to survive the trauma of delivery, he or she is often born alive. These little ones, however, are often left in stainless steel bowls or sinks, unattended, to die.

"The fifth procedure is often used in normal deliveries when the mother is having great difficulties with labor. It is the Caesarean Section. An abortionist may use this method to expose the child. Abdominal surgery is performed, the womb is opened, and the baby is lifted out. If its lungs are too immature to breathe, it will struggle for life, then die. If it does begin breathing, it is left unattended. In some cases, it has been reported that the babies have even been smothered by the abortionist or their attendants.

"As long as these abortionists are allowed to perform their grizzly tasks, it is a reproach to a once-honorable profession. Western medical professionals have held to the basic principles of Hippocrates from 450 B.C. until this century. The Hippocratic oath specifically condemns abortion. Yet American medical groups have joined other notorious doctors like those in Nazi Germany in disregarding basic life-protecting principles. I find myself deeply ashamed, at times, of my own profession. As people realize we have lost our basic commitment to save lives, how will they trust us at all?

"When pro-abortionists claim that they want freedom of choice, we should ask them, 'Choice to do what?' Every time they use the name 'pro-choice,' we should use it as an opportunity. Hitler was pro-choice. He wanted to exercise his choice to kill Jewish people. One of the arguments you will hear repeatedly from the pro-abortion side is that a woman has the right to do what she wants with 'her body.' But again, what are the facts? That baby is not a part of her body like an organ, or an arm, or even a tumor. The baby is actually separate though enclosed in her body. It has its own heartbeat, its own blood that is not necessarily of the same type as the mother's, and its own unique genetic code. After reaching a certain maturity, it is fully capable of sustaining life outside the womb. Medically, the baby is not part of the woman, but a separate, living human." With that closing comment, Dr. Mortensen returned to his seat. People exchanged whispers and uncomfortable looks as the doctor sat down.

David stood up and introduced the question time by telling the people there would be another meeting the following week for those interested in getting specifically involved in the struggle to protect life. This evening had been designed to provide information.

A woman about half-way back in the room stood up and said, "I realize that abortions have to be stopped somehow. But I'm wondering, if we succeed, what will happen to all those mothers, and fathers too, who have already done what can't be undone?"

David responded, "Part of the answer to that question we'll have to save for next week, but I do want to mention one important thing. Many of those people you just referred to haven't been helped by abortion. We are just beginning to find out the price that our society will have to pay for what has already gone on.

"Let me mention some alarming figures from a national survey. These statistics are explained in detail in a book by David C. Reardon entitled, *Women Exploited, A Nation Deceived,* in which he catalogs some of the physical after-effects of abortion.

"Of the women surveyed, approximately 50 percent complained of suffering from one or more physical complications following their abortions. Of those 50 percent who reported complications, 27 percent described the complications as minor, 30 percent said they were moderately severe, and 42 percent claimed to have experienced severe complications. Among the short-term complications were bleeding or infections after the operation. In some cases the abortion had been incomplete, and a second procedure was required. Among those who reported long-term or delayed complications, the results were most often severe: complete or partial loss of reproductive ability. Women reported complete hysterectomies, blocked Fallopian tubes, cervical cancer, and miscarriages all directly attributable to abortion-related complications.

"Even more widespread has been the reported psychological aftereffects of abortion. Again, Reardon records that 94 percent of women surveyed who had abortions reported negative feelings about their abortion experience. Seventy percent of these women described the negative psychological impact as severe. Here are just some of the long-term effects in these women's lives following abortion: almost all described a worsened 'self-image'; many listed guilt, depression, and lower self-worth; among other complaints were nightmares, insomnia, nervous breakdowns, fear of touching babies, fear of the abortion anniversary, anxiety, bitterness, loneliness, even promiscuity. About 80 percent of the women reported that complications from abortion had lasted three years or longer. The Reardon study concluded that 'Looking back on their lives from where they are today, 71 percent of the women surveyed believe their lives today are worse off because of their abortions.'"

David paused for a moment. He knew they were overwhelmed by the figures. But there was more to learn.

"I really don't think it is hard for us to believe that the mothers suffer. But, what about the father? He is often the one insisting on the abortion. Yet, deep within the soul of men there is a desire to have a son like themselves, and fair and beautiful daughters like their mother. Social laws, standards and legends have grown up around the place and privilege of the firstborn son. In all of recorded history, a man's firstborn was considered of special value.

"Can we imagine that a hedonistic society can undo the work of God's Spirit and thousands of years of history, and convince our sons and daughters that the concept of valuing children is a useless myth? Can we go along with the voices telling our children, 'Go ahead, put having momentary fun above all else, practice being irresponsible, kill the spirit within — cease being what God created you to be and you will suffer no harmful consequences?' We can't take that course without paying horrible consequences.

"The concentric circles of loss and heartache begin with the baby, include the parents and the rest of the extended family. God created the family as a nurturing web of relationships including aunts, uncles, cousins, grandparents. All of these are harmed by the killing of children. In fact, ultimately, every aborted child is an immeasurable loss to the world. At the very least, we have to consider the tremendous loss of talents and contributions that could have been made by those whose opportunity to live has been taken away.

"How many potential Billy Grahams, Mother Theresas, or Joni Eareckson Tadas have been kept from seeing the light of day? How many Einsteins, Handels, Washington Carvers, or Ethel Waters have been lost to a needy world?

"The Bible speaks about God's view that a land and a culture are actually polluted through the unlawful shedding of blood. Numbers 35:34 says, 'Do not defile the land where you live and where I dwell, for I, the Lord, dwell among the Israelites.' The pagan peoples in ancient times regularly sacrificed their children to their gods. The Lord God hated this practice then, and He hates it now. 'They have built the high places of Topheth . . . to burn their sons and daughters in the fire — something I did not command nor did it enter my mind' (Jeremiah 7:31).

"God also spoke through Jeremiah about the defiling, or polluting, of the very temple of God and He pronounced terrible judgment on the people because of these sins. It really isn't difficult to see the parallels between those sins of the past and the sins of today that equally pollute

God's temple. First Corinthians 3:16, 17 says, 'Don't you know that you yourselves are God's temple and that God's Spirit lives in you? If anyone destroys God's temple, God will destroy him; for God's temple is sacred, and you are that temple.'

"The birth of a baby is normally the center of great joy in an entire family. What is more beautiful and delightful to watch than the pride of all those in a family when a new baby is born and brought home? On the other hand, what is more devastating than the death of a little one? And yet, in our land, the killing of babies is big business. As a nation we are beginning to experience God's judgment.

"These are questions that haunt my life. Will history record that the church of Jesus Christ did little or nothing to stop one of the greatest atrocities ever committed by humans against other helpless humans? Could not the mass murder of innocent pre-borns be at least part of the reason for the increase in senseless and seemingly random violence that is growing in our society? News of women and children being brutally assaulted and abused; people being killed over petty arguments; or teenagers committing suicide when they should have more to live for than any previous generation; these are all signs of a desperate illness in our land. I think it's time we realize there is a connection among all these things. When life is cheapened in any area, eventually it will be cheapened in every area. The price of sin is more than we can afford to pay."

David stopped and looked around at his audience. Their faces were attentive. He felt he could almost read their hardening resolve toward action. He realized how encouraging their response was to his own commitment.

He smiled and said, "This has been a heavy experience, hasn't it?" A number of people nodded or murmured their agreement.

He went on, "I don't apologize for telling you the truth, but I do sympathize with those for whom this has been a first-time, eye-opening introduction to the realities of the abortion crisis. It's not easy to take it all in. But, even knowing part of the picture can be depressing." There were more nods.

"However, it is not a hopeless situation. We know there is a better way, and there are actions every one of us can take to help stop this modern holocaust and reaffirm the value of life. It's an important first step in proclaiming clearly the good news about the Lord of life!

"I want to personally invite all of you back a week from tonight to discuss some of those specific action steps. Dr. Mortenson will be back to answer questions, and you will have a chance to hear from several people who are already deeply involved in the struggle for life. My friend Mike here will have flyers at the door that you can take to invite others next week."

David turned the meeting back over to the local pastor who closed with a brief but passionate prayer. In it he asked God to build a real fire of concern and committed action in the lives of Christians in that church. He also asked God to use the two meetings to make a difference for good and for life in the community.

The people parted ways that night with a quiet seriousness and expectant attitude about the future.

Comment

Photographs and descriptions may be gruesome, but many do need to be shocked out of the attitude that abortion is just a word. The issues will not go away or solve themselves. For Christians, the abortion crisis does not offer the option of avoidance or involvement. We are involved. Intentional ignorance and fearful lack of action are not acceptable excuses. They are part of the problem! Sooner or later we must face and give a response to the crisis of abortion. Waiting until later will only increase our shame and guilt. Those who call themselves Christians need to be known again as people who love the Giver of life so much that they are willing to let go of their own lives that others might find real Life!

In the News

Under siege from protesters and largely isolated from medical colleagues, doctors who perform abortions say they are being heavily stigmatized, and fewer and fewer doctors are willing to enter the field.

Reflecting the public's ambivalence about abortion, many doctors on both sides of the issue say that they find abortions emotionally difficult and unpleasant.

A 1985 poll by the American College of Obstetricians and Gynecologists showed 4,000 of its 29,000 members reported that 84 percent said they thought abortions should be legal and available, but only a third of the doctors who favored abortions actually performed them and two-thirds of those who did abortions did very few.

About 4 percent of those polled performed 26 or more abortions a month. The researchers did not ask the doctors why they did or did not perform abortions.

"The term 'abortionist' still has a very heavy stigma," said Dr. Curtis E. Harris, an obstetrician in Oklahoma City who heads the American Academy of Medical Ethics, a group of 21,000 doctors that favors greatly restricting availability of abortions.

"Most gynecologists work to bring a child into the world in a healthy state," Harris said, adding that carrying out an abortion "is a real contradiction."

With few incentives to perform abortions, most obstetricians and gynecologists avoid them, medical experts say, and surveys of doctors report. Those who support abortion rights say the shortage of willing doctors makes it harder for women who sometimes have to travel hundreds of miles to find a doctor to abort a fetus.

Source: Kolata, Gina. "Doctors Shy From Abortion." *Daily Courier-News* (Elgin, IL), January 8, 1990.

&a. &a. &a.

Dear Editor,

The decision to have an abortion affects each woman differently. Let me tell you about my experience.

I never once thought of the life within me as a little baby. I knew, once it was born, it would be a baby, but for the time being, it was just a blob that had created a major disturbance in my life.

After receiving a shot in my cervix, the doctor would dilate it with a series of big instruments. After inserting some instruments, the doctor would determine the size of the fetus and the stage of my pregnancy. A vacuum machine would then suck the fetus out. The doctor would use another instrument to get any remaining parts.

The counselor didn't tell me that the remaining part would be the baby's head, and that the doctor would have to crush it to get it out. She didn't tell me that the vacuum machine would dismember my baby. She didn't tell me recognizable arms and legs, not just blobs of tissue, would be ripped from my womb. She also didn't inform me that any movement during the procedure could cause the doctor's instruments to perforate my uterus. In fact, complications were never mentioned.

Feeling my baby being torn from my womb was one of the worst sensations I've ever experienced. As the machine tried to suck out my insides, everything was trying to move up in my body to escape being pulled out. The vibration made me feel extremely nauseated. . . .

Coming out of the clinic, I felt as if I had just lived through a nightmare. I felt humiliated, patronized, ashamed, cheap, degraded, and ruined — the whole spectrum of the most negative feelings a woman could ever experience. I felt sick, not relieved. . . .

Source: *The Hillsdale Collegian,* Hillsdale College, Hillsdale, MI, February 22, 1990.

ﻬ ﻬ ﻬ

The controversial "Baby M" case and the recent Vatican document on "respect for human life and its origins" have prompted many in the religious world to face the ethical issues raised by the new reproductive technologies. Our understanding of the relationship between sex and procreation has been challenged by heretofore unimagined methods of reproduction.

On March 10, 1987, the Vatican's Congregation for the Doctrine of the Faith issued its "Instruction on Respect for Human Life in its Origins and on the Dignity of Procreation: Replies to Certain Questions of the Day," which expressed the Vatican's moral opposition to such practices as in vitro fertilization (IVF), artificial insemination by donor (AID), surrogate motherhood, embryo freezing, and artificial insemination by husband (AIH) when semen is collected through masturbation. The instruction was clearly attempting to influence the choices of infertile couples and to encourage a public call for government restrictions on reproductive technology.

Reproductive technology raises the question of whether it is proper for science to interfere with natural reproduction. Jerry Falwell argues against surrogacy on the grounds that "God's way is still the best way." The Vatican instruction argues that reproductive technology tempts man "to go beyond the limits of a reasonable dominion over nature."

Source: Greil, Arthur L. "The Religious Response to Reproductive Technology." *The Christian Century,* January 4–11, 1989, p. 11.

ᶻᵃ ᶻᵃ ᶻᵃ

If she had been born a decade earlier, the baby would not have lived. But in the summer of 1985, a modern medical miracle took place at St. Joseph's Hospital in London, Ont. It began when a woman gave birth to a baby girl a few days before reaching her 23rd week of pregnancy — 17 weeks short of a normal full term. Weighing only one pound, the baby was placed in an incubator linked by tubes and wires to an array of life-sustaining machines that have been perfected over the past 10 years. Until very recently, almost no babies born so young survived because many of their vital organs — especially the lungs — were not yet developed enough. But, for this tiny infant, there was hope for life — the result, said Dr. Graham Chance, a specialist in newborn care at St. Joseph's, of the new technology. Other hospitals across Canada have reported similar incidents. But the science that enables doctors to perform such feats also raises an ethical dilemma: if medicine can save a 23-week-old fetus, is it right to allow abortions to be carried out at the same stage of pregnancy?

Source: Laver, Ross. "The Debate About Life: Technology Alters the Old Rules." *McLean's,* Vol. 102, July 31, 1989, p. 20.

ᶻᵃ ᶻᵃ ᶻᵃ

A Wirthlin Group poll released Feb. 7 indicates most Americans hold positions which are pro-life, although some of them call themselves pro-choice, thus tipping the balance to the pro-choice side when only labels are being measured.

The survey explains, "When asked which of six statements best describe their personal stand on abortion, a majority of Americans (52 percent) take positions that can be described as pro-life, while 44 percent take pro-choice positions. . . .

"However, when asked later in the survey whether they consider themselves to be 'pro-life' or 'pro-choice,' a majority of respondents (50 percent) label themselves pro-choice while 40 percent say pro-life. Thus 12 percent of those taking pro-life positions shun the pro-life label.

"There is significant confusion on the abortion issue between circumstances and semantics. When the issue is debated on circumstances, a majority of Americans are pro-life. However, when the issue is debated on semantics, a majority are pro-choice."

A Milwaukee Journal poll of 400 Wisconsin residents conducted Feb. 1 illustrated the same phenomenon in more subtle ways. Although 61 percent called themselves pro-choice compared to 34 percent pro-life, only 54 percent opposed a father's consent requirement before abortion, while 81 percent favored parental consent for a minor's abortion. Thus greater numbers held to pro-life stances than actually admitted to the pro-life label.

Source: "Americans Favor Pro-Choice Label But Not Pro-Choice Beliefs, Polls Say." *American Life League News (Newsletter)*, February 19, 1990, pp. 1, 7.

ra ra ra

If adoption is to be chosen more often, we must begin to present it as the responsible and loving option that it is.

Myths and misconceptions must be addressed. Talk-show sensationalism aside, adoption works very well for the overwhelming majority. Contrary to the myth of birth mothers' endless grief, for instance, studies find greater life-satisfaction ratings as well as higher educational and financial attainment for relinquishers compared with nonrelinquishers. Data also counter the common notion that adopted children more often suffer mental illness: In fact, children adopted as infants display a more positive world view than nonadoptees, no higher rate of mental-health problems, greater educational and financial attainment, and even greater satisfaction with their parents than nonadoptees.

Educators can do much to help change stereotypes of adoption. Characterizing this choice as a loving option and eliminating such negative language as "children of their own," "real parents," and "giving away a baby" are good first steps, beginning at the elementary level. Presentations by adoptive parents, birth parents, and adoptees have proven effective tools for dispelling misconceptions. Challenging myths in the classroom can also help students examine the stigma unjustly attached to adoption.

Source: Krausman, Susan. "'Stereotypes' Of Adoption Are Inaccurate." *Education Week,* January 31, 1990, p. 32.

ta ta ta

"If my political career ended tomorrow, I'd still be damn proud of what I've done just on abortion," [Colorado Governor Dick] Lamm said (*The Denver Post,* May 31, 1970). He also used quite a few "I's" in a piece for the *Zero Population Growth (ZPG) Newsletter* (May, 1974) bragging about his accomplishments to curtail growth, particularly as the state representative who, in 1967, was the chief sponsor of the nation's first law legalizing abortion.

Population control was, and still is, his primary objective.

In 1972, a little group called The Good Death Fellowship was founded in Denver for the purpose of advancing euthanasia. One of the spokeswomen for the group was Elsie Garman, who advocated "one more pill" so that people over eighty might "go out with dignity," i.e., commit suicide easily. She told this writer that then-Representative Lamm believed in their cause, but that he had said the "time wasn't right yet" for euthanasia.

Abortion had to come first. If society would tolerate killing the most innocent and defenseless member of society, then the logical next step would be to eliminate the newborn defective ones and the elderly and other terminally ill, then others who did not have a "meaningful life."

With legalized living wills, they said, they could get rid of Down Syndrome children, "no-hope veterans" and all those "old bodies" in nursing homes. Those who were concerned about population growth thought this a good way to reduce population.

I think Lamm expressed his belief on euthanasia very well with his "We've got a duty to die" remark (March 27, 1984). He got more national media attention from that than anything he had said or done previously.

Source: *The Forum,* November/December, 1986, p. 3.

ONE GUY SPENT THE DAY PROTESTING OUTSIDE AN ABORTION CLINIC. THE OTHER SPENT IT INSIDE KILLING UNBORN BABIES. WHICH IS WHICH?

Key Quotations

If I profess with the loudest voice and clearest exposition every portion of the truth of God except precisely that little point which the world and the devil are at that moment attacking, I am not confessing Christ, however boldly I may be professing Christ. Where the battle rages, there the loyalty of the soldier is proved and to be steady on all the battlefield besides is mere flight and disgrace if he flinches at that one point.

Martin Luther

I praise you because I am fearfully and
        wonderfully made;
    your works are wonderful,
    I know that full well.
My frame was not hidden from you
    when I was made in the secret place.
When I was woven together in the depths
        of the earth,
    your eyes saw my unformed body.
All the days ordained for me
    were written in your book
    before one of them came to be.
How precious to me are your thoughts,
        O God!
    How vast is the sum of them!

Psalm 139:14–17

PRACTICAL ACTION

Key Question: What changes in attitude and action are required of Christians when we understand the abortion crisis?

Setting: At the informational meeting following the gathering, many practical suggestions are given for action.

D avid had prepared Mike and the others for a smaller turnout at the follow-up meeting. Actually, while there were fewer people there, David was encouraged by the size of the group. He had come to realize that people often hesitate to move from being informed to becoming involved. But here was a wide variety of people of all ages, from teens to grandparents, single adults to parents with children, some in three-piece suits while others wore T-shirts and blue jeans, all wanting to discover the best way to invest themselves in the abortion crisis on the side of life.

Some, in fact, were already deeply involved. David was aware that many of those he had invited to share their particular stories were scattered throughout the audience. Once again he was thrilled at all God was doing in the lives of people.

David introduced Mike as a student who was discovering that God could use him among his fellow students, and then asked him to open the meeting in prayer. In spite of the obvious seriousness of the reason for the occasion, there was a real lighthearted atmosphere in the room. It was as if people who had come together in a common commitment suddenly found they could relax with like-minded strangers.

"We are here to consider some specific ways we can become personally involved in the effort to stop the killing of pre-born children and promote life in our community," David began. "I want to take a moment to prepare you for what others will be sharing. After all, considering the size of the crisis of abortion in our society, and our own relative insignificance, the biggest hurdle for many of us will be answering the question: Can I really make a difference?

"Without a doubt, this is the most fantastic time to be alive and serving God of any time in history. On the one hand, we face gigantic and seemingly unsolvable problems; but on the other hand, we have opportunities and 'tools' to work with that would make Christians of the past green with envy.

"Let's think for a moment about what we have going for us. The life-style of even the lower classes of our society rivals that of kings of old in terms of medical attention, entertainment, freedom, and self-determination. We have worldwide communication at light speed, and laser technology that makes the accumulated knowledge of the ages instantly available on a personal computer. Satellites give detailed pictures of weather patterns around the world and warn us of danger. Robots build equipment and do mundane tasks, setting people free for more creative work. Common illnesses that once killed millions are now eliminated with a simple medicinal injection. The modern house is a marvel of comfort, air conditioning, microwave ovens, refrigerators, and electric blankets. And all this technology and comfort can be made available to everyone in the world through the use of other advances like solar power systems and earthquake-proof construction. We have good reasons to be excited about life in the twenty-first century!

"We don't deny that we have some serious problems to solve and large challenges to face. Nor do we pretend that obeying God and seeking to live life His way will automatically remove the threat of war or curb man's basic tendency toward greed and selfishness. The abortion issue itself, as serious as it is, is a symptom of deeper problems within our society. We desperately need God's help in the struggle ahead!

"However, what is the joy of life, having or achieving? Struggling to overcome and reach the top or being comfortable and relaxed? People climb mountains because they love challenges, not to seek comfort. We strive against great odds in all areas of life because there is joy in the struggle, not simply in having or arriving. In the struggle for life there are enough challenges to fit the skills and style of every person in this room for a dozen lifetimes.

"To respond to these challenges we have to realize that we've been deceived and misled by those who see no meaning in life and view man as just another animal who is born, suffers, and dies pathetically, and whose remains are thrown into a pit and discarded. They are wrong about man because they ignore the reality of God. How can they possibly appreciate the creation when they deny the Creator?

"But, we must honestly admit that the church has also at times lost track of its purpose and mission. For example, when we read what Jesus said about the gates of hell not prevailing against His church, most Christians see in their minds a small church surrounded by a large army of evil forces. The brave saints are holding on, waiting for the heavenly cavalry. This is an entirely wrong picture. Gates don't attack! Gates defend! It is the church that is to be attacking the fortresses of those bound for hell and it is hell's gates that Jesus said will not hold up under the attack of the church, empowered by God's mighty presence and weapons."

Several people clapped spontaneously and an older woman in the second row smiled broadly and said, "Amen," from the depths of her soul. David felt as if he'd been flooded with new energy.

"We need to discard the old concept and image of weakness and defeat as the church of Jesus Christ and put on the right attitude, one of victory and triumph. Yes, we must always remember that the victory comes through the Lord Jesus Christ as He works in and through our weaknesses. The attitudes we hold are basic. It's not who we are that is important; it's who we are part of that makes the difference. Is the Christ who lives in us a conquering king or a wimp?"

Like an echo, David could hear the word "King!" being whispered through the crowd.

"Are we victims, or are we responsible individuals in the service of an all-powerful God? If we say we believe He is the King of Glory, then we need to live as if He is.

"Let's be very clear. God does not lead His church to conquer as the world does. We advance and overcome by actually being servants who are willing to lay down our lives for others — not in some grand, flashy way, but right in the middle of ordinary, daily living. Jesus did not come to be served, but to serve. He conquered, but as a suffering servant, and He calls us to follow His example. We are also to serve.

"The question we're back to, though, is 'Can I do something that might make a difference?' Beyond giving a few dollars and becoming informed, can I actually do anything that will make a difference in the ultimate outcome? The answer, my friends, is yes, a thousand times, yes! God will use us ordinary people, in our ordinary lives, to accomplish His extraordinary plans and purposes!

"Even in apparent defeat, Christians need to have victory in their planning. We worship the God who will ultimately be victorious. He specializes in turning defeats into victory. We have many instances like Joni Eareckson's life in which a tragedy became the doorway to a unique ministry and countless changed lives that might never have been transformed without the price she paid. It's often difficult for us to understand God's ways, but there is simply no such thing as a worthless or unnecessary person in God's creation. Someone once said, 'God don't make no junk!' That's why we can never treat pre-born children as unwanted or unneeded. We honor God when we respect life. In God's hands, you can and will make a difference!

"Now, before we move into specific practical areas, let me add one thing. Start answering the question of what God wants you to do by deciding to be faithful right where you are. It may not seem like much, but it is a beginning. God doesn't repeat the phrases, 'fear not' and 'be of good courage' so often in the Bible without cause. If you decide to be faithful, there will be times when you will be afraid and lack courage. That's being human. But it is also then that you will discover God's presence and help. Even in times of fear and apparent failure, don't give up!"

David paused and said, "Well, I've just about said my piece for now. We want to open the floor to those of you who are already in the battle. Tell us what you are doing, and where you see the need for others to be involved. We're also open for any questions you might have. No one here is an expert, but this room is full of experience. Let's encourage each other."

Before David could sit down, there was already a woman on her feet. She had been seated on the front row. Turning to face the audience, she said, "I'm Martha Barnes and I work in the local crisis pregnancy center. I first went there for help some years ago when I felt guilty for not doing anything about the problem of abortion. I not only found help for myself, I also found a place I could help pregnant women find accurate information and a listening ear. I may not be a trained social worker, and I don't have formal education in counseling, but I've learned a lot from co-workers and experience. What I mean to say is that you don't have to be a professional to get involved with helping other people. Most of all you need to care, be willing to learn, and want to minister to women in need. We need people to answer the phone, counsel, take girls into their homes, and help in the office. For me, it has been a great experience. There have been plenty of times I was tempted to quit, but every time I see one baby brought into life, saved from death in the abortion mills, I know I have to go on. So, if this kind of ministry interests you, let's talk when the meeting is over."

"Thanks, Martha," David said. "I've known Martha for several years. She's a real veteran in the struggle who can teach all of us lots of practical skills in helping people see what it means to be pro-life."

A bearded man, dressed in blue jeans and a T-shirt, stood up and walked slowly to the front before addressing the group. He was carrying a worn but legible picket sign which simply said, "There ARE Alternatives to Abortion, Ask Me." He spoke softly, "Hi, my name is Darrel. I know that some of you would rather give about all you owned rather than walk a picket line in front of an abortion mill. At times, those of us who picket expect to be treated like we're odd. However, I want to tell you that picketing is another way, a way with an honorable history, in which people can make a difference. I'm not saying it's the only way, no more than Martha would tell you that what she does is the only way. You see, I don't make a lot of money to give, and I don't have many talents, but I can show up at the killing places and hold my sign up. I don't know how many babies my actions have saved, but I do know that now and then women do ask me for one of my pamphlets with information on where they can find alternatives to killing their babies. I do catch some flak from the abortion people and others who drive by, but I've also had a few women come back and thank me. In fact, just last month a woman brought her baby by and showed him to me. She told me it was this very sign that caused her to stop and turn away from killing that precious little baby."

He stopped and looked down as tears filled his eyes. He swallowed and continued in an even softer voice. "Just that one baby made it worthwhile for me and I'll continue picketing every chance I get. But there are many days when no one is available to carry a sign. You could be used to just hold a sign and give material to those who ask. We need you." With that he smiled at the group and quietly thanked them as he walked back to his seat, turning the sign so that the audience could now see the other side. It had a picture of a group of newborn babies with the words, *CELEBRATE LIFE.*

David thanked Darrel and said, "There's no question that peaceful picketing has been an effective way to cause many women to reconsider what they were about to do and it has also drawn attention to the killing centers. I read an article recently which stated that one reason we have allowed the little pre-born babies to be killed is because they are nameless. The author was suggesting that we should stand out in front of an abortion mill and ask each woman who comes in one simple question— 'What is your baby's name?' This question just might jar a woman into realizing that she is about to allow a living person inside her to be killed."

The next person to speak was a distinguished man who looked vaguely familiar to many in the audience. He seemed to be comfortable addressing a group. He looked over at Darrel's sign and said, "God bless you, Darrel, for being faithful at what you do."

Then he looked at the group and began, "I'm Jim Shogauer, an attorney and lobbyist at the state capital. I make my living through my law practice, but I find my greatest challenge is working as a legal volunteer to help stop the holocaust in our state. Frankly, our greatest need is for funds, but I also want to tell you some ways you can help at this level of the struggle. Letters to your elected officials do make a difference, especially when they come from the heart. Showing up at special hearings, court cases, and demonstrations are also important, especially when you make it a point to stop by at the same time and see your elected officials to express your concerns.

"But most of all, I want to encourage you to get involved in the electoral process. I know some of you think that politics are dirty, and you are right. But you are wrong if you think that good people shouldn't be involved in politics for that reason. In fact, politics will remain soiled until more Christians get involved and clean it up. Christians need to be active in every part of society, bringing the light of Christ with them. One of the most important places of involvement is right in your local precinct and county. I'm here to tell you folks that from a legal standpoint, the battle to stop the killing is actually going to be won or lost at the local level, not just in Washington. Now I realize that is a major change in thinking for many of you, but local political service is a significant way to make a difference. There are good materials and organizations to give you guidance if you decide to become active in this way. Ask me afterwards for key names to contact.

"We need a core of committed Christians who will learn to use the political process. Changes come slowly this way, but they are also important. The babies who will be saved are worth the trouble!" Jim sat down after thanking all of them for the opportunity to speak.

David in turn thanked him and expressed how difficult it was not to launch into another sermon. "Who's next?" he asked.

A moment later, halfway back in the room, a young girl stood up holding tightly to a bundled baby. "My name's Bobbie," she began. "If it's all right, I'll just stay back here. I'm not used to speaking to groups of people."

She looked around at the sea of encouraging smiles and was able to go on. "I made a bad mistake, and I almost made two of them. Fortunately, I went by the clinic and met Martha before making an even bigger mistake. The things she said about how important it is for people like me to have someone lovingly tell us all the facts about abortion are true. I hope some of you decide to help her. But I also want to talk about the couple that took me into their home while I waited for my baby." She looked down at the couple next to her. "Tom and Shelly took me in when I desperately needed a place to stay. I had been told to get an abortion or not bother to come home." By this time tears were flowing down her cheeks and her speech was halting. "And I have to admit that it really wasn't easy for them because at first I was very angry and selfish. . . ." Shelly reached out and put her arm around the girl's waist and held her. Bobbie wiped her tears away and went on, "I almost went ahead with the abortion, and I probably would have except for Tom and Shelly. But I'm so glad I didn't." She pulled back the pink blanket so that everyone could see the tiny girl she held. "I want to encourage some of you to think about taking a pregnant girl into your home. It won't be easy, because if they're anything like me, they'll have a lot to learn about everything. The thing is, though, you may end up saving a baby, and the mother too." She sat down and buried her face in the blankets around her baby and Shelly held her tenderly.

From where she was sitting, Shelly added, "It sure wasn't as bad as Bobbie made it sound. It does really change your routine when someone else is in your home after all the children have grown up, but Tom and I are glad Bobbie stayed with us. Now we have another daughter and another grandchild!" The group broke out in a spontaneous applause of joy. Those close to Bobbie reached over and touched her to demonstrate their love and support.

"There are many ways you can be involved," David commented. "Some of them require direct emotional and physical commitment, but there are ways those who can't provide that kind of support can still help. Jan, I expect your experience would help us here."

A sharply dressed woman in her thirties quickly walked to the front and turned to speak. "I'll make this quick. I'd like to push for more people to help educate others to the realities of abortion. The pro-death people scream and yell about the right of the woman to choose but they neglect a basic point: a good decision requires objective truth and facts. I'm sorry to have to admit that, as a supposedly educated person, I didn't know the facts. They didn't tell me I was killing a baby in my womb. They didn't tell me about the guilt and regret, they just said my career would suffer if I didn't end the pregnancy. I was assured their 'procedure' was the right choice. Well, it turned out to be the wrong choice and I now live with the consequences.

"What I'm doing so that others don't have my experience is getting the word out to young people about the whole picture so they can make informed choices. Please feel free to pick up literature from my table in the back and share it with your children and neighborhood young people.

"And one more thing. I'd like to point out a giant inconsistency that may alert you to some of the tactics you'll run into. Have you noticed that when the same pro-death people get involved pushing to save the baby seals they don't hesitate to show us pictures of baby seals being clubbed to death? Or they show us whales being harpooned. Or they plead for peace by graphically showing the horrors of war. But, when they are pushing for their views on abortion, they show women picketing for their right to choose. They hold up their coat hangers, implying that women will have to resort to them if we make abortion illegal. They don't show us pictures of cut-up and burned little babies in trash cans, or the bloody hands of the abortionist, or the stabbed little babies those coat hangers were used to bludgeon. And yet, they accuse us of censorship and of being narrow minded and trying to suppress the rights of women and their freedom to choose. If that isn't hypocrisy, I don't know what is." She realized that she had gotten somewhat carried away. She smiled self-consciously then said, "I guess I can't help getting emotional sometimes, too." The group warmly applauded her as she took her seat.

"Thanks, Jan," said David, "we do need to get the word out to people. It's amazing, with all our communication abilities and technology, that so many people don't know the facts. And of course one of the most effective means of communication is still one person telling another. The means can vary from conversations, to pamphlets, to audio cassettes, or videos. When it comes from someone they know, there's a good chance they'll pay attention.

"Claudia and Bill, you play a very important part in this overall battle. Would you please share with the group what has become your ministry?" An older woman, with white hair and a grandmotherly look slowly stood and faced the group. "Bill and I are retired. It's hard for us to drive at night, so we can't get to many meetings or events like this. But as we thought and prayed about how we could serve God and tiny babies, we came to realize that God has given us a lot of free time to pray. Prayer doesn't cost any money, and doesn't require any special equipment or organization, but that doesn't mean it's easy! Maybe praying is hard because it works. The one who is behind the killing of babies doesn't want us crying out to God on their behalf.

"But we've been learning. And praying has been rewarding. We've had to decide to turn off the T.V. and deal with other distractions. Praying for others has clarified our own relationship with God. And it really is a joy to bring the needs of people and groups to God. We have seen God answer prayer. Please pray with us, even if there are other things you are doing."

"Thank you, Claudia," said David. "I happen to know that you have a standing invitation at your home for times of prayer, and that applies to anyone here who would like to join you. Every one of the opportunities we've heard about tonight involves prayer also. Prayer keeps our attention on God, where it should be." Claudia was nodding her head vigorously.

David paused to let anyone else speak, but, seeing no one, he continued, "We've heard some challenging and practical ideas, and a wide variety of opportunities that should appeal to just about everyone here. I'd like to remind you of something I heard a missionary say at the end of an inspiring presentation. I've been encouraged by the words whenever I am faced with more challenges than I can possibly meet. He simply said, 'We can't do everything, but we can do something. And what we can do, we will do by the grace of God!'

"We have been trained to think that if anything significant is going to happen, it has to happen in Washington, D.C. and be accomplished by 'important' people. There is no denying the significance of decisions by the Supreme Court, or actions by federal and state governments. It's also true that the media and the public school system exert great control over what people think and do. However, I want to remind you that, in this struggle between life and death, the most powerful determining factor in our society is what people like you and me think, are, and do in the context of our everyday lives. We do count! Whatever good happens in society must first happen within us. As we allow the living God to change how we live our daily lives, those changes need to be reflected in every area of life.

"If we are to win this battle for life in our society at this point in history, we must set aside the things that divide and separate us and learn to work together. We can continue to be called by whatever name we choose, but let's make sure we agree that we are together in this struggle of life over death. God may be using this very issue to demonstrate the unity which should exist in His church.

"As we work and struggle, remember that the God who created us is a living God who means for life to triumph over the forces of death. We will suffer temporary setbacks, which some will gleefully call defeats. But, this war will be won. There will come the day, and we pray it comes soon, when the killing of the pre-born will stop and babies will again be valued and loved as God intended."

On the way home that night, it would have surprised everyone to find out how often the phrase, "We can't do everything, but we can do something," was echoed in conversation. And no one could seem to dismiss from their minds that well-worn but beautiful picket sign with the babies' pictures and the two words that seemed to capsulize the entire mission — *CELEBRATE LIFE.*

Comment

Books end, but wars go on. In the big picture, the struggle between life and death is the war of the ages. It will go on until God decides it's time for a new heaven and earth. Until that time, we are called to be obedient. The place is probably not as important as the obedience. Seeking to obey God, to do "something instead of everything" has a way of leading to the right places. There are practical opportunities for involvement around every corner and part of every day. Knowing more, we are now responsible for more. Realize again that God never asks us to do everything, but He certainly has something in mind for each of us to do!

In the News

Legislating Death: The U.S. Senate is considering a bill called the Patient Self-Determination Act — National Living Will bill, for short. The lawmakers get their philosophy from folks like Philip Sharpe, Jr., who says too much money is being spent on care of the elderly.

"When the distribution of a limited resource such as health care is based solely on age," Sharpe said, "it is not only irrational, it's immoral. No one has the guts to say 'no' to seniors' insatiable demand for services."

Sharpe served as special counsel to the Senate Committee on Labor and Human Resources, chaired by Sen. Ted Kennedy.

Oklahoma Doctors Acquitted: Four Oklahoma physicians are free after admitting they withheld treatment from babies born with spina bifida. The doctors said they used a mathematical formula to decide whether 60 newborn babies with spina bifida should be treated or allowed to die. The formula included how much money the parents had, how intelligent the parents were and how close they lived to a treatment facility. 24 children were sent to an unlicensed shelter where they died.

Source: *Washington Report,* March 1990.

ﻬ   ﻬ   ﻬ

"Let's keep abortion safe and legal" is the cry from the N.O.W. organization. Legal Action for Women, a Pensacola, Florida group has targeted N.O.W.'s cries for safety by coming up with a legislative packet. This packet offers legislation for individual states, calling abortion centers to task.

Legal Action for Women also has two new pamphlets. "Aborting the Myth" provides the so-called "fact" sheet obtained from N.O.W. plus Legal Action for Women's own "fact" sheet, documented and bibliographed. Another pamphlet, "Quick Facts," delves into the myths of the abortion lies. Legal Action for Women offers these pamphlets and legislative packets along with two books, *Aborted Women Silent No More* by David Reardon and *Every Woman Has the Right to Know the Dangers of Legal Abortion* by Ann Saltenberger as a fund-raising packet. The above materials can be obtained for a specified donation plus shipping and handling. This information is invaluable in becoming knowledgeable when arguing in favor of life and protecting the lives of all human beings, born and unborn.

Source: "Legal Action for Women Offers Help." *Legal Action for Women,* September 5, 1989.

ᴥ ᴥ ᴥ

New York (AP): A pro-choice resolution approved by the American Bar Association's governing body is dividing the lawyers' group and testing its members' capacity for professional detachment.

Despite opposition from the ABA's president, president-elect, secretary and treasurer, its governing body last week approved a resolution endorsing a woman's right to an abortion.

"Some of the very best people in the ABA are in agony over this resolution, and I'm sorry for that," said Sandy D'Alemberte, a supporter of the measure who probably will become ABA president next year.

The resolution was criticized by Attorney General Dick Thornburgh, who contended that it raises questions about the ABA's ability to honestly render advisory opinions on the professional competence of judicial nominees.

The resolution says the ABA "opposes legislation or other government action that interferes with the confidential relationship between a pregnant woman and her physician or with the decision to terminate the pregnancy at any time before the fetus is capable of independent life."

As a result of the resolution's passage, ABA groups will be able to file briefs in abortion cases and work against proposed state laws that would restrict abortion rights.

Source: "Pro-Choice Stand Splits Bar Group." *Joliet Herald-News,* December 14, 1989.

ᴥ ᴥ ᴥ

One assumption common to people on both sides of the abortion debate is that the pro-choice position is the very essence of feminism. Strong though this belief may be, the early feminists objected strenuously to abortion.

An abortion debate raged during the Victorian era. *The Revolution,* the suffragist paper put out by Elizabeth Cady Stanton and Susan B. Anthony, refused to run ads for patent medicines because these were frequently thinly disguised abortifacients. Victoria Woodhull and Ten-

nessee Claflin, the notorious free-love advocates, held to the same policy in their newspaper.

Why did they oppose abortion? They knew enough about embryol-
ogy that they could make an ethically significant distinction between
contraception and abortion: The former practice did not take a human
life but the latter one did. Anthony referred to abortion as "child-mur-
der." Stanton classed it with the killing of newborns under the single
term "infanticide."

Mattie Brinkerhoff commented that women were as much victims of
abortion as fetuses were. It was not feminism but anti-feminism which
caused abortion.

Few of us have known that for the Victorian foremothers of modern-day feminists, abortion was an atrocity forced on women by a male-
dominated society which denied them real sexual and reproductive freedom. It is time that we all learned about, and learned from, these
pioneering champions of female and fetal liberation.

Source: Derr, Mary Krane. "When Feminists Opposed Abortion." *The Detroit
News,* December 7, 1989.

ॐ ॐ ॐ

Feminist ideology according to Simone de Beauvoir, Gloria Steinem,
Betty Friedan, Kate Millett, and Germaine Greer teaches that men, especially husbands, are awful creatures and that a wife is just an unpaid
servant-mistress.

Now, at last, through the meticulous research of one of the 20th
century's greatest historians, Paul Johnson, I have discovered where
these feminists got their nutty notions. His newest book, *Intellectuals,*
makes it clear that the leftwing intellectuals of the last two centuries
really did treat their wives and mistresses like unpaid servants and usually treated their children even worse.

The intellectuals on whom Johnson reports were not just artsy celeb-
rities who could assume the public would accept an immoral lifestyle.
They were writers who arrogantly presumed to diagnose the ills of society, to prescribe cures, and to tell mankind how we should all live our
lives and how society should be structured.

Jean-Jacques Rousseau, the French philosopher who wrote prolifically about "truth" and "virtue," kept an illiterate laundress as his mistress for 33 years, treating her like an unpaid servant, while he continued his affairs with many other women. He wrote that he "never felt the least glimmering of love for her . . . the sensual needs I satisfied with her were purely sexual and were nothing to do with her as an individual." He forced his mistress to abandon their five babies at birth on the doorstep of a foundling home.

Karl Marx, who had more impact on actual events than any other intellectual in modern times, made his wife's life a nightmare. He kept her and their children destitute while he disdained work and seldom bathed. He denied his daughters an education and vetoed their careers because he thought women were suitable only to be clerical assistants. He kept a female slave in his household from the age of 8, never paid her a wage, used her as his mistress, and refused to acknowledge their child.

Bertrand Russell, who ground out a steady stream of advice on almost every political and social issue from disarmament to religion, was one of the leading names in the 20th century movement to "emancipate" women from Victorian morality through "free love." He portrayed women as victims of an antiquated system of morality, while hiring lawyers to give his ex-wives as little support as possible. He had three wives and seduced almost any woman who was available, including chambermaids, governesses, and daughters of friends he happened to be visiting.

Jean-Paul Sartre, a professional philosopher who presumed to preach to a mass audience, aligned himself with the Communists. When he seduced Simone de Beauvoir, he said his credo was "Travel, polygamy, transparency." Sartre used her as his mistress, cook, laundress, seamstress, and housekeeper, all the while boasting of affairs with younger and younger women until he got to teenagers. He treated her like a slave, and didn't even leave her any money. But Simone de Beauvoir was an educated and able woman and she didn't have to live like a servant-mistress unless she chose that lifestyle.

Fortunately, the bizarre feminist theories about men and marriage are true only as to the crowd they associate with.

Source: Schlafly, Phyllis. "Insights into Feminist Ideology." *The Phyllis Schlafly Report,* December 1989.

⁂

Companies that donate to Planned Parenthood, the nation's best-known advocate of abortion rights, have become targets of campaigns by pro-life groups.

Inundated by letters and calls from vocal, well-organized abortion foes, several companies have cut off contributions to Planned Parenthood. J.C. Penney Co. stopped giving in 1988, when it moved from New York to Dallas. Robin M. Caldwell, manager of corporate contributions, says that "as long as Planned Parenthood supports abortion, we won't support them, because the country is too torn up about it right now."

The vast majority of Planned Parenthood's corporate sponsors plan to continue their funding. Still, though corporate grants account for just 1.5 percent of Planned Parenthood's $65 million overall fund-raising budget, they're now only half what they were in the 1970's, says Peter T. Wilderotter, Planned Parenthood's vice-president for resources.

Source: Tierney, Barbara. "Planned Parenthood Didn't Plan on This." *Business Week,* July 3, 1989, p. 34.

⁂

Anti-abortion activists have been fixtures in the halls of state capitols for years, and their grass-roots head start may still give them the clout to restrict abortion rights in some states. Right-to-life candidates have won four of six elections for state legislative seats since Webster. At a movement-wide strategy session in Washington this week, anti-abortion activists will set an ambitious agenda for the state capitals.

That doesn't mean pro-choice candidates in both parties are marching with Molly Yard of the National Organization for Women. Just the opposite. It seems the key to using the abortion issue is to tie it in to other themes and target voter appeals with precision.

Source: Fineman, Howard. "Pro-Choice Politicking." *Newsweek*, October 9, 1989, pp. 34–35.

Key Quotations

If you do not fight for what is right when you can easily win without bloodshed, if you do not fight when the victory will be easy and not too costly, the moment may come when you will have to fight with all the odds against you and with only a precarious chance of survival . . . you may even have to fight when there is no hope of victory, for it is better to perish than to live as slaves.

Winston Churchill

If my people, who are called by my name, will humble themselves and pray and seek my face and turn from their wicked ways, then will I hear from heaven and will forgive their sin and will heal their land.

2 Chronicles 7:13–14

CELEBRATE LIFE OUTREACH
"Giving Your Name for the Nameless"

Washington, D.C. is a city of monuments that memorialize our heroes and remember our history. By preserving our past, we can better prepare for the future.

One monument, in particular, has become a unique place of remembering and healing. It's the Vietnam War Memorial, a 500-foot-long granite wall that has engraved on its surfaces the names of almost 58,000 men and women who gave the ultimate sacrifice for their country. Each had a distinct personality, history, and potential. Each is identified by name. Many who visit the wall cry and hug a loved one, someone nearby, or even a stranger. Many also have experienced a healing of scarred memories and received inspiration and a sense of purpose in living from having been to the wall. It is a fitting and significant memorial.

In 1973, toward the end of the Vietnam War, another tragic war began that is still ripping our country apart at its moral foundation. It's a war between conflicting value systems, and as in all wars, there are casualties. But in this war, it is innocent babies who are being killed daily. The victims in this war far outnumber those killed in the bloody Vietnam War. In fact, there are more victims of this war in two weeks than there were in the twelve years of the Vietnam War. If we were to build a memorial wall similar to the Vietnam memorial, the wall would be over forty-four miles long!

How can one grasp the true tragedy of legalized abortion? Its victims don't have names. They never marched off to war because they never even learned to walk.

During the height of the Vietnam War, *LIFE Magazine* printed the pictures of all the people killed in one typical week of fighting. As you turned page after page, you could look into their eyes and see them as individuals. The truth was heartbreaking—these fine young people were now dead.

The media doesn't want to print pictures of the victims of the abortion war. They don't want to let people see the tiny torn or burned bodies. They can't list their names because they are nameless. They have been discarded in trash bins with the hope the truth will be forgotten.

But the Bible asks a key question, "Can a mother forget the baby at her breast and have no compassion on the child she has borne?" And it answers, "Though she may forget, I will not forget you. See, I have engraved you on the palms of my hands; your walls are ever before me" (Isaiah 49:15–16). And neither must we forget these murdered babies. By remembering, we will be moved to work to stop this continued slaughter. By remembering, we will work to bring healing to the wounded mothers, fathers, and families. By remembering, we can work to restore the moral foundation to our country.

How can we help people to remember? How can we stop the killing and change our society from a "death-style" obsession to a "life-style" celebration?

First, the abortion tragedy must be personalized. It may be impossible to grasp the tragedy of millions of babies who have been killed, but to identify with just ONE baby is possible. And because this baby was nameless, we are asking you to give your name to one baby. The Celebrate Life Outreach, a ministry of The Christian Connection, has set a goal to collect one person's name for each of the nameless babies who has been killed by abortion since 1967 (when abortion was first legalized in this country, in the state of Colorado). We also have a goal to build a Celebrate Life Center in Washington, D.C. in which all these names will be recorded for posterity. This will help educate future generations to the horrors of abortion so that this atrocity will never be repeated. It will serve as a place of healing for those scarred by abortion and other manifestations of the death mentality. It will also be a rallying point for the rebuilding of the moral and spiritual fiber in our nation. This memorial will call each generation to seek a life-style that protects, cherishes, and continually celebrates life.

Therefore, this center will serve as a memorial, a museum, and an institute, built with an unashamedly Christian foundation.

A Memorial

A memorial is a special tribute, and this will be a tribute to the millions of innocent babies who were killed by abortion. After we have collected one name for each nameless baby, these millions of names will be displayed in the architecture of the memorial in such a way that viewers will be emotionally shaken by the immensity of the abortion holocaust. Visitors to the center will be greatly moved by the fact that literally millions of human beings were murdered legally. A closer look will reveal the names of millions of people who stood for life. In this majestic and solemn structure, we trust that there will come the conviction that we must never again allow death to reign in our land, whether in the form of abortion, teen suicide, or euthanasia, or any other manifestation of a "death-style" mentality.

A Museum

A vital part of the center will be a museum displaying the history of the death mentality. While our current focus is primarily the abortion issue, the purpose of the museum is to show that the problem is far deeper than just abortion. Abortion is one outgrowth of a preoccupation with death that comes from rejecting God's design for His creation. The museum will graphically display the historic struggle between the "life-style" and "death-style" views. It will show how Satan has led people in all cultures in the history of man to devalue life. Visitors will also be shown how secular education and media have played a major part in the devaluation of life in our society and how they promote a death mentality.

Death through abortion is central to the current struggle; therefore, visitors will be educated on its social, political, and spiritual ramifications. A theater with film and video histories of actual events and people involved in the pro-life struggle will be available — including testimonies from those who experienced the pain of having killed their own baby, and testimonies from doctors who turned from doing abortions back to practicing their profession of saving lives. Above all, there will be a dynamic visual presentation showing the beauty of life from the moment of conception until natural death.

A chapel will be available for prayer. A counseling and referral center will be open in order to help hurting people who were deceived and scarred by having, performing, or assisting in the abortion holocaust.

An Institute

The Celebrate Life Center will be a place where people can find research material to study the entire history of the battle for life. We know that simply ending legalized abortion or abolishing death education will not end the overall struggle for life. People must discover how to better manage God's creation. As social and political realities change, The Celebrate Life Center will be able to provide education and leadership for historically and Biblically sound solutions to contemporary problems.

A Christian Center

The center must be a place that openly and unashamedly acknowledges that the only way people can know the highest values of life and experience true liberty is through knowing "the way, the truth, and the life" as revealed in the Lord Jesus Christ. This will be a Christian memorial.

When abortion is finally made unlawful, we will have won an important battle in the overall war of restoring and promoting life in our society. This will be a significant victory and a time to mark the beginning of a return to our country's moral foundation. The center must point each generation to the deeper and more significant problem: humanity's rejection of God. Then we must introduce them to God and show them His solutions to contemporary problems. We must not be ashamed to openly declare that God revealed the guiding truths for life in the Bible. Our basic sin as a people has been our rejection of God. We can only be restored to our true potential by following the truths revealed in the Bible.

How can all this come to pass? God has already laid this vision on many hearts, and as the idea spreads, we are trusting God to raise up the architects to plan the structure, the realtors to find the property, and others who will give generously to spread the vision and raise the funds.

Millions of individuals were murdered because of the pride and arrogance of human nature. We must not forget the nameless generation. Therefore, as we fight the battles that must be won to overturn legalized abortion, remove death education and the devaluation of life from public education, and to stop all moves toward legalized euthanasia, we call on all who support life to band together around this goal of providing a national Celebrate Life Center in our nation's capital.

There are three ways you can become involved:

1. You can donate and give your name for a nameless baby. If you are able to give $100 or more, you will be listed as a founding member of the memorial. If you are able to give $50 or more, we will send you a complimentary copy of this book, *Celebrate Life,* that you can share with a friend. For a minimum gift of $15, you will have your name listed in the memorial. These gifts will provide immediate resources for the expansion of the national Celebrate Life Outreach and the establishment of the Celebrate Life Center in Washington, D.C.

2. Every month when you pay your normal long-distance phone bill, you can be making a significant contribution to the cause of life. Since the divestiture of the telephone companies, it has become possible for new marketing companies to privately market long-distance telephone services. Telecom Xpress Inc. of Schaumburg, Illinois was one of the early companies, organized in 1984. The men and women who started this company are committed to helping fund the work of Celebrate Life.

Telecom Xpress provides all the same services that you are presently getting, and possibly even better ones. On a residential or business telephone, it is probable you would save money over your current carrier and still provide a generous percentage of your paid bill to The Celebrate Life Outreach. Your calls will continue to go over the fiber optic lines of major carriers, using the latest in digital equipment and computer technology. Simply use the following form to have your phone service upgraded to Telecom Xpress and begin to provide ongoing support for the cause of life without it costing you one extra penny.

3. You can personally become involved in a leadership capacity by spreading the message and mission of Celebrate Life to others. We will equip you with the information and tools you need to introduce Celebrate Life to others. Just check the appropriate box on the detachable form facing this page. We look forward to working with you to whatever extent you can become involved and together influencing our world to once again Celebrate Life.

Yes, I want to participate in

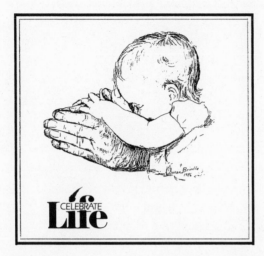

By giving my name for the nameless.

Here are three suggested levels of participation:

1. For a donation of $100 or more, you will be listed as a Founding Member of the Washington Memorial and receive a complimentary copy of this book, *Celebrate Life: Hope for a Culture Preoccupied with Death.*

2. For a donation of $50, your name will be listed in the Memorial, and you will receive a complimentary copy of this book, *Celebrate Life: Hope for a Culture Preoccupied with Death.*

3. For a minimum donation of $15 per name, you will be listed in the Memorial.

Here is my name and donation for $ _____

Name(s): _____

Phone: (   ) _____

Address: _____

City:State:Zip:_____

All donations are tax deductible. Return this sheet and your donation with checks payable to Celebrate Life, P.O. Box 59100, 717 East Golf Road, Schaumburg, IL 60173.

☐   I am interested in helping to promote Celebrate Life Outreach. Please send me information.

CELEBRATE LIFE
Long-Distance Phone Service Application

Please Print or Type

Date: _____

Name: _____

Street Address: _____

Mailing Address:_____

City, State, Zip:_____

S.S. or Fed I.D. #:_____

Present Long Distance Company: _____

Estimated Monthly Long-Distance Bill:_____

Main Telephone Number: (   )_____

Additional Numbers: (   )_____

(   ) _____ (   ) _____

Number of Travel Cards Required: _____

Yes, I support Celebrate Life. I authorize Telecom Xpress, Inc. (TXI) to act as my agent in providing "Dial One" service for the telephone numbers listed above, and agree to pay all charges billed to these numbers. Only one long-distance company may be designated for each telephone number and will be selected by TXI at the time my request for service is processed. I understand that the rate charged by TXI will reflect competitive prices and that all customer service, including my monthly phone bill, will be provided by Telecom Xpress, Inc.

Authorizing Signature: _____

☐   I would like information on Telecom Xpress's business services.

Mail to: Celebrate Life
                           P.O. Box 59100
                           717 East Golf Road
                           Schaumburg, IL 60173
                           (708) 843–8855

Yes, I want to participate in

By giving my name for the nameless.

Here are three suggested levels of participation:

1. For a donation of $100 or more, you will be listed as a Founding Member of the Washington Memorial and receive a complimentary copy of this book, *Celebrate Life: Hope for a Culture Preoccupied with Death.*

2. For a donation of $50, your name will be listed in the Memorial, and you will receive a complimentary copy of this book, *Celebrate Life: Hope for a Culture Preoccupied with Death.*

3. For a minimum donation of $15 per name, you will be listed in the Memorial.

Here is my name and donation for $ _____

Name(s): _____

Phone: (   ) _____

Address: _____

City:State:Zip:_____

All donations are tax deductible. Return this sheet and your donation with checks payable to Celebrate Life, P.O. Box 59100, 717 East Golf Road, Schaumburg, IL 60173.

☐   I am interested in helping to promote Celebrate Life Outreach. Please send me information.

CELEBRATE LIFE
Long-Distance Phone Service Application

Please Print or Type

Date: _____

Name: _____

Street Address: _____

Mailing Address:_____

City, State, Zip:_____

S.S. or Fed I.D. #:_____

Present Long Distance Company: _____

Estimated Monthly Long-Distance Bill:_____

Main Telephone Number: (   )_____

Additional Numbers: (   )_____

(   ) _____ (   ) _____

Number of Travel Cards Required: _____

Yes, I support Celebrate Life. I authorize Telecom Xpress, Inc. (TXI) to act as my agent in providing "Dial One" service for the telephone numbers listed above, and agree to pay all charges billed to these numbers. Only one long-distance company may be designated for each telephone number and will be selected by TXI at the time my request for service is processed. I understand that the rate charged by TXI will reflect competitive prices and that all customer service, including my monthly phone bill, will be provided by Telecom Xpress, Inc.

Authorizing Signature: _____

☐ I would like information on Telecom Xpress's services provided for business.

Mail to: Celebrate Life
                          P.O. Box 59100
                          717 East Golf Road
                          Schaumburg, IL 60173
                          (708) 843–8855

ABOUT THE AUTHORS

S teven A. Carr became involved in social issues in 1975 after he and his wife Peggy counseled a fifteen-year-old who was considering an abortion. In January 1987, he began the ministry of The Christian Connection, an organization that specializes in networking in the three arenas of ministry, social issues, and business. Today he is the president of this ministry.

Mr. Carr has been actively involved with college student Bible study and evangelism groups. He has been a church planter, a political strategist, and a businessman for many years.

Steve, Peggy, and their daughter, Elizabeth, live in the Chicago area.

❧ ❧ ❧

Franklin A. Meyer, vice president of The Christian Connection, has a varied background of Christian service. Besides serving as a pastor (he is a retired Evangelical Presbyterian Church minister), Frank has been a businessman, taken graduate courses in radio and TV production, and directed a video production ministry.

His current responsibilities for The Christian Connection include development and production of new products as well as an extensive training program to help Christians apply Biblical principles in all areas of life.

Frank and his wife, Judith, have two grown sons, Erich and Aaron, and live in the Chicago area.

The typeface for the text of this book is *Times Roman*. In 1930, typographer Stanley Morison joined the staff of *The Times* (London) to supervise design of a typeface for the reformatting of this renowned English daily. Morison had overseen type-library reforms at Cambridge University Press in 1925, but this new task would prove a formidable challenge despite a decade of experience in paleography, calligraphy, and typography. *Times New Roman* was credited as coming from Morison's original pencil renderings in the first years of the 1930s, but the typeface went through numerous changes under the scrutiny of a critical committee of dissatisfied *Times* staffers and editors. The resulting typeface, *Times Roman*, has been called the most used, most successful typeface of this century. The design is of enduring value to English and American printers and publishers, who choose the typeface for its readability and economy when run on today's high-speed presses.

Editing:

The Livingstone Corporation
Wheaton, Illinois

Cover Design:

Steve Diggs & Friends
Nashville, Tennessee

Page Composition:

Xerox Ventura Publisher
Printware 720 IQ Laser Printer

Printing and Binding:

Maple-Vail Book Manufacturing Group
York, Pennsylvania

Cover Printing:

Weber Graphics
Chicago, Illinois